D1525403

Inclusive Education and the Issue of Change

Policy and Practice in the Classroom

Series Editors: **Richard Race**, School of Education, University of Roehampton, UK; **Barbara Read**, School of Education, University of Glasgow, UK; **Alaster Scott Douglas**, School of Education, University of Roehampton, UK

This series will publish monographs exploring issues to do with education policy and practice in relation to classroom settings, with each book examining the implications of its research findings for educational policy and practice. Themes explored include teaching and learning; youth identities; inclusive education; education policy-making; de-schooling; student teachers; the primary classroom; and science teachers.

Titles include:

Alaster Scott Douglas
STUDENT TEACHERS IN SCHOOL PRACTICE
An Analysis of Learning Opportunities

Michael Singh and Bobby Harreveld
DESCHOOLING L'EARNING
Young Adults and the New Spirit of Capitalism

Anastasia Liasidou
INCLUSIVE EDUCATION AND THE ISSUE OF CHANGE
Theory, Policy and Pedagogy

Policy and Practice in the Classroom
Series Standing Order ISBN 978–1–137–26856–3 Hardback
978–1–137–26857–0 Paperback
(*outside North America only*)

You can receive future titles in this series as they are published by placing a standing order. Please contact your bookseller or, in case of difficulty, write to us at the address below with your name and address, the title of the series and the ISBN quoted above.

Customer Services Department, Macmillan Distribution Ltd, Houndmills, Basingstoke, Hampshire RG21 6XS, England

Inclusive Education and the Issue of Change

Theory, Policy and Pedagogy

Anastasia Liasidou

Assistant Professor, European University Cyprus, Cyprus

First published 2015 by
PALGRAVE MACMILLAN

Palgrave Macmillan in the UK is an imprint of Macmillan Publishers Limited, registered in England, company number 785998, of Houndmills, Basingstoke, Hampshire RG21 6XS.

Palgrave Macmillan in the US is a division of St Martin's Press LLC, 175 Fifth Avenue, New York, NY 10010.

Palgrave Macmillan is the global academic imprint of the above companies and has companies and representatives throughout the world.

Palgrave® and Macmillan® are registered trademarks in the United States, the United Kingdom, Europe and other countries.

ISBN 978–1–137–33369–8

This book is printed on paper suitable for recycling and made from fully managed and sustained forest sources. Logging, pulping and manufacturing processes are expected to conform to the environmental regulations of the country of origin.

A catalogue record for this book is available from the British Library.

Library of Congress Cataloging-in-Publication Data
Liasidou, Anastasia.
  Inclusive education and the issue of change : theory, policy and pedagogy / Anastasia Liasidou.
    pages cm. — (Policy and practice in the classroom)
  Summary: "This book critically examines transformative change within the context of inclusive education policy and practice. Exploring the theoretical, policy and classroom (pedagogical) dimensions of the process of transformative change, this book documents the ways in which ideological presuppositions and professional practice should be transformed in order to meet learner diversity in effective and non-discriminatory ways. The distinctiveness of the book lies in its analytical approach, which aims to blend diverse perspectives and disciplinary lenses to provide a comprehensive understanding of the ways in which transformative changes aligned with the tenets of an inclusive discourse can be theorized and enacted. The sheer complexity and interdependency of the perspectives underpinning the process of change, necessitates adopting a multiperspectival and multidisciplinary approach to theorizing educational change." — Provided by publisher.
  ISBN 978–1–137–33369–8 (hardback)
  1. Inclusive education. I. Title.
  LC1200.L529 2015
  371.9'046—dc23

2015002379

Contents

Acknowledgements   vi

1 Introduction   1

2 Neoliberal Reforms and the Crisis of Education   5

3 Inclusive Education Policymaking and the Question of
   Change   26

4 Theorizing Educational Change within the Context of
   Inclusion: Socio-cultural and Whole-School
   Considerations   50

5 Inclusive Classrooms and the Issue of Change   89

6 Sustainable Inclusive Education Reforms   105

7 Disability Studies at the Crossroads of Critical,
   Feminist, Anti-racist Theories and the Issue of Change   116

8 Educational Leadership and Socially Just Change   135

9 Disability Studies and the Issue of Change: The Voices
   of Disabled People/Students   151

10 Conclusions   163

Bibliography   168

Index   190

v

Acknowledgements

The author gratefully acknowledges the help of Dr Richard Race and Dr Alaster Scott Douglas.

1
Introduction

Inclusive education is a recent internationally mandated policy phenomenon that stipulates all students' right to quality mainstream education by means of promoting effective educational approaches and strategies to respond to learner diversity. Given that the notion of diversity extends to include various markers of difference, the analytical edge adopted in this book concentrates on disability-related differences, along with their intersections with other sources of social disadvantage linked to race/ethnicity, social class and gender (Liasidou 2013a). While acknowledging that prolonged reform efforts have largely been ineffective (Branson 2010) and even pernicious, for they corroborated rather than challenged exclusionary and discriminatory educational regimes (Lloyd 2008; Tomlinson 2012), the book attests to the importance of reconceptualizing and reimagining the process of educational change within the context of inclusion.

Inclusion is a prodigious task that cannot be materialized through facile policy rhetoric and practices intended to 'patch up' the educational system (Weddell 2008). Inclusive education can only be understood and analysed against concerns about initiating radical, comprehensive institutional and ideological reforms so as to challenge the special education status quo, along with the paraphernalia of its deficit-oriented practices, and facilitate inclusion (Thomas and Loxley 2007). Consequently, the issue of educational change is at the core of an inclusive education agenda (Ainscow 2005a, 2005b; Slee 2006, 2008; Liasidou 2007; Barton 2008) aimed at challenging power inequities and enhancing the learning and participation of disenfranchised groups of students.

The book aims to critically explore the issue of change within the context of inclusive education policy and practice. This involves exploring the theoretical, policy and classroom (pedagogical) dimensions of the process of transformative change, with a view to documenting the ways in which ideological presuppositions and professional practice should be transformed in order to meet learner diversity in effective and non-discriminatory ways. In terms of the theoretical dimension of the process of educational change, the book is given over to exploring the varied facets and underpinnings of inclusive education reforms, and analysing the ways in which systemic dynamics as well as issues of power, privilege and oppression are involved in the pursuit of transformative change. Emphasis is also given to the cosmopolitan nature of the change process by exploring the ways in which international politics as well as global policies and dynamics are reciprocally related and have a significant effect on national reform efforts (Ball 2012).

The distinctiveness of the book lies in its analytical approach that aims to blend diverse perspectives and disciplinary lenses, with the aim of providing a comprehensive understanding of the ways in which transformative changes aligned with the tenets of an inclusive discourse can be theorized and enacted. In discussing the sheer complexity and interdependency of the perspectives underpinning the process of change, the book draws insights from scholarly work on education policy, teaching and learning, disability studies, critical pedagogy, feminist theory, critical race theory and educational leadership so as to forge and exemplify links with inclusion, and to advance a comprehensive analysis of the theoretical and critical aspects of an inclusive education reform agenda.

The complex and multilayered nature of inclusive education necessitates a multidisciplinary and multiperspectival approach to theorizing educational change, an approach that this book aims to present and critically analyse. Theoretical compartmentalization and disciplinary fragmentation prohibit constructive dialogue and reflection on a number of common issues and concerns that surface across distinct disciplinary camps. These diverse disciplinary perspectives need to be correlated, concretized and contextualized with a view to enhancing current understandings of the ways in which inclusion interrelates with, and concomitantly is distinguished from, other disciplinary theorizations and academic discussions concerned with the issue of transformative educational change.

Common issues, considerations and debates that emerge across distinct disciplinary camps and bring to bear a significant impact on the process of change are thus highlighted, explored and interrelated in the light of the attempts to precipitate reforms aligned with the theoretical and philosophical underpinnings of inclusion. Owing to the multidisciplinary and multiperspectival approach adopted, a number of recurrent themes dealing with issues of 'difference', social justice and emancipatory forms of pedagogical discourse arise throughout the book, which are discussed in different contexts as well as from different theoretical perspectives and analytical lenses. The thematic similarities and overlapping considerations that arise reflect the shared 'theoretical ground' and common analytical perspectives deployed by distinct disciplinary camps in dealing with the notion of educational change and learner diversity. Such a multidisciplinary and multiperspectival approach aims at developing critical and reflexive understandings of the assemblage and multiplicity of ideas, factors, dynamics, ideological contestations and institutional conditions that impact upon the process of transformative change within the context of inclusion.

The cross-fertilization of diverse insights and perspectives germane to the politics of difference and diversity and the process of educational change can potentially strengthen and rationalize arguments in favour of inclusion, while also rationalizing and further developing political and socio-cultural perspectives on conceptualizing issues of difference and diversity on the grounds of special educational needs and/or disabilities (SEN/D). To this end, the book gives particular emphasis to the ways in which issues of difference and diversity on the basis of various markers of difference linked to race/ethnicity, gender and social class have been framed and theorized across distinct disciplinary camps and academic domains, in order to extend, contextualize and diversify them, without, however, losing sight of the ways in which disability-based differences relate to, and differ from, other sources of social disadvantage. The distinctiveness of disability-based needs should be both acknowledged and theorized in order to devise sound pedagogical strategies and designs to effectively respond to diversity on the basis of disability. At the same time, it should be noted that the notion of distinctiveness does not equate with reductionism; hence any deficit-oriented and individual pathology perspectives are problematized and jettisoned in view of emerging understandings of disabled students' intersecting identities (Liasidou 2013b).

The book also takes the view that developing critical and informed understandings of the complex and contested nature of inclusion necessitates a global discussion on disability and difference that does not homogenize and silence the peculiarities of diverse geopolitical contexts. While being cognizant of the perils of the policy-borrowing process (Watson 2001), which are associated with the complex and unanticipated ways in which global and local dynamics interact and impact upon policy formulation and implementations across distinct geopolitical contexts (Green 2002), policy snapshots from different socio-political contexts such as Finland, the United Kingdom (UK) and the United States of America (USA) are presented, so as to explore and contextualize current policy/practice trends and developments, and put abstract ideas and theorizations into practice. These snapshots derive from the literature, but they are also presented as part of a case study approach concerned with exploring the differing ways in which inclusive education policies are formed and implemented across diverse socio-political contexts. This approach highlights the cross-cultural dimension of change and the ways in which the latter is contingent on socio-political and historical dynamics (Barton and Armstrong 2007). The globalizing discourse of inclusion necessitates taking into consideration idiosyncratic conditions and localized struggles that mobilize and impact upon the process of educational change (Liasidou 2012a). Implications for educational policy, classroom practice and research are discussed and reflected upon.

2
Neoliberal Reforms and the Crisis of Education

Introduction

This chapter is concerned with exploring the intricate relationship between inclusive educational policymaking, politics and the economy. In particular, emphasis is placed on discussing the ways in which neoliberal ideologies impact on the process of education policy formulation and implementation, and influence the aims and outcomes of national educational reform agendas. Global and local dynamics interact in complex and unanticipated ways, and bring to bear a significant impact on the ways in which market-driven ideological and institutional dynamics influence the process of educational change across differing socio-political systems.

While analysing the complexity and multiplicity of educational policymaking, Ball (2012) refers to the emergence of new policy networks that are constituted by local and global forces against which national policies are formulated and enacted. Dominant policy networks work towards disseminating particular discourses that contribute to the propagation of neoliberal reforms across the globe. These reforms have significant social justice implications for disabled people, their advocates and the general population.

As Barnes (2012:21) put it:

> Since the coming of capitalism inequality within and across nation-states has escalated. This has been exacerbated over recent years by a succession of deepening global economic crises....Consequently as we move further into the new

millennium economic and political stability in all countries is likely to be increasingly fragile and the struggle for a fairer and inclusive global society more difficult

The above considerations have particular implications for the ways in which disabled people experience their impairments (Thomas 1999). The experiential aspects of disability are to a significant extent dependent on disabled people's level of access to social and material resources. Currently, a large proportion of disabled individuals are increasingly denied access to these resources, in both the developed and developing world due 'to the globalization of a particular materialist world view that prioritizes the pursuit of profit over equality and social justice' (Barnes 2012:20).

The emergent neoliberal-driven policy and ideological imperatives, along with their impact on disabled and non-disabled people alike, raise a number of important issues that need to be urgently addressed in the light of ecumenical pleas and legal mandates promoting the necessity to advance more democratic and egalitarian communities (United Nations 2008). Even though multiculturalism, citizenship, equal opportunities, human rights and diversity are the lexical flagships that characterize contemporary political discourse and epitomize progressive thinking, the existence of actual practice that works against neoliberal governance is far away from official rhetoric, which is occasionally simply spouted for electoral purposes and for attracting media interest (Race 2015). Thus, in spite of the fact that rhetorical attacks on neoliberal discourse abound, transformative action is scarce and inconsistent; hence the mobilization of the reform process should be primarily directed towards intensifying and reinforcing political action aimed at transforming neoliberal preoccupations across social, political and educational domains. McLaren and Farahmandpur's view (2001:144) is very apposite: 'We simply are saying that without overcoming capitalist relations of production, other struggles will have little chance of succeeding.'

This chapter takes the view that the current crisis of capitalism reflects a wider social, political and educational crisis, which necessitates questioning, re-evaluating and repositioning the ideals of 'casino capitalism' (Giroux 2012) underpinning the dominant social, political and educational discourse. That said, it is suggested that the recent fiscal crisis necessitates developing an informed understanding of the relationship between the state and capitalistic modes of pro-duction, along with its implications for the intricately interwoven ways in which education and the market-based society are shaped (Woods 2011). As Giroux (2012:32) so appositely writes, the current crisis of capitalism is more than an 'economic or political prob-lem: it heralds a crisis of education that is part of a broader crisis of democracy itself'. A change in this reciprocal relationship can be mobilized by an education system that advances alternative values and principles, which are not an appendage to corporate ideals.

Neoliberal reforms and evocations for a discourse around values

Woods (2011:64) uses the metaphor of 'meta-governance' in order to portray the environment within which education policy and practice is formulated and enacted. 'Marketizing meta-governance' is what currently dominates in the UK, the USA and other Western-centric socio-political contexts, which steer 'education in the direction of people formation for the economic system'. This metaphor epito-mizes the propagation of corporate-driven regimes that mimic the highly competitive, individualistic and profit-oriented marketplace. Framed against the wider context of 'marketizing meta-governance', educational change initiatives have been largely abetted by the ascendancy of neoliberal ideologies that have placed a pronounced emphasis on choice and competition as a means of raising standards in public service. Education is thus meant to be subject and sub-servient to the mode of production, while the hierarchical division of labour is replicated and reproduced in current schooling.

In recent years, the vast majority of education policy developments in Western-centric socio-political systems have been increasingly subsumed within capitalistic modes of thinking that favour preoccu-pations with increased competition, individualism and quantitative measures of effectiveness (Ball 2009, 2012). Despite acknowledg-ing that '[p]olitical and cultural exigencies in places such as Russia, China, and the United States, for example, necessarily lead to dif-ferent instantiations of free-market capitalism' (Dudley-Marling and Baker 2012:2), neoliberal imperatives have had similar implications for education policy and practice across different geopolitical juris-dictions. Ball (2012:12), for instance, discusses the ways in which neoliberal policy reforms do not only take place locally but 'are also "carried" and spread globally through the activities of transnational advocacy networks...'. Western policy discourses are thus diffused and embedded in diverse policy contexts and bring to bear a prodigious impact on localized struggles for educational reforms. Neoliberalism has thus become a globalized discourse as it has been variously intertwined with diverse geopolitical cultures, ideologies and socio-economic exigencies. A global conversation on educational change and inclusion presupposes a concomitant analysis of the ways in which neoliberal ideological and policy imperatives undermine the process of mobilizing and sustaining socially just reforms for learner diversity. As this is a very influential ideological presupposition, understanding the theoretical underpinnings and policy implications of neoliberalism is crucial, if we are to challenge the status quo and to galvanize the process of transformative change.

The values of the marketplace are enshrined in educational institutions, which are called upon to produce 'human resources' in order to fulfil the demands of the global economy, thereby relegating to the margins those students who are allegedly deemed 'unfit' to meet the demands of corporate modes of schooling (e.g. disabled students). Under the light of this kind of global 'meta-governance', education is reduced to indoctrination with market-oriented values that are 'merely connected with gaining manual or technical skills for getting a job or being employable' (Sargis 2005:8), while the contention that '[e]ducation is the best economic policy' (Brown 2007:1), has gained momentum around the world.

Thus, the recent financial turmoil has not only exposed the bankruptcy of capitalism, but has also contributed to the resurgence of values-based considerations that necessitate questioning and re-evaluating the ideological and institutional infrastructure of social and educational domains. The circumstances of the crisis reaffirmed the fundamental importance of questioning the purpose of public schooling, along with the ways in which it has both contributed to and been affected by the bankruptcy of capitalism. Some years ago, Sargis (2005:1) posited that 'the system of public education is fundamentally flawed; that its purpose is not, as common belief has it, to educate, to enlighten, and thereby to produce citizens who act in both their own and in their society's best interests, that is, citizens for a true democracy'. A couple of years later this assertion proved its veracity amidst the turmoil of the global crisis of capitalism.

The patent failure of the market-driven model has instigated resurgent concerns about the necessity to formulate education policies that are informed by a 'discourse around values' (Woods 2011:3) in mobilizing democratic and socially just reforms as a response to the ascendancy of market-based education policy imperatives that legitimize, reproduce and reinforce wider social inequalities. As one head teacher has very adroitly described, 'the spiritual emptiness of capitalism' has precipitated a renewed interest in what another educational professional called a 'discourse around values' (Woods 2011:3) that brings to the fore the necessity to embrace social democratic approaches to education policy and practice (Hursh 2007; Giroux 2012). Such a reflective and critical approach highlights the importance of promoting alternative values, emanating from more democratic and inclusive ideals, as the antidote to the proliferation of monolithic market-driven governance regimes.

Even though concerns about fostering more democratic approaches to human relations and conditions are not new, as these have prevailed in theoretical discussions and debates, the recent fiscal crisis has exacerbated inequality (Hursh and Henderson 2011) and made even more visible 'the denting of the superiority of the private business/markets model' (Woods 2011:2). The crisis thus provides the impetus to challenge the ways in which schools reproduce wider social inequalities, and routinely silence 'the historical, economic, moral, and social political debts owed to disenfranchised communities' (Bass and Gerstl-Pepin 2011:928).

Education constitutes a critical site within which wider changes can be envisaged and enacted as the role of education is crucial in formulating and influencing the ideological and institutional bases of distinct socio-political systems. In the aftermath of the recent global financial turmoil, educational change thus should be seen as a precursor for more fundamental social, economic and cultural transformations predicated on alternative values and priorities. These considerations make imperative, according to Goodson (2010:775), the need to 'seriously scrutinise the neo-liberal orthodoxy in the field of education' precisely because the corporate-driven educational restructuring attempts of recent years have distorted the role of schooling and have adversely affected educational outcomes. In a similar vein, Hargreaves and Shirley (2012) are scathingly critical of the neoliberal nature and direction of recent educational reform initiatives. As they write: 'market oriented reforms that are designed to yield short-term economic returns are clearly the wrong strategy, headed in the wrong direction. Another kind of change is needed . . . . What might that be?' (Hargreaves and Shirley 2012:4).

Determining the kind of change required is a major and timely issue, which needs to be taken into consideration when designing and implementing education or wider social policy reforms. Education policy and practice is not only embedded in and affected by a myriad of exogenous ideological and institutional dynamics (Berkhout and Wielmans 2001), but it also variously affects and shapes these dynamics. Quoting Hargreaves and Shirley (2012:1): 'It's not just the world that's changing education now. An orchestrated shake-up of every aspect of education is starting to change the world.'

Countries such as Finland, which have somehow resisted neoliberal imperatives, and maintained a strong focus on a social democratic vision in education policy and practice, have managed to achieve higher educational standards and more equitable educational outcomes for learner diversity (Hargreaves and Shirley 2012). While explaining the nature of Finnish educational reforms, Sahlberg (2010) points to the fact that the country has not been influenced by the global education reform movement (GERM), which has emerged from the interests of supranational development agencies and has been geared towards introducing high-stakes accountability regimes for schools. Having resisted market-driven educational reforms, the Finnish educational system maintained a focus on a social justice discourse in educational developments. This discourse has been concerned, according to Sahlberg (2010:332), with providing 'equal opportunities for all, equitable distribution of resources rather than competition, intensive early interventions for prevention, and building gradual trust among educational practitioners, especially teachers'. Simultaneously, the role of schools has been (re)framed against attempts to 'focus on deep, broad learning, giving equal value to all aspects of the growth of an individual's personality, moral character, creativity, knowledge and skills' (Sahlberg 2010:333).

Given the above considerations, the following sections concentrate on exploring the ways in which the notion of educational change has hitherto been conceptualized in Western-centric socio-political systems, with a view to discussing alternative ways of what this 'change might be' within the context of an inclusive education reform agenda.

Neoliberal policy reforms and the role of schooling

As already discussed, corporate-driven ideologies have monopolized educational reforms in Western-centric socio-political systems. What currently prevails is the propagation of neoliberal education policies intended to promote reforms to increase efficiency and accountability under globalization. These developments have been manifested in the ascendancy of the 'perfomative' culture of public schooling (Ball 2004), which promotes an instrumental approach to teaching and learning embodied in a 'teaching to the test' pedagogical culture. In the name of erroneously conceived understandings of raising standards and proclaimed intentions to close the gap between privileged and vulnerable groups of students, key policy reforms have introduced and consolidated a market-based approach to current schooling (Hursh 2009). Policy initiatives such as the No Child Left Behind (NCLB) in the USA stipulate a number of market-driven reforms that promote accountability regimes, payment-by-results criteria, high-stakes testing, choice and competition. These corporate-based reforms have been supported by consecutive political administrations, thereby suggesting their influential role in determining diverse political agendas and implementation strategies (Dudley-Marling and Baker 2012).

International performance indicators such as PISA (Programme for International Student Assessment) have instigated a shift from policies concerned with alleviating inequalities experienced by vulnerable groups of students to policies that promote high-stakes testing, accountability and corporate-driven systems of parental choice. (Smith 2012). Students have been increasingly viewed as profit-maximizing pawns in the service of an 'audit culture', whereby a school's 'effectiveness' is measured against simplistic and superficial assessment procedures akin to corporate rationality. For instance, Dudley-Marling and Baker (2012:3) refer to the US context to discuss the ways in which students 'are transformed into "commodities"....who bring more or less value to charter schools. Students with high test scores enhance the reputation and, hence, the marketability of charter schools. Students who do not score well on tests threaten charters' competitiveness – and, ultimately, their survival'. Neoliberalism advances individualism and, as a result, failure to achieve socially and academically is attributed to individual pathology. The notions of collegiality and social solidarity are substituted by concerns about enhancing the ability of individuals to act in their self-interest so as to achieve economic, social and educational well-being.

While analysing the nature of educational reforms in seven European countries, Goodson (2010:767) is critical of the ways in which these educational reforms have been driven by neoliberal imperatives, and makes the astute observation that '[o]ne area where the financial crisis has shown the limitation of neo-liberal thinking is the area of educational reform'. The author exemplifies the ways in which these reforms have been characterized by a preoccupation with choice, effectiveness, competition and value for money as the organizing principles underpinning social and educational domains.

In particular, these market-driven educational reforms, most notably manifested in countries such as the USA, the UK and Germany, have concentrated on introducing high-stakes accountability regimes for schools, which according to Sahlberg (2010:330) have been:

> closely tied to the processes of accrediting, promoting, inspecting, and, ultimately, rewarding or punishing schools and teachers. Success or failure of schools and teachers is often determined by standardized tests and external evaluations that devote attention to limited aspects of schooling...

For instance, in England, the new Labour government in 1997 endorsed a corporate-driven educational culture that was heralded in the 1988 Education Reform Act, whose avowed focus on 'raising standards' was touted as a means of enhancing the educational opportunities of high- as well as low-performing students. Nevertheless, the beguiling rhetoric of equity has never come to fruition because the standards agenda was solely linked to standardized high-stakes testing outcomes and league-table rankings (Ball 2009).

While commenting on the implications of the neoliberal orthodoxy, the Rose Report (DCSF 2009c) and the Cambridge Review

(Alexander 2009) in the UK discuss the 'educational damage the apparatus of targets, testing, performance tables, national strategies and inspection is perceived to have caused for questionable returns' (Alexander 2009:2). Similarly, Ainscow et al. (2009:172) have been especially concerned about the 'disjuncture between reform efforts and equitable outcomes' and discussed the ways in which educational reforms have created 'an educational market place' that privileges forms of thinking and acting that give rise to the market forces underpinning current schooling. These kinds of educational reforms are patently antithetical to attempts to foster more equitable and socially just forms of schooling (Sindelar et al. 2006; Ainscow 2010), as they have placed the 'burden of decades of inequity on current students, teachers, and school administrators' (Bass and Gerstl-Pepin 2011:913), and silenced concerns about the ways in which the achievement gap between advantaged and disadvantaged groups of students results from the intersecting effects of social and cultural disadvantage (Mittler 1999; Dyson 2001a; Bass and Gerstl-Pepin 2011).

In analogous ways, educational reforms in the USA have also introduced and cemented a corporate-driven educational system, and disregarded the ways in which the achievement gap between advantaged and disadvantaged groups of students can be attributed to a significant extent to the intersecting effects of social and cultural, as well as educational injustices experienced by these groups of students (Mittler 1999; Dyson 2001a; Bass and Gerstl-Pepin 2011). Notwithstanding ample rhetoric on raising standards, Hursh (2009:166) provides evidence to suggest that, as a result of the NCLB agenda in the USA, 'the achievement gap between white students and students of colour is not narrowing as quickly as pre-NCLB', while its emphasis on test scores has ignored the longstanding cumulative social inequality that accounts for inequitable educational outcomes (Bass and Gerstl-Pepin 2011:909).

In the context of the USA, Giroux (2012) discusses the ways in which another policy initiative, namely the 'Race to the Top' agenda, mandates radical educational reforms which are aligned with ill-defined notions of educational effectiveness. This agenda is characterized as 'a contest that mimics the new more ruthless, market-based ideological agenda at work in removing barriers for the privileged while narrowing the opportunities for the vulnerable, particularly poor minorities of color' (Giroux 2012:41). As a result, the notion of the public good is blatantly denounced in a context that favours individual responsibility and entrepreneurship to meet that individual's own needs. Wider social injustices and income disparities are reproduced within schools in the name of insular notions of educational effectiveness and tarnished understandings of equality and democracy abetted by neoliberal ideologies. In this respect, the individual is called upon to flourish in order to compete and excel in the free market, and schools are regarded as being the preparatory sites towards this end. Markets are presented as being the most rational and democratic way of organizing current schooling, while corporate understandings of social justice and equality of opportunity have ascended and permeated dominant educational discourse. As a result, the educational experiences of disenfranchised groups of students are systematically marred by the bigoted culture of corporate rationality which positions students as 'human resources' rather than 'resourcefully human' (Bottery 2000:59). In this respect, a student's worth is gauged by the extent to which she can contribute to the corporate modes of production, a perspective that is especially problematic for certain groups of students whose 'perfomative worth' (Ball 2009:42) is not compatible with the neoliberal discourse of educational success.

The values of the marketplace are unproblematically transplanted into educational institutions, which valorize students' identities according to the extent to which they fit into the new ontological category of neoliberal 'normality', incarnated in 'docile bodies' (Foucault 1977:138) deemed 'fit' and 'capable' enough to contribute to the labour market. In consequence, schools privilege certain 'student-subjects', while devaluing others who are regarded as being a threat to the unfettered quest for effectiveness, efficiency and value for money in order to raise standards and attainment (Armstrong and Barton 2007). These students, who are perceived as being incapable of meeting such expectations, are usually from ethnic minority groups and deprived socio-economic backgrounds, as well as students designated as having SEN/D, who are routinely relegated to the margins of the educational and social domains (Ball 2009).

Simultaneously, given the neoliberal constructions of the 'ideal student', the characteristics that construe this kind of student within the context of neoliberal educational reforms are used as a normative device against which the 'non-ideal student' is identified and managed (Harwood and Humphry 2008:380). In the light of such a mediocre and individualistic social and educational context, special education and the paraphernalia of the segregating and assimilationist practices associated with it, are used as a neoliberal 'safety net' for schools to single out those students who are considered as being a threat to normative and exam-driven attainment thresholds. These 'filtering' procedures exert disciplinary power on those students who are deemed 'less than docile bodies' in meeting the demands of the global marketplace.

Within this context, educational institutions epitomize a repressive ideological device that rationalizes discriminatory and subjugating practices on the basis of presumed deviations from sacred and quintessential ideals of mental and corporeal supremacy (Watts and Erevelles 2004). As Tomlinson (2012:2) writes, while discussing the paradoxical resurgence of a 'special education industry', despite rhetoric on the necessity to promote an inclusive discourse:

> Yet governments of all political persuasions bowing to a variety of economic, professional and parental vested interests, have acquiesced in the expansion of SEN industry, implicitly conceding its importance in dealing with potential groups, who, while being offered some education and training appear increasingly surplus in 'knowledge economies' and/or are in need of social control from an early age ...

In this respect, current schooling becomes 'a site in which bodies are compared, differentiated, hierarchized, diagnosed; in which judgments of normality and abnormality are made' (Sullivan 2005:29) for the sake of meeting short-term and narrowly conceptualized performance indicators. Under the light of neoliberal governance, current schooling acts as a political site, reproducing social hierarchies with a view to reinforcing and legitimizing the existing relations of power in a way which is commensurate with capitalistic modes of production. As Lakes and Carter (2011:110) write with reference to Western-centric educational systems:

> Classrooms once devoted to the preaching of tolerance, acceptance of difference, and the achievement of civic responsibility are fading out of existence. Our education institutions have become

reterritorialized with business-driven imperatives that legitimize the symbolic capital of entrepreneurial and individualized selves.

At the same time, the pastoral role of schools is undermined, as concerns for developing the 'whole person' (Best 2008) are subordinated to the demands of the market-driven fabrications of successful schools (Ball 2001). The 'terrors of perfomativity' and their mono-dimensional emphasis on producing 'measurable and "improving" outputs and performances' (Ball 2003:222) give rise to 'gaming strategies' (Ross and Berger 2009), which are increasingly adopted by schools in an attempt to marginalize and exclude groups of students who are thought to be a major threat to a school's performance indicators. Simultaneously, daunting epithets of 'named and shamed' schools that are in danger of being placed in 'special measures' – as promulgated by the inspectorate body of the UK (OFSTED) – and of 'useless' teachers, who do not succeed in teaching the 'unteachable' (Smith 2012:41), have become an endemic aspect of the public discourse of education that haunts and demoralizes educational professionals.

In a related fashion, Ross and Berger (2009:470) explore issues of equity and leadership in the USA and discuss the proliferation of 'strategies that involve "gaming" the accountability system'. The practice of 'gaming' generates a number of discreet and inconspicuous practices and procedures in order to marginalize and exclude certain groups of students, who are regarded as a counterforce to a school's quest for educational excellence. The intention is, amongst other things, to prevent these students from adding negative value to a school's performance indicators in relation to minimizing the achievement gap that is attributed to a student's racial, cultural and linguistic characteristics, ability and gender (Ross and Berger 2009; Graham and Jahnukainen 2011). Rather than being the result of individual pathology, the achievement gap between advantaged and disadvantaged students should be attributed to the ways in which the latter are entangled in multiple and overlapping forms of social disadvantage linked to their racial, cultural, linguistic and other characteristics (see Chapter 7).

Practices of 'gaming' also have a pervasive effect on adopting particular teaching strategies and assessment regimes that are more concerned with the outcomes of high-stakes assessments than with an inclusive education reform agenda. Given this perspective, the teachers' pedagogical role is restricted to teaching to the test (Sindelar et al. 2006), whilst the moral and emancipatory dimensions of their professional praxis are silenced (Giroux 2012).

Given the above considerations, it is imperative that the notion of educational change is radically reconceptualized and redefined by shifting the focus on to engaging with a critical re-evaluation and reconsideration of the aims and ideological underpinnings of current schooling that valorize certain 'student-subjects' while devaluing others (e.g. disabled students) (Yuddel 2006). To this end, Francis (2006:197) highlights the imperative to pursue 'a critical analysis and deconstruction in order to make visible the discursive "sharp blades" of delineation and pathologization at work in neo-liberal education policy.... [and] also identifying and illuminating the ways in which neo-liberal policy demonizes vulnerable groups'.

This critical and questioning perspective is embodied in current debates on inclusive education aimed at challenging individual pathology perspectives by means of valorizing students' multiple and overlapping identities that go beyond dominant arbitrations of corporeal, cultural and class ideals. As Giroux (2012:40) so aptly suggests, the real danger of neoliberal education policy and practice is 'political illiteracy that views difference rather than bigotry as a great threat to learning and democracy'. Bigotry is reflected in every aspect of current schooling (Hursh 2007; Giroux 2012), which views learner diversity as a threat to the unfettered quest for effectiveness, efficiency and value for money: principles that are starkly incompatible with recognizing difference as an endemic and valuable aspect of human experience.

Educational reforms and neoliberal understandings of inclusion

As alluded to earlier, corporate-driven current schooling advances Western-centric and neoliberal constructions of the 'ideal student'. Concomitantly, this process evokes the constitution of the 'non-ideal' students (Harwood and Humphrey 2008:371), who are plagued by their alleged individual, social and cultural pathology. At the same time, concerns about human rights, social justice, collegiality and the common good have been substituted by the ideologies of the global economy embodied in the quest for competiveness, profitability and increased productivity (Hursh and Henderson 2011). This ideological *mélange* has inevitably altered the purpose of education and, as a result, the 'learning of meanings' has been transformed into the 'learning of earnings' (Zajda 2011:144). As the previous section has shown, the 'learning of earnings' has reduced education to a technical issue of data-driven quality indicators that measure specific aspects of educational excellence and yield superficial and short-term results.

Rather than questioning whose values and interests shape dominant educational discourses that oppress and marginalize certain groups of students (McLaren 1998), the emphasis is mono-dimensionally placed on students' alleged individual and family pathology. Graham (2008:2) provides an insightful analysis of the socially mediated ways in which schools construct 'disorderly objects' which are predominantly the result of 'disorderly social conditions'. As she explains:

> ….'social construction' comes to be read simplistically as: the disorders of society create disorders in our children. Whether our children really have disorders…, what is and who decides what constitutes a disorder…, and whose interests 'disordered-ness' serves…are arguments that remain, on the whole, isolated to the academy and to increasingly marginalised fields within it.
>
> (Graham 2008:2)

By isolating learning from its wider social and cultural context, the 'achievement gap' between privileged and vulnerable students is unproblematically presented as being the result of varied bodily, mental and psychological deficits, without paying due attention to the social, curricular and instructional injustices (Westwood 2001; Dyson and Kozleski 2008) experienced by disenfranchised groups of students, who are entangled in overlapping forms of social and educational disadvantage (Artiles et al. 2006; DCSF 2009a; Bringhouse 2010) (see chapters 7 and 8).

Neoliberal versions of inclusion are aligned with the standards agenda abetted by the ascendancy of market-based imperatives (Dyson 2001, 2005). Roulstone and Prideaux (2008) posit that inclusive educational policies are occasionally informed by the assumption that disabled students, as well as other disenfranchised groups of students, can be included insofar as this is compatible with school efficiency indicators. Under the constraints of neo-special education discourse, the educative process has thus become a normal-izing and 'filtering' device with the aim of producing approximations of the 'ideal student' favoured by the neoliberal discourse (Dyson 2005) while marginalizing and singling out the 'non-ideal' student. The curriculum and pedagogy are tailor-made for the 'able, pro-ductive, skilled, accountable individuals, who are ready and willing to lead developments within the classroom' (Goodley 2007:321), while concerns about the 'socially toxic' conditions (Watts and Erevelles 2004:290) and educational inequalities (Westwood 2001) experienced by students who are perceived to deviate from 'the quintessential construction of the modernist, unitary, humanistic subject' (Goodley 2007:321) are blatantly ignored. What prevails is a damaging preoccupation with students' alleged pathology, while there is no interest in exploring the host of power imbalances and dis-criminatory regimes underpinning dominant educational discourse (Liasidou 2012b).

In this way, the notion of social justice is reconceptualized and redefined in terms of a mediocre perspective (Artiles et al. 2006) whereby 'equity is no longer a value in its own right within pol-icy' (Ball 2009:191), as it becomes an appendage to the economy. As Rizvi and Lingard (1996:15) write, 'social justice is no longer "seen as linked to past group oppression and disadvantage" judged histor-ically, but represented simply as a matter of guaranteeing individual choice under the conditions of a "free market" ' (cited in Artiles et al. 2006:263). Even in countries such as Norway, which traditionally have a strong focus on social democratic ideals, recent education policy reforms promote neoliberal versions of inclusive schooling through an increased emphasis on competencies, differences and individualization. As Arnesen (2011:196) writes:

> Traditionally, the Norwegian version of inclusion has been built around the notion of social community (*fellesskap*), and a strong commitment towards including 'all' children in mainstream schools. These values are less pronounced in recent reforms. Despite rhetoric on inclusion in policy documents, it seems that there has been a turn away from sensitivity towards diversity and

individualised teaching within a social community towards teaching the individual (Carlgren et al. 2006). 'The competent child' is defined in political texts as the motivated child, the self-governing child, the 'child with stamina' with responsibility for his or her own learning.

While recent policy developments in Norway prioritize concerns about enhancing 'entrepreneurship, reading, creative learning, mathematics, natural science and technology, participation for language minorities, foreign languages and competence for development', the notion of inclusion is blatantly ignored (Arnesen 2011:197). Even though there is some reference to the necessity of enhancing participation for language minorities, students designated as having SEN/D are excluded from official rhetoric on difference and diversity. As Arnesen (2011:197) writes: 'Inclusive education is not implicitly or explicitly prioritised in general policy texts, and neither are the children and young people who are defined as "special" or at risk of falling outside the mainstream school.'

The question of educational placement and participation for disabled students in mainstream settings is sometimes considered as being irrelevant, provided that these students have access to the most appropriate common enterprises of learning, irrespective of where these enterprises are located in either special or mainstream schools (e.g. Farrell 2009; Warnock 2005, 2010). Inclusion is thus equated with attempts to engage hitherto disaffected groups of students in the learning process with the aim of rendering them more productive in terms of the demands of the global economy. As Warnock (2005:36) has forcefully asserted in her anti-inclusionist pamphlet, which was published by the Philosophy of Education Society of Great Britain in 2005 and which stirred heated debate due to the unsubstantiated and naïve nature of her claims: 'It is the right to learn that we must defend, not the right to learn in the same environment.'

By subscribing to this kind of thinking, the validity and effectiveness of special education thinking and practice are acclaimed and rationalized. The neoliberal constructions of inclusion consolidate and perpetuate the notion of 'special educational needs' and the paraphernalia of individual pathology perspectives associated with it, while ignoring the ways in which 'personal troubles' are intertwined with, rest upon and emanate from 'public issues' (Mills 1967). Special education is thus skilfully presented as being part of an inclusive reform agenda, while inclusion becomes a policy veneer to disguise the regeneration and consolidation of the status quo in special educational that lead us to what Dyson (2001) has termed 'inclusion backlash'.

At the same time, neoliberal meanings of social justice, whereby the idea of 'fairness' is defined 'as giving people what they deserve, a "fair reward for talent and effort"' (Smith 2012:5), are manifested in current educational initiatives to enable the most outstanding schools to become more autonomous in terms of their admissions policies and the curriculum, as well as teachers' pay and conditions (Smith 2012). The implications of these anticipated changes are not difficult to envisage, along with their impact on vulnerable groups of students and teachers' professionalism. As we have seen, schooling has been increasingly transformed into a calibration and arbitration site of 'identifying' and 'singling out' those students who are deemed incapable of contributing to the neoliberal demands and expectations of the global economy (Harwood and Humphrey 2008; Lakes and Carter 2011).

In terms of teachers' pay and conditions, it is proposed that payments should be commensurate with educational outcomes, something that will inadvertently make teachers reluctant to teach vulnerable groups of students (Hursh and Henderson 2011). Giroux (2012:43) provides virulent criticism on similar policy initiatives, informed by the payment by results caveat that 'emphasize[s] market driven notions of competition and choice, putting teachers against each other through the use of monetary rewards for teachers and students who meet allegedly objective, performance-based goals.' Interestingly, tenure rules in relation to teaching have also been questioned by a judge in California recently, on the grounds that tenure rules are accountable for failing to sack bad teachers who, allegedly, harm poor students and infringe the state's constitution. It is suggested that an ineffective teacher has a 1 in 125,000 chance each year of being dismissed for incompetence. Even though teachers' unions fiercely opposed and criticized this legal verdict, the US education secretary endorsed it (*The Economist* 14 June 2014).

The ascendancy of this kind of punitive and demoralizing culture has significantly undermined teachers' job satisfaction and professional autonomy, while forcing many teachers to leave the profession

(Hargreaves and Shirley 2012). The 2012 MetLife Survey of the American Teacher (cited in Hargreaves and Shirley 2012) documents that teachers' professional satisfactions has markedly declined, while 29 per cent of teachers consider leaving the profession. As Hargreaves and Shirley (2012:3) note, the 'modal (most commonly occurring) number of years experience in teaching in the United States is now just one year'!

Under these circumstances, and while the educative role of schooling is transformed into a selective process of singling out those students who are considered as a counterforce to the quest for quantifiable measures of effectiveness, teachers have reportedly become apprehensive about the prospect of having disabled as well as other vulnerable groups of students in their classrooms, a phenomenon that is expected to become even more prominent if the payment by results caveat gains more momentum. The following quote is indicative of the reasons why a teacher is reluctant to teach particular students:

> If my job depends on their test scores … I don't want those kids. I do because I am a teacher and went into teaching to help kids. But if my job depends on it … my car payments depend on it … my apartment payment depends on it … I don't want those kids ….
> (Koelpin 2006:141 cited in Dudley-Marling and Baker 2012:14)

The reductionist pedagogy advocated by corporate-driven models of education, along with its pernicious effects on teachers' morale and disabled students' education, needs to be substituted by a critical pedagogical approach to questioning and challenging the ways in which neoliberal templates of normality undermine the educative and democratic role of current schooling. What is urgently needed, therefore, is to instigate a paradigm shift from a reductionist pedagogy to an interdisciplinary analytical approach to questioning individual pathology perspectives that subjugate groups of students on the grounds of their alleged deviations from neoliberal constructions of the 'ideal student' (Harwood and Humphrey 2008:380). This interdisciplinary analytical approach denounces theoretical dogmatism and conceptual monopolies, which generate and sustain neoliberal templates of normality and negative connotations of difference, and seeks to challenge the ideological orthodoxies and institutional dynamics that oppress and marginalize certain groups of students. What is fundamentally needed is to question the arbitrary fabrications of the 'ideal student' that isolate students' identities from their socio-cultural context and disregard the host of injustices that impact upon students' lives and educational trajectories (Liasidou 2013a).

The next chapter discusses the ways in which inclusive education can provide this interdisciplinary analytical approach to challenging the domination of neoliberal discourse in constructing students' identities and determining the aims of current schooling. Inclusion embodies new kinds of 'meta-governance' (Woods 2011), which prioritize alternative models of educational provision and accountability regimes to facilitate the generation and enactment of socially just, participatory and equitable forms of schooling. Conceptualized as a human rights and social justice issue, inclusion constitutes the political, ethical and pedagogical response to the pathologizing and medicalizing perspectives that disempower groups of students on the basis of their alleged deviations from corporeal, class and ethnic ideals favoured by modernist and neoliberal assumptions of normality (Campbell 2008, 2009). Inclusive education is, therefore, discussed as a way of reaffirming the imperative need to proceed to a radical overhaul of existing educational regimes, in order to advance new forms of being, thinking and acting to foster participatory, socially just and democratic communities for learner diversity (Artiles et al. 2006; Liasidou 2013a).

While acknowledging the vast and multifaceted challenges endemic in its pursuit, inclusion should be seen as an ethical and political project that involves 'exercising the desire for something other than the status quo' (Allan 2005:293), with a view to challenging unequal power relations and discriminatory regimes that emanate from the ways in which the market-based ideals of current schooling valorize certain student subjects while devaluing others (Youddel 2006). This process necessitates commitment, vision and action, as well as an informed recognition of the perennial character of the struggles 'to create spaces for new knowledge and forms of action to emerge' (Barton 2001:1), so as to foster 'emancipatory' and 'potentiating' learning communities for all (Claxton and Carr 2004; Goodley 2007).

Conclusions

Educational reforms during the last few years have been characterized by market-based considerations allegedly intended to raise standards and to provide enhanced learning opportunities for all. The hegemony of neoliberal ideologies has created marginal student subjects, whose educational worth has been calibrated in light of narrow performance indicators and market-driven audit procedures. Schools have increasingly become unwelcoming places for a sizable number of students, who are deemed incapable of contributing to the demands of the educational marketplace. The curriculum and pedagogy have been geared to the needs of the 'ideal student' (Harwood and Humphry 2008), while issues of class and culture as well as disability frequently have been excluded from the dominant pedagogical discourse (Giroux 2012).

This chapter has explored the ways in which the crisis of capitalism necessitates questioning, re-evaluating and repositioning the market-based ideals underpinning current schooling. The financial turmoil has exposed the bankruptcy of capitalism and, concomitantly, contributed to the resurgence of the 'discourse around values' that necessitates a thorough revaluation of the underlying values and structure of society. While concurring with the view that 'the most radical organisational reconfigurations and social innovations will tend to occur during a post-crisis recession' (Hartley 2012:789), the chapter has articulated the necessity to re-evaluate the nature of current schooling in order to advance alternative conceptualizations of education that are informed by values-based considerations.

Evocations of 'a discourse around values' need a name, along with a conceptual and pedagogical framework, so that they transcend rhetorical exhortations and effect transformative changes to the existing forms of schooling which mimic neoliberal arrangements and conditions of the free market. Branson (2010:107) has rightly suggested that '60 years of leading educational change has been largely ineffective', partly owing to the lack of 'a new paradigm, a new strategy, and a new way to see how to bring about long lasting and effective change'. Having said that, he concludes by advancing the view that '[w]e desperately need a new paradigm' as 'a compelling alternative to the status quo'. Arguably, inclusion embodies and is embodied in a new epistemological and pedagogical paradigm in order to precipitate transformative change. Fostering inclusive policies and practices can provide conceptual and practical 'counter-narratives' (Thomas 1999), which acclaim the emancipatory potential of pedagogy in mobilizing democratic and socially just reforms. The next chapter is given over to exploring the ways in which the quest for inclusion is primarily a quest for transformative change so as to challenge a myriad of ideological and structural impediments that undermine the process of change. In order to understand this conceptual link, it is imperative to disentangle the hybrid nature of inclusion and the ways in which such inclusion is occasionally used as a veneer to reinforce rather than to challenge the status quo in special education.

3
Inclusive Education Policymaking and the Question of Change

Introduction

This chapter is concerned with exploring the notion of inclusive education, along with the various discourses that surround it, in order to forge and exemplify links with the notion of educational change, while providing an enhanced understanding of the ideological and institutional preconditions of an inclusive education reform agenda. While alluding to the interconnectedness and reciprocity of the two notions, Norwich (2010) locates some of the debates, problems and dilemmas pertaining to inclusive education within the context of educational change. Hence, the chapter concentrates on exploring the two notions and suggests that inclusion cannot be achieved unless there is radical educational and social reform based on a human rights and social justice approach to disability and difference.

The notion of change is a ubiquitous concept that underpins all aspects of social domains and relations. The dynamic nature of the social world is manifested in the myriad of changes that are constantly effected on practices, processes and human relations. The field of education does not constitute an exception as it both mirrors and embodies wider societal changes. The complexity and multiplicity of the process of change is evidenced in attempts to promote a rights-based approach to human relations and conditions within the context of inclusion (Kenworthy and Whittaker 2000; Artiles et al. 2006; United Nations 2008; Rioux 2010). This process has been very appositely characterized by Barton (1997:232) as being 'a difficult and disturbing task', which requires a profusion of conceptual and practical impediments to be overcome so as to achieve and sustain transformative change.

As already discussed in Chapter 1, the influence and legitimacy of 'marketizing meta-governance' (Woods 2011) has come to an impasse, in part because of the patent bankruptcy of capitalistic modes of production to regulate social and economic relations. According to Giroux (2012:41), the circumstances of the current fiscal crisis reaffirm the fundamental importance of questioning the purpose of public schooling that subordinates, if not undermines, democratic goals 'by an emphasis on policies, values and social practices that mimic the market-driven values of the existing mode of casino capitalism' (Giroux 2012:41).

The global economic crisis necessitates transcending political inertia and complacency by prioritizing new forms of 'meta-governance' with a view to re-evaluating and re-assigning new meanings to social conditions and relations. As a result of this broader crisis, Woods (2011:42) posits that educational reforms should be aligned with 'democratic entrepreneurialism' that is not only focused on effective and creative change, but extends to include issues of meaningful participation, democratic relations and socially just ways of pedagogical thinking and acting. To this end, Giroux (2012:14) suggests that 'students should be educated for democratic citizenship, engaged in debates about public values and ethics, and taught the knowledge and skills necessary to support economic opportunity for all instead of just a few.'

In view of the above considerations, the process of educational change should be radically reconceptualized and redefined so as to align it with more democratic and critical approaches to current schooling. That said, Hargreaves and Shirley (2009) provide an insightful analysis of the 'fourth way' approach to bringing about transformative change. In stark contrast to the 'third way' approach, which has largely become an appendage of the market by attempting to bring together social democratic and free market ideals in education (Dyson 2005; Ball 2009), the 'fourth way' approach envisages bringing about change.

> through democracy and professionalism rather than bureaucracy and the market. It transfers trust and confidence back from

the discredited free market of competition amongst schools and reinvests them in the expertise of highly trained and actively trusted professionals. At the same time, it reduces political bureaucracy while energizing public democracy.

(Hargreaves and Shirley 2009:72)

The six dimensions of purpose and partnership advocated by the 'fourth way approach' are closely aligned with the axioms of an inclusive education reform agenda, which envisages the radical democratization of education policy as a response to the encroachment of market-based ideologies within educational domains. The process of democratization of education policy includes:

Genuine community participation and democratic decision making; looking for ways to eradicate, avoid or mitigate repressive pressures, to work towards social justice, and to form spaces where authentic freedom can be exercised; encouraging multiple communication flows which create cultures of openness and transparency; and exploring innovative ways in which the personal and the social can be rescued from being appendage to the market.

(Woods 2011:42)

The above considerations chime with community understandings of inclusion, which are at the core of a human rights and social justice approach to difference and diversity. The quest for inclusion necessitates creating participatory communities that are characterized by the values of collegiality, equality of opportunity and democratic decision-making. Axiomatically, segregated forms of provision violate disabled students' rights to participate in non-discriminatory, socially just and quality forms of educational provision on an equal basis with their non-disabled peers. As Naraian (2011:965) puts it:

Regardless of such diversity of meaning, an important construct with which inclusive education has come to be strongly affiliated is the notion of *community*. The successful participation of students with disabilities in a general education classroom is premised on the creation of classroom communities that can nurture the qualities of equity and care.

Given the definitional plurality of inclusion, this chapter is concerned with discussing the idea of inclusive education, along with the various discourses that surround it, in order to forge and exemplify links with the notion of change with a view to fostering socially just and democratic learning communities. To this end, the analysis concentrates on exploring the intricately interlinked nature of the two notions and suggests that inclusion cannot be achieved unless there is radical educational and social reform based on a human rights approach to difference and diversity.

The politics of inclusion and the notion of change

Being an essentially political act, inclusive education policymaking is contingent on a dynamic and intricately intertwined discursive framework within which the 'will to power' is reconfigured as the 'will to truth' (Foucault 1984). Powerful social agents such as policymakers and other professionals vie to impose their own 'will to truth' according to their beliefs and vested interests (Fulcher 1999). That said, the policymaking process is characterized by 'a discursive assemblage of contesting and unequal power relations subjected to incessant reconfiguration and reconstitution' (Liasidou 2009:108). Given the complexity and the ideological multiplicity of the policymaking process, fostering greater inclusive policies and practices entails dissecting and establishing relations, structures and interactions which impinge upon this process (Berkhout and Wielemas 1999). Transformative change cannot be achieved unless we foreground and challenge the dynamic and reciprocally related web within which inclusive policies are formulated and disseminated (Liasidou 2012a).

The dominant policy landscapes are in constant flux, as different ideological and discursive dynamics emerge and influence the policymaking process and the discursive struggles associated with it in multiple and unanticipated ways. The interplay amongst practices, policies and actors should become the focal point of social analysis (Ball 2009, 2012). Notwithstanding the fact that the quest for inclusion is a rather elusive and never-ending process, inclusive education is a feasible pursuit, provided that there is ideological and institutional convergence towards this end. Central to the process of transformative change is the notion of human agency that is embodied in the policymakers' and educational practitioners' role in policy constitution and implementation.

Even though human agency is a pivotal aspect of the process of change, nevertheless, it is largely influenced, albeit not determined, by structural conditions and processes. The theory of structuration, articulated by Giddens (1986) and exemplified in the work of Archer (1982), eschews dichotomous considerations that prioritize structural conditions over political agency and vice versa, and presents an integrated account depicting the interplay between action and institutional and structural conditions. Priestley and Miller (2012) draw on the work of Archer (1988) to provide a succinct theorization of the process of educational change with reference to policy changes within a particular socio-political system. The process of change is articulated as a multifaceted phenomenon that is contingent on three dynamically interwoven constitutive elements underpinning a given social situation, namely, culture, structure and agency. The distinctiveness of Archer's work, in relation to Giddens' structuration theory of articulating the reciprocal and interactive relationship of agency and structure in the process of change, lies at the discernible line that is drawn amongst the various elements, so as to provide a more nuanced analysis of the constituent role of each element during particular instances of the process of change. This dynamic and interactive cycle of the changing process can result in three typical outcomes that are exemplified as follows: (a) 'morphogenesis' to denote instances where the old idea is substituted by the new one; (b) 'morphostasis' when old ideas are maintained and the new ones are rejected; and (c) the blurring of new and old ideas thereby leading to a hybrid social situation where the old ideas co-exist with the new ones in a paradoxical discursive assemblage, whilst there is, concomitantly, some kind of morphogenesis. The three typologies can explain different facets of the process and nature of change within the context of inclusion.

Real change in terms of a rights-based approach to inclusion requires 'morphogenesis' that infers a radical subversion of the special education status quo. Inclusion constitutes a paradigm shift from special education and the assimilationist integrative practices associated with it (Thomas and Loxley 2007; Lloyd 2008). The process of 'morphogenesis' should be directed to all constituent elements, namely, structure, culture and agency. However, given the contentious nature of the notion of inclusion and the multiplicity of educational arrangements that purport to be 'inclusive', all typologies can be applied in explaining current versions of inclusion.

It is, for instance, frequently the case that special education and segregated forms of provision are presented as being part of the inclusion agenda, thereby manifesting instances of 'morphostasis'. At other times, vestiges of special educational thinking and practice are regenerated and reconfigured under the banner of inclusion and advance hybrid forms of inclusion whereby old and new ideas and practices are conflated in hybrid forms of inclusive discourses (Liasidou 2012), especially under the governance of neoliberal imperatives as discussed in Chapter 1.

The paradoxical co-existence of hybrid discourses of inclusion can potentially lead to the propagation of inconspicuous forms of exclusion, despite laudable rhetoric on the necessity to promote inclusion. For instance, Powel (2011) draws on data from Germany and the USA to point to the paradoxical increase of segregated forms of provision, notwithstanding policy proclamations advocating the realization of an inclusive discourse. As he writes:

> Despite the plethora of reform efforts to implement inclusive education the group of students participating in traditional special education settings in both countries have grown and continues to increase.
>
> (Powell 2011:271)

The same phenomenon was reported in the UK context. Croll and Moses (2003) report on data from a number of local authorities, which were allegedly committed to foster the 'fullest' possible inclusion, to highlight the increase in the number of students in segregated forms of provision. More recent research evidence from a two-year enquiry initiated by the Children's Commissioner into illegal exclusions in UK schools suggest that a great percentage of children designated as having SEN/D are currently illegally excluded from their schools (Children's Commissioner 2013). These children have been reportedly sent home for trivial reasons; for instance, because the specialist teacher was not available. Illegal exclusions do not only affect disabled students but also a large percentage of other students, who are arbitrarily excluded from the school premises, sometimes for extended periods of time, even in cases when children are thought to have 'the wrong haircut' (e.g. boys with long hair). The Children's Commissioner characterizes these illegal exclusions as a 'source of shame to the education system' and suggests that there should be legal sanctions for schools which insist on wrongdoing (Children's Commissioner 2013). Exclusion also acts in surreptitious and seemingly more legal ways by means of allocating students 'into "streams", "tracks", "sets", and so on in terms of their performance. These placements and categorical ascriptions may function as "special classes" without the official label of "special class"' (Armstrong et al. 2010:110). As it has been suggested:

> practices that are nominated as being 'inclusive' are in essence practices within which a plethora of inconspicuous forms of exclusion are operating. These practices restrict inclusion to its spatial dimension by adopting assimilationist perspectives and compensatory measures of support in order to 'normalize' certain individuals through expert intervention and remedy, thereby promoting 'internal' exclusive practices to take place in terms of streaming or grouping of pupils.
>
> (Liasidou 2012a:112)

Inclusive education and the question of change

Given the ways in which concerns about equity and social justice are currently subsumed within economic considerations (Ball 2009), and while experiencing the aftermath of a global fiscal crisis, Bass and Gerstl-Pepin (2011) take the view that the bail-out initiatives undertaken by governments to rescue financial institutions should not be limited to the latter, but rather:

> Just as the government stepped in to 'bail out' financial institutions, the government should recognize the failure of states in creating equity in education, and likewise, effectively bail them out.
>
> (Bass and Gerstl-Pepin 2011:923)

Arguably, a crucial element of this bail-out process is recognizing the necessity of fostering more inclusive forms of pedagogical thinking and acting in order to re-evaluate and reposition the role of education. As Ball (2007:191) has put it:

> We need to struggle to think differently about education policy before it is too late. We need to move beyond the tyrannies of improvement, efficiency and standards, to recover a language of and for education articulated in terms of ethics, moral obligations and values.

As already discussed in Chapter 1, the transformative process necessitates cultivating a 'discourse around values' (Woods 2011:3), with a view to creating global citizens, who valorize human diversity as a means of achieving individual and collective self-actualization. It is axiomatic that 'inclusive schooling is a precondition of democratic education' (Slee 2010:161), hence, it should be prioritized in debates and policy developments concerned with eliminating social injustice. As Barton (1997:235) writes, inclusive education is concerned with developing 'a vision of democracy through difference'. This process involves embracing and celebrating learner diversity on the grounds of various markers of difference, and challenging the multiple and intersecting sources of social and educational disadvantage that render certain groups of students vulnerable, and put them at great risk of educational failure (Ainscow et al. 2006).

The realization of inclusion is, however, an arduous task fraught with challenges, ambiguities, resistance and impediments. The process of change is both complex and contested; hence, the quest for inclusion is a painstaking endeavour that cannot be reduced to theoretical blueprints and implementation recipes. As already pointed out, this can be partly attributed to the fact that there is a terminological messiness and conceptual opacity around the notion of inclusion, for it can be understood and enacted in varied ways. The conceptual *mélange* around inclusion is multifaceted and contradictory, something that is reflected and embodied in the ways in which an inclusive reform agenda is envisaged and enacted. Occasionally, the proposed reformist agendas pertaining to inclusion merely corroborate the special education status quo in inconspicuous yet powerful ways. Thus, in spite of the fact that the historical isolation and institutionalization of disabled students has been challenged to a considerable extent, discriminatory and segregating practices are still present in covert yet pervasive ways. Harwood (2010) uses the metaphor of 'mobile asylums', which exclude, marginalize and isolate certain students, who are considered as a threat to the normal functioning of modern schooling. The metaphor of 'mobile asylums' denotes the ways in which disciplinary power is not only exerted through the processes of institutionalization and incarceration, but is also surreptitiously exerted through a number of assimilationist and compensatory measures of support which emerge under the banner of inclusion (Lloyd 2008). Inclusion might thus operate within a system of concomitant exclusion, thereby creating a hybrid context in which discourses of inclusion/exclusion co-exist in a paradoxical discursive assemblage that further compounds the process of transformative change. As Armstrong et al. (2010:112) state: 'The same school that removes barriers or provides additional support to facilitate the participation of some students adhering to existing anti-discrimination disability may operate in other ways that create student identities that lead to exclusion.'

Understanding inclusion and exclusion

Inclusion is informed by a variety of divergent and occasionally contradictory discourses with a multiplicity of meanings and ideological connotations, which are occasionally rhetorically embellished in order to disguise exclusionary attitudes, process and practices (Armstrong 1999). Given the 'discursive multiplicity' of the notion (Taylor 2004), the ensuing institutional arrangements have ranged from segregating placements to more inclusive arrangements. Inclusion has been rightly characterized as 'an inherently troubled and troubling educational and social project' (Slee 2010:161). As we have seen, it has taken many configurations ranging from full inclusive arrangements to 'exclusionary' ones, whereby traditional special educational practices have been inconspicuously regenerated and reconfigured within current schooling. As discussed in the previous section, a major cause for concern is the subtle ways in which the exclusion of students designated as having SEN/D has been variously masqueraded under the banner of inclusion. Thus, even though inclusion is rhetorically applauded, there is considerable scepticism around the interpretation of the concept and the optimal educational arrangements that can effectively meet the needs of all children (Farrell 2009; Norwich 2010; Warnock 2010).

As Ainscow and Miles (2009) suggest, there are two 'superordinate' factors that can foster greater inclusive policies and practices if they are pursued in tandem. One of these factors concerns the necessity of clarifying the definition of inclusion so as to devise a conceptual and action-oriented framework for change. In a similar vein, Hargreaves and Shirley (2012:21) point out that: 'Knowing what to change comes before knowing how to change'. Hence, the 'semantic multiplicity' of inclusion, which is occasionally used as a rhetorical facade to disguise exclusionary and discriminatory practices, needs to be critically analysed and deconstructed so as to provide an informed understanding of the conceptual and practical dimensions of an authentic and rights-based inclusive education reform agenda. Such an informed understanding involves a comprehensive knowledge base with regard to the ethical and theoretical as well as the political underpinnings of inclusion (Mills and Lingard 2007). Consequently, understanding the political nature of inclusion and clarifying its political intent are crucial aspects of mobilizing the desirable kind of transformative change envisaged by the proponents of a human rights approach to disability and difference (Barton 1993; Rioux 2010).

The definitional and conceptual clarification of inclusion, however, is not a simplistic and straightforward endeavour because inclusion also needs to be understood in relation to exclusion. Slee (2011:11) takes the view that 'defining inclusion might be a distraction' and the real challenge lies at the necessity to 'detect, understand and dismantle exclusion as it presents itself in education'. This is particularly important when it is apparent that 'much of the activity advanced in the name of inclusive education has exclusionary effects'. Concerns about inclusion presuppose the existence of exclusion, the elimination of which necessitates a perennial critical engagement with an assemblage of micro- and macro-dynamics that sustain and perpetuate a number of special educational imperatives, disguised under the banner of inclusion. As Graham and Slee (2008:85) point out, it is imperative to understand the 'conjoined nature of inclusion and exclusion', while interrogating 'the normative assumptions that lead us to think we can even talk of "including"'.

At the same time, a definitional clarification of inclusion necessitates adopting a cross-cultural approach to understanding its culturally and socially mediated character. The globalizing discourse of inclusion involves a critical discussion and analysis of the hetero-geneity and idiosyncrasy of diverse socio-political contexts, especially in countries of the South, where a great percentage of students are denied access to education. A cross-cultural approach to exploring the notion of inclusion is necessary in order to 'interrogate the ways that the "cultural politics" of inclusive education policymaking are played out, contested and manifested within distinct socio-political contexts' (Liasidou 2012a:137).

Inclusive education as a human rights issue

The process of educational change within the context of inclusion should be understood as being a highly political pursuit that goes beyond procedural and organizational considerations, which can be linked to school effectiveness research (Dyson 1999; Ainscow 2005b). This process involves addressing questions of power implicated in the attempts to deal with a dynamic network of intertwined and reciprocal related ideological and structural elements (Power 1992) that undermine the quest for transformative change. This kind of change entails mobilizing political action, in order to challenge the status quo and to precipitate transformative changes towards more equitable and just forms of educational provision for learner diver-sity (Choules 2007; Evans 2007). As Howes et al. (2009:31, 32) write: '... inclusion involves a discussion of values. We are drawn to a prin-cipled definition of inclusion, and a view that inclusion necessarily involves working out those principles in action'.

Inclusive education epitomizes a values-based approach to school-ing; it is concerned with the education we value and the society we envisage creating, while advancing new conceptualizations of stu-dents' diversity, abilities, learning, emotional development, human rights, citizenship and social justice (Barton 1993; Artiles et al. 2006; Wedell 2008; Rayner 2009). A values-based approach to human rela-tions and conditions (Armstrong and Barton 2007:6) can provide theoretical and practical tools in order to acclaim the emancipatory potential of pedagogy in instigating socially just reforms.

Exemplified as a human rights and moral issue, inclusion is based on a democratic approach to social conditions and relations, with a view to redressing the power imbalances and social hierarchies that subjugate vulnerable groups of students (Roaf and Bines 1989; Rioux

2002; Cigman 2006). To that end, an inclusive education reform agenda is essentially an endless pursuit of fostering more socially just and equitable ways of pedagogical thinking and acting, with the aim of creating schools and societies that valorize and respect human diversity. Creating an inclusive education system is the precursor for achieving an inclusive society whereby all individuals realize 'their social, political and civil rights of citizenship' in non-discriminatory and democratic ways (Barton 1997:235).

Notwithstanding the fact that the above considerations are not new, as they are at the heart of critical pedagogy with which inclusion shares close theoretical affinities (Liasidou 2012b), the distinctiveness of the debates in the context of inclusion lies in the pronounced emphasis placed on individuals with SEN/D. This group of individuals has been ignored to a significant extent in critical pedagogy's theorizations about the oppressive effects of pedagogy on marginalized and disenfranchised groups of students (see Chapter 8).

Fostering inclusive cultures and pedagogies necessitates ideological transformation of longstanding individual pathology regimes that essentialize difference and diversity on the grounds of disability. Inclusion subscribes to new theorizations of disability whereby the latter is redefined as a multifaceted form of social oppression. These new theorizations of disability transcend fixed and essentialist understandings of 'disabled identities' (Thomas 1999), and foreground 'situational' or 'intersectional' understandings of the self (Makkonen 2002:18), which highlight the ways in which disabled students identities are fluid, multifaceted and constantly re-authored and reframed according to emerging and changing socio-political conditions and exigencies. Cole (2009:175) criticizes psychologists and other psy-complex professionals who are inclined 'to see certain identities as totalizing and determinative, as trumping all others' thereby ignoring the fluid and intricately complex nature of people's identities, whose formation and (re)formation depends on an interactive web of exogenous dynamics. In this respect, the individual pathology perspective and the paraphernalia of its assimilationist and normalizing practices are substituted by an institutional pathology perspective centred upon initiating radical and sustainable educational reforms (Pather 2007; Eckins and Grimes 2009) as well as challenging a host of power inequities and discriminatory regimes that create subordinated subjectivities.

In view of the above considerations, the aim of inclusive education reforms is to achieve revolutionary pedagogical and curricula changes to accommodate students' diverse needs. Albeit crucially important, this dimension of change is very restricted because it fails to identify and challenge power inequities and discriminatory regimes that construct subordinate human identities. Thus, notwithstanding the imperative need to effect radical pedagogical and curricula changes in order to meet learner diversity on the basis of disability (Norwich and Lewis 2001; Howley and Rose 2007; Mitchell 2008), it is equally important to focus on issues of power, domination and oppression (Johnson 2004; Knoll 2009) so as to redress inequalities and discriminatory regimes that adversely affect the lives and educational trajectories of disenfranchised individuals.

Hence, it is crucial that, apart from dealing with the bureaucratic and technical issues of current schooling (Riehl 2000), the emphasis should also be placed on ethical and critical dimensions of the attempts to foster greater inclusive policies and practices (Riehl 2000; Allan 2005; Lingard and Mills 2007). For instance, it has been suggested that universally designed pedagogies are incomplete unless supplemented by critical perspectives and considerations linked to concerns about subverting asymmetrical power interplays and hierarchical social relations that impact upon accessibility issues.

The implementation of universal design for learning principles (UDL) has concentrated on the introduction of curricula (Doyle and Robson 2002) and teaching methods (Thousand et al. 2007; Burgstahler 2012) that improve teaching and learning, and facilitate educational accessibility on the basis of ability, race/ethnicity and other markers of difference, without the need to introduce specialist interventions and accommodations (such as special educational needs accommodations) (Thousand et al. 2007). The ideas of UDL originated in the field of architecture and were developed by the Center for Applied Special Technology (CAST) in the USA (Burgstahler and Cory 2008) with a view to designing universally accessible environments and minimizing the necessity of providing specialized interventions and compensatory measures of support (Rose and Meyer 2002; Burgstahler and Cory 2008).

Despite the immense importance attributed to UDL in creating accessible learning environments for all, a mono-dimensional emphasis on accessibility ignores issues of difference and inequality in order to facilitate the empowerment of marginalized groups of students (Burbules and Berk 1999). Crucially, the emphasis should be concomitantly placed on subverting discriminatory conditions and disabling practices that oppress and marginalize disenfranchised groups of students. This necessitates questioning and challenging a profusion of structural and systemic contextual dynamics which create power inequities and exclusionary practices for a great percentage of the student population, with a view to achieving 'socially just change' (Hattam et al. 2009:304) and promoting a fair distribution of and accessibility to educational resources for learner diversity. As Knoll (2009:124) succinctly states:

> To apply only universal design or individual accommodation would either leave gaping holes in access to academia and courses, by not seeing and addressing the intersecting dilemmas of privilege and oppression within the disability experience; conversely, it could situate the problem and solution as residing in individual bodies and environments, thereby reinforcing the false notion that disability is an individual problem (rather than a socially created barrier that can be, and often is, interconnected with additional forms of privilege and oppression).

Changes should thus extend beyond institutional modifications to include challenging the power imbalances and hierarchical social relations experienced by disenfranchised groups of students on the basis of their corporeal, racial, linguistic and other characteristics. The construction of 'the slow learner' or 'disabled child' is a highly political phenomenon that needs to be deconstructed, questioned and ultimately challenged. As Armstrong et al. (2010:109) have expressed in relation to the steady increase of special education identification and referral numbers:

> ... there is evidence that increasing numbers of students are being identified as having 'special educational needs' in many systems. Whether this is due to increased awareness, improved identification and assessment procedures, and the introduction of legislation that provides support, or is a result of schools trying to manage through special education practices students that do not

'fit' in terms of their academic and/or behaviour performance is a contested issue.

Political activism in favour of disabled people and their advocates envisages creating more democratic and socially just forms of schooling, with a view to subverting the ways in which certain groups of students are construed and positioned as 'abnormal' and 'deficient' in need of special education interventions and placements. This kind of political action necessitates understanding inclusion as a values-driven quest with the aim of exposing and challenging social hierarchies and exclusionary regimes. Ultimately, the aim is to render current schooling 'a transformative and positive experience for all as opposed to an exclusionary process, where commitments to equality and diversity are not just respected ideas but enacted practices' (Gibson and Haynes 2009:1).

The 'inclusion backlash'

Notwithstanding laudable progress in mainstreaming moves across the world, exclusion is occasionally reconfigured and disguised under the rhetorical facade of inclusion (Slee 2011). This is a pernicious turn that needs to be critically exposed and challenged, if the rhetoric of inclusion is to be translated into practice. As already discussed, inclusion is occasionally used as a euphemism for sustaining and propagating segregating practices (Barton 1998), thus reflecting an ambivalent and essentially unchanged policy orientation. Vislie (2003:30) warns against superficial educational reforms allegedly intended to represent a shift towards more inclusive forms of educational provision. This kind of superficial change regenerates special education practices within mainstream settings and fails to challenge deep-seated assumptions and discriminatory regimes that construct inferior student subjects on the basis of their alleged deviation from monolithic and insular conceptualizations of the 'ideal student'. As he writes: 'The real challenge is the reproduction of special education paradigms and rituals in regular education as represented by the trend towards mainstreaming SEN students' (Vislie 2003:30).

Stainback and Stainback (1992) coined the term 'maindumping' to describe the superficial attempts to place disabled students in unchanged and monolithic mainstream schools. These perfunctory integrative attempts have been solely oriented towards introducing a number of normalizing special education practices and compensatory measures of support in order to enable students with SEN/D to adapt to unchanged educational contexts (Lloyd 2008). The professional gaze has concentrated on the 'impaired self' that has been subjected to a host of disciplinary and diagnostic rituals in order to adapt to the social and educational status quo (Foucault 1977a). Schools have thus become the embodiment of repressive and discriminatory ideologies that legitimized and rationalized oppressive practices informed by an individual deficit model of pathology and difference. Slee (2012) discusses the ways in which special education paradigms have been skilfully disguised and presented as being part of an inclusive education reform agenda. The real danger is 'complacency' that results from ostensible instances of 'progress' towards the realization of an inclusive discourse, which in essence work towards corroborating the special educational status quo and safeguarding professional vested interests in the field. As the following quote suggests:

> We can tread the traditional special educational path and call it inclusion but we will create more strangers, more surplus children and more exclusion. This means that we need to carefully examine proclamations of inclusive education. Many of those who describe themselves as inclusive educators are not looking for education or social reform to build engaging communities; they need clients to practice on
>
> (Slee 2012:12)

In this way inclusion has become 'a form of governance' (Slee 2010:163), which not only conceals but also rationalizes therapeutic and deficit-oriented approaches. Attempts to safeguard 'the efficient governance of difference' give rise to 'greater calibration and categorization' (ibid.), while traditional special education discourses are reconfigured through hybrid discourses which are placed alongside inclusion to signal an alleged radical paradigm shift from traditional special education practices. Thus even though the rhetoric of inclusion and its association with educational change have been extensively utilized as a means of declaring progressive thinking and praxis in every aspect of social and educational domains, special educational imperatives are still rife. For instance, Slee (2010:164) makes the astute observation that: 'Special education conferences frequently select inclusion as their organizing theme. Special Education textbooks, the "big glossys" as Brantlinger (2004) refers to them, have acquired an additional chapter on inclusion.'

Special education and its segregating practices are also occasionally evoked and extolled in order to foreground an anti-inclusionist ideal by lamenting the alleged shortcomings and catastrophic orthodoxies of a rights-based approach to difference and diversity on the grounds of disability. Some advocates of special schooling go so far as to provide alternative ways of promoting an inclusive discourse. It is, for instance, suggested that inclusion can be realized in special schools (see also neoliberal understandings of inclusion in Chapter 1). This can happen when non-disabled children are placed in special schools alongside their disabled peers. This is what they call 'inverse inclusion' (Kassah and Kassah 2013). Actually, this is not a bad idea but why call this 'inverse inclusion' when the aim should be to jettison educational dichotomies (mainstream vs special schools)? The annihilation of the bipolar couplet of special/regular schooling, and the creation of a school for all are issues at the core of a human rights approach to disability and difference, for example, the United Nations Convention on the Rights of People with Disabilities (UNCRPD) (United Nations 2008).

Going even further, while attempting to rationalize the existence of special schooling, it has also been suggested that the placement of disabled children in special schools can be 'liberating' in certain cases because some of these children might come from impoverished homes and stereotyping communities that adversely affect their 'lived experience' of disability. Consequently, their enrolment in special schools can be 'liberating' in terms of saving children from hunger and other forms of social disadvantage (Kassah and Kassah 2013). This line of argument concurs with the ways in which some Education for All (EFA) initiatives, especially in developing countries, have been criticized on the basis that these initiatives have occasionally resulted in the propagation of segregating and lower-quality forms of provision for disabled children. These forms of provision have been presented as a panacea for meeting the needs of these children (Miles and Singal 2009).

Segregating forms of provision and initiatives focused exclusively on the notion of disability run the risk of accentuating stigma and discriminatory practices, while ignoring the ways in which disability intersects with other sources of social disadvantage (Miles and Singal 2009). Hence, it is imperative that EFA initiatives should draw upon the notion of intersectionality (see Chapter 7) so as to develop strategies that take into consideration the ways in which disability intersects with other sources of social disadvantage (Makkonen 2002). These observations necessitate a critique of policies and institutional arrangements that account for the emergence and sustenance of varied and overlapping forms of social disadvantage that adversely affect the lives and educational trajectories of certain groups of individuals (see Liasidou 2013a).

Disabling discourses and international human rights law

It is occasionally the case that laudable policy rhetoric articulated in ostensibly progressive policies and legal mandates promoting a human rights approach to disability and difference is characterized by textual hybridity and linguistic obscurity, thereby contributing to the resurgence and consolidation of a special education discourse in covert yet powerful ways. The symbolic power of language and its discursive embodiments play a prodigious role in creating social hierarchies and exclusionary matrices through legislation and education (e.g. Liasidou 2008a, 2011, 2014a). While acknowledging the ontological power of language, it is crucial to develop a reflective and reflexive understanding of the ways in which language is utilized to frame meanings that embody negative connotations of difference and diversity, and construct subordinated and marginal social identities (Luke 1996, 2002).

Despite the predominance of a human rights discourse in current debates about difference and diversity on the basis of disability, Byrne (2012) points to the ways in which international human rights law pertaining to disability issues is characterized by ambiguities, omissions and contradictions that undermine its role in safeguarding disabled students' right to inclusive education. This paradox denotes the resilience of special education thinking and its paraphernalia of normalizing practices that pervade to a considerable extent these rights-based international legislative initiatives, while silencing the necessity to pursue radical curricula and pedagogical changes to meet learner diversity. As Byrne (2012:5) puts it:

> International law in its various forms has sought to address the question of educational placement of children with disabilities. Its success in effectively doing so is questionable and, it is argued, constitutive of hidden contradictions and conditional inclusion; that is, the burden of change continues to be placed upon children with disabilities, their 'ability' to adjust to naturalized pedagogies, to 'cope' and overcome their impairment to become 'one of us' as opposed to a somewhat burdensome 'minority one'.

Prominent attention should thus be placed on the symbolic power of language in forming discourses of inclusion and exclusion in international as well as national human rights law. Occasionally, the discourses of inclusion, integration and special educational needs co-exist and are used interchangeably, thereby obscuring their immense philosophical and conceptual disparities (Vislie 2003). This terminological fusion is indicative of an unchanged and ambiguous orientation that undermines the quest for the realization of a human rights discourse.

The critical analysis of language and its constituent discourses can make transparent the inconspicuous ways in which the 'political elasticity' of language (Slee 1996) is responsible for the 'smoke and mirrors' (Byrne 2012:10) that sometimes characterizes international human rights law. One example frequently deployed in anti-discrimination legislation is the use of a phraseology that portrays disability as an individual problem in need of 'reasonable accommodations', rather than a systemic problem that emanates from asymmetrical power relations and discriminatory regimes (Guillaume 2011).

The 'smoke and mirrors' metaphor (Byrne 2012:10) can also apply to the ways in which nation states, which ratify human rights conventions and laws, delete stipulations they do not like or render them 'non-self executing'. One recent example is the case of the USA and the UNCRPD. Although the USA has ratified the Convention, it is speculated that the Senate will render it 'non-self executing', meaning that its implementation will be contingent on separate laws. The USA is not the only country to adopt the 'Yes but' caveat to treaties;

this is a very frequent phenomenon. It is reported that one third of the countries that ratified the United Nations (UN) Conventions on the rights of women, children and racial minorities had included caveats so as to exclude areas where treaties will not be implemented (*The Economist* 23 November 2013).

An unconditional and binding international human rights law can potentially force all state parties to abide by the proclamations of the law and eradicate all forms of exclusion currently experienced by a great percentage of students designated as having SEN/D. Even though Article 35 of the UNCRPD is explicit on the necessity that state parties 'submit to the Committee a comprehensive report on measures taken to give effect to its obligations under the present Convention and on the progress made in that regard, within two years after the entry into force of the present Convention for the State Party concerned' (Article 35), empirical evidence from the following case study on the implementation of the UNCRPD points to the necessity of introducing more robust and reliable monitoring mechanisms to ensure national implementation strategies.

For instance, a critical analysis of the first report of Cyprus on the implementation of the UNCRPD (Department for Social Inclusion of Persons with Disabilities/Ministry of Labour and Social Insurance 2013) brings to the fore the covert and overt ways in which the rhetoric of inclusion is reduced to deficit-oriented discourses. Even though the report ostensibly presents a rights-based and inclusive orientation by asserting that the Republic of Cyprus has 'a modern and powerful legal framework for the protection and promotion of the rights of persons with disabilities, including general and specific laws in every aspect' (Department for Social Inclusion of Persons with Disabilities/Ministry of Labour and Social Insurance 2013:3), a critical analysis of the current policy and legislative landscape suggests quite the opposite. For example, in spite of the fact that the preamble of the 'Persons with Intellectual Disability Law of 1989 (117/89)' stipulates that 'decent livelihood and social security is a fundamental human right' for all people including people with 'learning difficulties', a term preferred by disabled people and their organizations (e.g. People First in the UK) as well as analysts within disability studies (e.g. Goodley 2000), the legislative document still uses the unacceptable term 'mentally retarded people' to refer to this group of people (see Liasidou 2014).

The use of this kind of language in this legislative document constructs inferior subject positions and marks out this group of people in a negative sense as different from the rest of the population. Identity politics concerned with recognizing disabled people's subject positions on an equal basis with their non-disabled peers constitute an important dimension of a human rights discourse (Slee 1993). Gale and Tranter (2011) refer to the notion of 'epistemological equity' to denote the legitimization of certain kinds of knowledge at the expense of others. Dominant forms of 'knowing' valorize certain human identities while devaluing others. The effect of the 'able-bodied order' pervades social understandings that valorize certain kinds of normalcy and create inferior and marginal subject positions (Campbell 2008, 2009).

The 'able-bodied order' works in synergy with the individual pathology approach that is enshrined in the legal document, which patently ignores the ways in which social and educational barriers contribute to the creation of 'learning difficulties' and other needs. In stark contrast to the UNCRPD's definition of disability as an 'evolving concept' that results from and depends on a reciprocal web of socio-political dynamics, in this policy document individuals with 'learning difficulties' are marked by their own individual deficiencies and inadequacies, thereby ignoring the contextual dynamics that impact upon these individuals' identities and educational trajectories. The document consolidates a deficit-oriented perspective while silencing the fact that disabled peoples' identities are culturally and socially mediated constructs (Liasidou 2013c, 2014a).

The same observations apply to current special education law (Ministry of Education and Culture 1999) of the Republic of Cyprus, whereby disability and 'special needs' are construed as individual pathology problems, notwithstanding bold statements that are aligned with inclusion and attest to the commitment of the government to safeguard the rights of students designated as having SEN/D by providing them the necessary opportunities to develop their potential to the greatest possible extent within mainstream settings (Liasidou 2008a). Paradoxically, both legislative documents are cited by the report as examples of the 'modern and powerful legal framework', something that raises even more questions about the ideological presumptions and philosophical orientations that underpin the implementation process of the Convention within the context of Cyprus.

In order to enshrine liberatory and egalitarian political activism in educational praxis for positive social change, particular emphasis needs to be given to the formulation and implementation of a robust and unequivocal human rights policy framework as well as to the establishment of monitoring and evaluation mechanisms of implementation. As Rioux (2010:107) states in relation to the education policy and practice implications of a rights-based approach to difference and disability:

> To implement a rights-based approach to education requires using human rights as a framework for pedagogical theory, for access to places of learning, for testing of capacity and for measuring success. It makes principles of human rights integral to the design, implementation and evaluation of policies and programmes, and it means assessing the human rights implications of education policy, programmes and legislation.

A human rights framework needs to form an integral aspect of school development initiatives aimed at providing more effective and socially just education communities for learner diversity. To that end, it is imperative to establish new accountability measures as well as school effectiveness indicators in order to create incentives for schools and teachers to focus resources on students who are plagued by cumulative and intersecting forms of social and educational disadvantage (Artiles et al. 2006; Bringhouse 2010). At the same time, it is important to introduce and continually monitor data on the quality of the learning support provided to students designated as having SEN/D, along with the impact of this support on students' progress. This kind of data is crucially important in order to ensure accountability with regard to the educational outcomes of students with SEN/D.

Nevertheless, notwithstanding the importance of applying a human rights framework in education policy and legislation, Slee and Cook (1999) point out that 'of itself, the Law is not capable of eliminating disability discrimination'. Along similar lines, Stonemeier et al. (2013) write about the oxymoron of inclusion and the resurgence of special education paradigms in the USA context where, notwithstanding the civil rights agenda that precipitated an educational equity movement during the last decades, there are still great numbers of disabled students who are systematically marginalized and excluded from mainstream educational settings. As Stonemeier et al. (2013:2) point out:

> Brown v. Board of Education is often cited as the landmark Supreme Court case of the civil rights movement The Brown decision of 'separate is NOT equal' is arguably the link that connects the civil rights movement with the education equity movement. However, more than 60 years after that decision, research continues to show that our schools are more racially segregated now than at the time of the decision. Further, nearly 40 years after the passage of education civil rights legislation directed to disability, significant numbers of students with disabilities are either not included, or only partly included, in the general education activities in schools.

Even though international human rights law by itself cannot mobilize an inclusive education reform agenda (Barton 2009), it is nevertheless a crucial element in this process. By no means should the right of disabled children to attend their local mainstream schools be jeopardized by conditional discourses of inclusion, which place the onus on children to adjust to existing institutional and pedagogical arrangements. Disabled students' right to inclusive education should be unequivocally promoted and enacted in a radically transformed educational system, where all kinds of exclusion are subject to legal sanctions.

Conclusions

Emanating from socio-political perspectives on disability and difference, inclusive education is inexorably linked with the notion of educational change as it involves systemic institutional and ideological reforms commensurate with a rights-based approach to disability and difference. In stark contrast to the assimilationist and normalizing character of integration, inclusion celebrates learner diversity and focuses on organizational rather than individual pathology. As a fundamental first step, the realization of an inclusive discourse presupposes a radical ideological and pedagogical departure from the special education status quo and its associated policies and practices, which place disabled students in subjugated hierarchical subject positions. Hybrid policies and legislative documents along with their resulting segregating and discriminatory practices are used as a veneer in order to 'transplant the failings of mass education into the minds and bodies of disabled children' (Goodley 2010:138). Simultaneously, the political dimensions of teaching (Goldstein 1995) and the ways in which social and cultural dynamics interact with students to construct their identities are silenced (Liasidou 2012b). The failure to understand the embedment of schools in the wider socio-political context and the multifarious interactions that are at play, according to Slee (2008:108), undermine 'the capacity to shape inclusive education as a comprehensive education and social reform agenda'.

To that end, the notion of transformative change within the context of inclusion should not be limited to systemic and operational changes (Ekins and Grimes 2009) but should extend to include critical and value-based considerations that need to be addressed in politically informed ways. A human rights approach to inclusive education proclaims the importance of initiating socially just changes, so as to make mainstream schools accessible to all students without stigmatizing them on the basis of their biological characteristics and biographical experiences. Such an approach entails exploring the ways in which schools become sites 'for disciplinary power via the "ab-normalisation"' (Graham 2006:2) of those students who are perceived as being a threat to the unfettered quest for insular conceptualizations of educational excellence (Ball 2003), as discussed in Chapter 1.

This kind of transformative change can be achieved by challenging the conceptual and pragmatic dynamics that create hierarchical relations of power by either devaluing or privileging certain groups of individuals. Inclusion valorizes individual differences and celebrates learner diversity by shifting the focus to institutional rather than individual pathology perspectives, which single out certain students as 'different' on the grounds of their alleged deviation from corporeal, ethnic, linguistic and other kinds of social 'norm'.

4
Theorizing Educational Change within the Context of Inclusion: Socio-cultural and Whole-School Considerations

Introduction

Having identified and rationalized some of the reasons why inclusion is synonymous with the notion of educational change, the aim of the fourth chapter of this book is to provide a comprehensive understanding of the ways in which the process of educational change can be facilitated within the context of inclusion. The chapter provides theoretical, critical and research-based insights into the process of transformative change, and locates them within the context of inclusive education. The analysis also concentrates on the socio-cultural aspects of the process of educational change (e.g. Sahlberg 2010).

   The realization of an inclusive discourse requires discursive 'ruptures' (Liasidou 2012a:140) intended to radically change the *modus operandi* of social relations and current schooling in both conceptual and practical terms. These discursive 'ruptures', however, can only be achieved through continuous and sustained transformative action. Change, according to progressive politics (Foucault 1978), is accomplished slowly and gradually, for it entails challenging a profusion of contextual dynamics at the macro- and micro-level that undermine the process of transformative change. Even minor loci of resistance in all 'arenas' of educational policymaking (Fulcher 1999) can significantly contribute to challenging political inertia and stagnation so as to galvanize the process of change. Hence, even the tiniest attempt to challenge the status quo can have a massive impact on mobilizing the process of transformative change.

Institutional perspectives on the process of educational change

Fullan (2010:126) suggests that the process of change should be underpinned by two interrelated elements: 'pressure and support'. Despite the fact that '[a]bsence of pressure honors inertia' and perpetuates the status quo, punitive forms of pressure such as zero-tolerance policies (Kennedy and Lewis 2014) are counter-productive for they can engender a culture of fear, distrust and professional burnout. Simultaneously, 'pressure without support' is a futile measure that can easily lead to frustration and perpetuate inertia.

For instance, the proposed payment-by-results scenario (as discussed in Chapter 1), reflects characteristics of a punitive culture for those educational professionals who allegedly fail to meet certain 'perfomativity standards'. This scenario, however, fails to take into consideration the imperative to provide support to these professionals in order to improve their teaching and to maximize the learning outcomes of their students. Any kind of pressure, as a means of facilitating the process of positive change, is thus meaningless and even pernicious, unless it is ushered in by appropriate and adequate measures of support and strategic planning. Fullan (2010) cites the example of the NCLB agenda in the USA, which despite providing laudable rhetoric about the necessity for every child to reach world-class performance thresholds in literacy, numeracy and science, has not articulated a concrete strategy to this end. At the same time, this policy initiative has been characterized 'as the largest underfunded federal education mandate in the US history' (Blase and Bjork 2010:239), for it received no substantial financial support from the government for its implementation.

According to Fullan (2010), there are five forms of positive pressure which need to inform the process of educational change. These forms of positive pressure will be explained with reference to the implementation of an inclusive education reform agenda. The first form is concerned with developing 'a sense of focus urgency' by getting people's attention and communicating a conscious and informed understanding of the necessity to challenge the special education status quo that undermines attempts to initiate socially just and effective changes for learner diversity. This sense of focus energy should be clearly articulated in educational policies and pronouncements, as well as in legal mandates, so as to enable educational professionals to understand the imperative of becoming actively involved in the process of change, provided that there are the means and the supportive networks to do so, along with the mechanisms to put pressure on prioritizing and sustaining strategies and ensuring implementation progress.

The notion of 'urgency' does not convey moral panic; rather it gradually builds upon the system and intensifies with time, thereby ensuring the continuation of the process of change. It should be noted, however, that in order to develop 'a sense of focus urgency', it is crucial to give equal emphasis to the micropolitical processes underpinning the 'political culture' of schooling that is accountable for the perpetuation or subversion of the status quo (Blase and Bjork 2010). This point is related to the second form of positive pressure, which is concerned with developing strategies that encourage peer interaction and peer learning in order to achieve improvements. Central leadership, embodied in the role of the head teacher as well as the role of the special educational needs co-ordinator (SENCO) (Liasidou and Antoniou 2013, 2015, in press; Liasidou and Svensson 2013), can play a crucial role in nurturing a sense of leadership, as well as navigating and monitoring the process of change, encouraging positive working relations and creating effective channels of communication within an organization (see Chapter 8 on educational leadership).

That said, the success of inclusion is contingent on creating communities of learning as well as 'joined-up' or integrated services, by means of encouraging intra-professional collaboration and collective problem-solving regimes, so as to advance effective forms of provision to accommodate the needs of vulnerable groups of students. Hartley (2010) provides an example suggesting that, despite huge developments in information and communication technology, there has been a lack of communication amongst social care agencies in the UK, including education. This has led to some unfortunate events involving young children (including, for example, the deaths of Victoria Climbié and Baby Peter), who have been abused and died at the hands of those who were supposed to protect them (i.e. family members). The first tragic incidence led in a way to the introduction of the Every Child Matters agenda in 2003, which sought to address the holistic development and well-being of children and young people, including those with SEN/D, through a multi-agency approach. Notwithstanding policy reforms and laudable rhetoric on the necessity to overhaul children's services in both the UK and elsewhere, the promulgated process of change has been solely characterized by concerns to create more 'businesslike' and 'outcomes oriented' children's services. This has resulted in a reduction in direct work with families and has generated a family pathology perspective embodied in the idea of 'the problem family' (Garrett 2009:9) that supplements the idea of the 'problem child' favoured by the neoliberal discourse. The preoccupation with the individual pathology perspectives, along with the patent failure to provide seamless and co-ordinated services, have considerably undermined proactive and systemic approaches to developing well-rounded individuals through the pastoral and educative role of current schooling (Best 2008).

In order to address the problems ensued by disjointed and fragmented services, which fail to provide effective child welfare support, some local government authorities in the UK have recently established 'community' or 'full-service schools' and provided joined-up educational and social services through an integrated 'Children's Services' department (Topping 2012). At the same time, recent changes in the UK Special Educational Needs and Disability Code of Practice (from 1 September 2014) (DfE and DOH 2014) are expected to further enhance intra-professional collaboration, as the Code includes guidance on facilitating co-operation between education, health and social care services in order to provide comprehensive support for children, young people and their families. To that end, a co-ordinated assessment process has been introduced for children and young people with more complex needs, as well as a new 0–25 Education, Health and Care Plan (EHC plan) to replace statements and learning difficulty assessments (LDAs).

Another form of positive pressure that can facilitate the process of transformative change lies in establishing 'transparency of data' that consists of two interrelated elements, namely, transparency of student achievement and transparency of practice. Students' achievement/outcomes are consistently recorded and monitored in order to identify groups of students who underperform and need additional support and instructional interventions. Schools are expected to examine and become adept at identifying the causal link between certain instructional strategies and students' learning. It is important to note that, in order to achieve transparency of practice, learning outcomes should be widely accessible, along with the strategies of learning that engendered these outcomes. As a means of positive pressure, schools are expected to compare their current learning outcomes with the previous ones and design a strategic action plan for further improvement. Schools can, for instance, adopt a non-punitive strategy of comparing themselves with other schools with similar conditions and circumstances, through a 'statistical neighbours' database in order to be able to monitor their own performance and to learn from good practice elsewhere. In so doing, schools can devise strategies to achieve better results through a reflective and comparative approach (Fullan 2010).

An example of transparency of practice is stipulated in the revised UK Special Educational Needs and Disability Code of Practice, whereby schools have to accurately record and regularly update the provision made for pupils with SEN/D. The school inspectorate body (OFSTED) will seek to see evidence of the support provided along with its impact on students' progress. Simultaneously, all schools will be legally mandated to publish information on their websites about the implementation of the governing body's or the proprietor's policy for pupils with SEN/D (DfE and DOH 2014). The importance of evidence-based practice within the context of inclusion is also raised by Goransson and Nilholm (2014), who discuss the dearth of evidence-based research in inclusive education. As they point out:

> Studying change in an inclusive direction, we believe, must involve comparing a baseline with at least one later point in time. Clear indicators of the level of social and academic inclusiveness should be obtained in order to provide evidence for change in an inclusive direction. At a minimum, such indicators should provide some kind of objective data. It is not enough to merely claim that an environment has become more inclusive; nor does it suffice that teachers believe an inclusive change has occurred.... Objective data in the case of academic inclusion could consist of grades, tests or similar evaluations, for example portfolio evaluations. As concerns social inclusion, data can be obtained by interviewing children, using questionnaires and/or sociograms, or through observations, the records of which must include the number of observations, their representativeness and the ways in which they are expressions of social inclusiveness.
>
> (Goransson and Nilholm 2014:267)

However, the three forms of positive pressure presented above are not powerful enough unless they are carried out in a culture of non-punitive accountability. Accountability can act as a two-fold sword: punitive accountability can be pernicious, for it creates disincentives and demoralizes educational practitioners. Apart from the imposition of high-stakes accountability regimes, other measures of negative pressure can include increasing the rigour of renewing teacher licensure requirements, extending the school day and so on. These kinds of accountability regimes and procedures are both suppressive and counter-productive because '[r]ather than ensuring responsibility, they are imposing non-responsibility' (Branson 2010:119).

In contrast, in a culture of non-punitive accountability, underperforming schools are put under scrutiny in non-judgemental ways, as they are not blamed but supported in order to enhance their capacity-building potential. To this end, schools are held accountable for the quality of teaching by enhancing 'internal accountability' rather than imposing external accountability regimes. As Harris (2010:699) points out: 'The key to improving schools in challenging circumstances is building internal capacity and that is best achieved by securing greater coherence and agreement amongst teachers about expectations and effective instructional practices'. Teachers are thus responsible for enabling all students to reach the peak of their learning ability through collaborative professional practice and effective pedagogical interventions.

The synergetic existence and simultaneous enactment of 'internal accountability', along with all previous forms of positive pressure, can energize and sustain the process of positive change. Positive measures are intended to create a 'culture in which the system is committed to and engaged in improving' (Fullan 2010:129), thereby creating a self-transforming school that is committed to constant development and improvement (see Chapter 6 on sustainability). In order to reach the point of self-transformation, schools need to develop self-awareness in terms of their organizational and relational inadequacies and fallacies. Self-awareness can mobilize the dynamic process of self-transformation, as a means of achieving constant organizational development and improvement. For Branson (2010:125), a 'failing school' is basically a school that 'lacks sufficient access to itself'; this means that its interpersonal and interdependent relations are deficient and hence inept at instigating, monitoring and sustaining the process of change. In order to achieve positive change, a school needs to be able to learn more 'about itself from itself'. The learning process is instantaneously a development process by identifying organizational 'weakness' and ideological distortions. This is particularly pertinent within the context of inclusion, whereby school leaders are expected to promote 'community self-discovery' through a new moral vision. This moral vision needs to be clearly articulated, communicated and strategically framed so as to provide the conceptual backdrop against which the struggles for change can be framed and mobilized (Branson 2010). The Index for Inclusion provides a detailed collaborative self-review process for developing inclusion. The school development planning cycle consists of five phases, the second of which is concerned with a process of self-discovery (finding out about the school) so as to identify and subsequently address systemic and attitudinal barriers to inclusion (Booth and Ainscow 2002).

The role of educational professionals

Teachers and other educational professionals constitute important policymakers within their context of practice and their contribution to implementing novel policies and practices should be both acknowledged and theorized (Fulcher 1999). Arguably, legislative changes aligned with an inclusive agenda are incomplete, unless understood and acted upon by educational professionals. To this end, the latter should be empowered to gain ownership and become actively engaged in the process of transformative change.

Fullan (1993) attributes the failure of certain policies to their 'top-down' character that ignores educational practitioners' perspectives and encumbers their active engagement and participation in the policymaking process. Educational professionals are not inimical to the process of change per se but rather to the way in which top-down, or otherwise labelled, mandated changes are imposed on them. Blase and Bjork (2010:242–243) highlight

> the significance of teachers' political involvement in school-wide and interorganizational relationships: when teachers participated in negotiating a redefinition of roles, building trust, setting agendas and standards, and confronting sources of conflict, they frequently facilitated reform.

Barton (2008:xix) also highlights the necessity of active involvement in the process of change and alerts practitioners and researchers to be aware of their own contribution to the attempts to introduce transformative change. As he writes: 'Within our own work contexts and societies there is so much that is unacceptable and exclusionary and needs to be fought over and change and we must be part of the critical engagement.' In order to do this, however, individuals should understand their own significant contribution and role in this process, without subscribing to pessimistic allusions about the grim possibilities of a reform agenda given the existing institutional rigidities and adversarial ideological preoccupations.

It is suggested that the process of fostering inclusive pedagogies is contingent on teachers' 'knowing', 'doing' and 'believing' (Rouse 2009). Teachers' 'knowing' involves an informed knowledge base around the complex and contentious nature of inclusion. As we have seen, the debates around inclusion are constituted within a multi-disciplinatory realm of diverse values, understandings and insights. Hence, inclusion should be constantly problematized and interrogated in relation to the multiplicity of meanings ascribed to it as well as the contextual dynamics impacting on it (Liasidou 2012a). In so doing, educational professionals can become aware of the disabling ideological and institutionalized structures, which sustain and reproduce the special education status quo (Goodley 2007). Teachers' 'doing' refers to teachers' ability of 'doing' by turning their theoretical knowledge into pedagogical action so as to create effective and socially just learning environments for learner diversity (see Chapter 5). The third constitutive element of the triptych refers to teachers' 'believing'. 'Believing' infers teachers' unwavering commitment to inclusion that is driven by an unequivocal acceptance and concurrence with the ethical and pedagogical underpinnings of an inclusive discourse.

The conceptualization of policy as text (Ball 1994) recognizes the autonomy of educational practitioners to interpret and act upon policy in multifarious ways according to their 'regimes of truth' (Foucault 1984). From this perspective, teachers acquire a pre-eminent position in the policymaking process, as policy interpretation and hence implementation rests on their 'implicit systems'. Foucault (1989a:71) talks about the pervasiveness of the 'implicit systems in which we find ourselves prisoners' (cited in Blades 1997:95), which act obscurely, albeit incisively. Hence, the contradictions and dilemmas inherent in the policy agendas are mediated through teachers' 'implicit systems', thereby adding to the complexity of their role to be responsive to the 'intellectual, social and emotional complexities of schools in challenging circumstances' (Day 2005:575). Hence, top-down changes and mandated policy initiatives have minimal possibilities for success, unless taking into consideration the three factors pertaining to teachers' theoretical, pedagogical and ideological/ethical predispositions and preparedness to facilitate the process of change. For Veyne (1997:231), 'the self is the new strategic possibility', hence, educational professionals should be enabled 'to see themselves as the main source of transformation, rather than as passive subjects waiting for a more structural or material change' (cited in Allen 2005:283–284).

Another possible barrier to the process of change, articulated by Fullan (2001:21) is the fact that teachers are routinely presented with a large number of changes that are sometimes contradictory. This results in 'innovation overload' as there is no time for teachers to understand and rationalize these changes. In consequence, they experience stress and negative feelings and, as a result, resist the process of change. In addition, teachers occasionally experience punitive forms of accountability, an issue that also adversely affects their willingness, motivation and capacity to be actively and constructively involved in the process of change.

In particular, Hargreaves and Shirley (2012:xiv) suggest that the process of educational change presupposes 'professional dynamos which generate and transform people's energy for change'. The 'dynamos of educational change' cannot exist 'without the commitment and capability of thousands of classroom teachers and their leaders who have ultimate control over how they teach their own students every day' (p. xvi). While exemplifying the reasons as to why the Finnish educational system has succeeded in creating an effective and comprehensive educational system, the authors point to the immense contribution of teachers towards this end. In the Finnish educational system every child is considered as being a 'special educational needs child' and receives quality teaching and proactive support without the need to be categorized and labelled on the basis of an alleged 'pathology'. 'Specific interventions' for struggling students are not the result of sophisticated special education bureaucratic procedures, but rather are the result of teachers' 'personal knowledge, personal care for all students, and focused discussions within learning communities that meets together regularly' (Hargreaves and Shirley 2012:53). As far as intensive early interventions and prevention are concerned, it should be noted that these practices are provided on a proactive rather than a reactive basis. Hence, the school does not wait for the student to 'fail' in order to provide additional learning support. Another important point is that this support is available for every student who, for various reasons, might encounter learning difficulties, without the need for an 'administrative decision' or 'diagnosis'. In this way, the Finnish educational system has managed to foster, as Graham and Jahnukainen (2011:279) suggest, 'a more inclusive system by default by establishing an effective "fully comprehensive school"' (cited in Liasidou 2012:52).

Moreover, it should be noted that teaching in Finland is considered a very prestigious profession that attracts competent and committed individuals who take a personal and ethical responsibility for their students' learning. All prospective teachers are interviewed in order to identify their level of emotional intelligence and their moral commitment to enhancing all students' learning and participation. The subsequent training of the successful candidates (the selection success rate is one in ten individuals) is a rigorous and life-long process (Sahlberg 2010; Hargreaves and Shirley 2012) that combines university-based learning with school-based training and research-oriented practice (e.g. Douglas 2014).

The aim of this comprehensive and life-long educative approach is to inculcate and enhance teachers' 'professional capital'. The latter is referred to as ' the assets among teachers and in teaching that are developed, invested, accumulated and circulated in order to produce a high yield or return in the quality of teaching and student learning' (Hargreaves and Shirley 2012:49). The process of transformative change is invariably contingent on teachers' 'professional capital' that embodies their understanding of and commitment to the values and pedagogical underpinnings of inclusion. Building and maximizing 'professional capital' for inclusion is a *sine qua non* in attempts to mobilize and sustain transformative change in line with the axioms of an inclusive discourse.

While alluding to the importance of professional development for inclusion, Slee (2012:11) is critical of the ways in which 'we rush to fill inclusive education programmes at teacher training institutions with more special education, so that teachers can name differences and be able to recite etiologies and symptomatologies as they rush for specialist help'. At the same time, Slee laments the propagation of books that are supposed to give teaching recipes (what he calls education do-it-yourself manuals). These kinds of books make educators 'eschew analysis' and simultaneously 'forfeit the educational potential to the allure of quick fixes for the symptoms of education in a complex world. They do not offer tools for building inclusive schools and classrooms' (Slee 2012:2). Hence, another important dimension of building up 'professional capital' for the realization of an inclusive discourse is related to teachers' ability and willingness to be actively involved in research inquiry as a means to improving their educational praxis in increasingly complex and demanding classroom situations, where the learning of all students is an ethical pursuit and a professional responsibility.

Nurturing reflective professional practices

Apart from radical organizational reforms, the process of transformative change presupposes fundamental conceptual and attitudinal changes informed by an explicit attempt to reflect upon and interrogate personal beliefs about teaching and learning, disability and difference (Carrington 1999). This is an important, albeit underestimated and occasionally ignored dimension of the process of change. As Branson (2010:110) so appositely put it: 'Too often within educational change we have forgotten the human side. We have concentrated on the objective, the observable elements and ignored the subjective, invisible, elements.'

Along similar lines, Ainscow (2005:177) prioritizes the necessity 'to develop the capacity of those within schools to reveal and challenge deeply entrenched deficit views of "difference" '. This process entails questioning hegemonic conceptualizations of normality that play a crucial role in creating ontological categories and excluding groups of people who are constructed as deviant and abnormal (Yuval-Davis 2006). This kind of critical engagement can potentially interrogate and deconstruct the multitude of disabling pedagogies (Goodley 2007) that exclude certain groups of students, thereby reinstating teaching as an ethical project (Allan 2005) that envisages mobilizing socially just change. Cultivating positive connotations of difference and problematizing presupposed constructions of ontological normalcy are instrumental in deconstructing the status quo and its underpinning of individual pathology discourses (Campbell 2008, 2009).

A constituent and interrelated element of 'professional capital', discussed in the previous section, is 'decisional capital' that rests upon teachers' ability to make good judgements so to reflect upon and resolve their professional problems and dilemmas in complex situations. One key professional dilemma within the context of inclusion is the 'dilemma of difference' (Norwich 2008a, 2009) that refers to the ways in which 'difference' can be conceptualized and acted upon in educational settings. On the one hand, it has been suggested that the recognition of difference runs the risk of 'labelling' and 'stigmatizing' some students, thereby contributing to their marginal and subordinated status within mainstream settings. On the other hand, there is a counter-argument that failure to recognize difference runs the risk, through pedagogical homogeneity, of ironing out individual 'differences', thereby failing to address and provide for individual needs (Norwich 2008a).

Resolving the dilemma of difference, as well as a number of other vexed dilemmas that characterize educational praxis (Pollard 2012), necessitates good judgement and sustained professional growth, and development that results from extensive practice and reflection. Quoting Hargreaves and Shirley (2012:55) in describing the attributes of effective teachers in terms of their decisional capital:

> These teachers patiently improve their practice and solve their professional problems together in a spirit of continuous improvement and collective responsibility. This is the essence of professional capital. The capacity to make good judgements is accrued through lots of practice, but not through practice alone. Reflecting on that practice and taking the time to learn from it are indispensable to the quest of improving over time.

Reflexivity constitutes an integral part of the formation of the self, especially in instances whereby individuals face dilemmas in their daily educational praxis. Burkitt (2002) attempts to explicate the 'technologies of the self' by deploying Dewey's ideas of reflexivity and habit, the latter of which can be defined as the habitual teaching practices and pedagogies that teachers use in their classrooms. The multiple dilemmas that teachers face in their daily practice (Pollard 2012) can thus be considerably compromised, if not resolved, through reflexivity, as educational professionals can resolve their dilemmas and effect change upon themselves and their pedagogies, in order to promote the realization of an inclusive discourse. Starting from the notion of 'pedagogies of the self', this space can enable teachers to adopt deconstruction and reflection (Gore 1993) as a means to enhance their pedagogical effectiveness in relation to the needs of learner diversity. To that end, teachers need to be empowered to become autonomous and self-determining agents, who can challenge the impositions and subjugating structures that affect their ability to achieve 'professional mediation', either by themselves or with the help of 'critical friends', the aim being to 'disrupt conventional knowledge about "special needs"; (…) to question what they know themselves, to "ask what determinations and intensities [they] are prepared to countenance" (Roy, 2003, p. 91) and to abandon what seems unreasonable' (Allan 2004:424).

The triptych underpinning the act of professional mediation is primarily directed to the self and the ethical dilemmas, uncertainties and doubts that act as pervasive 'technologies of power' (Foucault 1977, 1980a, 1980b) and are accountable for the emergence of a host of 'disabling pedagogies' (Goodley 2007). Foucault dedicated much of his work on the 'technologies of power' and the ways that they 'determine the conduct of individuals and submit them to certain ends of domination'. Nevertheless, despite these pessimistic allusions, in his later writings, Foucault also acknowledges the productive rather than the subjugating effects of power, and introduces the 'technologies of the self' defined as the various 'operations [of individuals] on their own bodies and souls, thoughts, conduct and way and being' (Foucault 1988:18 cited in Burkitt 2002:221). The realization of an inclusive discourse can primarily be achieved through the 'technologies of the self' aimed at 'setting up and developing relations with the self, for self-reflection, self-knowledge, self-examination, for deciphering the self by oneself, for the transformation one seeks to accomplish with oneself as object' (Foucault 1985:29 cited in Burkitt 2002:220). In this respect, professional mediation should be ever present during 'those moments when habit breaks down or when habits clash and the self is forced to reflexively monitor itself and the context in which it is acting in order to meaningfully reconstruct with others both self and situation' (Burkitt 2002:220).

Given the productive effects of power, teachers can be empowered through professional development opportunities and 'professional mediation' activities to interrogate their own values and beliefs that engender disabling pedagogies. For instance, there has been extensive discussion about the 'discourse of professionalism' (Fulcher 1999) or 'professional knowledge' that necessitates scrutinizing and critically analysing professional practice that is routinely presented as being value-free and closely aligned with the 'best interests' of disabled individuals (Tomlinson 1982). Challenging the simplistic and unproblematized assumptions and projections of 'professional neutrality and benevolence' entails developing 'self-practice or ethical work' which relate to the process of 'deconstruction, criticism and reflexivity, all of which will help to undermine or subvert the "ideology of expertism" ' (Allan 2005:289).

Allan (2005) cites Lowson's (1994) work which invites professionals to use a reconstructive strategy in order to 'scrutinize' their own 'clinical symptoms' as a professional development activity. For instance, they might be encouraged to recognize and remove the ' "rigidity, imperviousness, and defensiveness" (Lowson cited in Corbett 1996:40) in their language and practices'. While acknowledging the symbolic power of language on SEN/D legislation and professional praxis, it is imperative that educational professionals interrogate and dismantle the pervasive material effects of language on their pedagogical practice. This reflective and reflexive approach can problematize and challenge the discourse of disability and SEN/D that undermine the process towards the realization of an inclusive discourse.

Lingard and Mills (2007) talk about the necessity to provide teachers 'space for professional mediation' in order to reflect upon the ways in which their pedagogies can create sites of justice or injustice for disabled children and all children who might find schooling challenging and oppressive. This personal mediation process ultimately will be an interrogation of their stance towards issues of social justice and equality, aimed at bringing out the potential of those students who are a priori doomed to fail given the neoliberal trends endemic in contemporary schooling. The professional journey of cultivating reflection and reflexivity, as a way to enhance critical self-awareness, should constitute an indispensable component of the attempts to foster greater inclusive policies and practices and can be significantly facilitated through in-service training (INSET) and continuing professional development (CPD) programmes, primarily intended to target change at the level of individuals.

It needs noting, however, that the above considerations do not suggest uncritically and naïvely that professional mediation and reflexivity constitute a panacea. Arguably, even though this is pivotal change that is urgently needed in order to challenge the pedagogical status quo, this critical endeavour is just one aspect of the multifaceted structural and ideological struggles endemic in the attempt to challenge the special educational status quo and foster inclusion (Nayler and Keddie 2007). At the same time, it needs to be acknowledged that, realistically, the rhetoric of professional mediation is often untenable in Western-centric educational systems due to the difficulties teachers have in setting aside time to be engaged with reflective acts of individual or collective professional mediation (Howes et al. 2009).

Apart from the empowering effects of professional mediation in challenging disabling assumptions and pernicious ideological predilections, particular emphasis also needs to be given to the extent to which institutional dynamics are conducive to the process of change. Research evidence suggest that, notwithstanding the educational professionals' level of commitment to inclusive education and related experience, 'educators lose direction and compromise their way back to segregating students' when 'district and school policies and practices are not centered on inclusion...' (Capper and Young 2014:162). 'Professional mediation' is difficult to achieve since teachers are also 'pathologized' by the neoliberal discourse (Beck 1999; Karlsen 2000), as they have increasingly become accountable to meet certain 'performance indicators' gauged against mono-dimensional and arbitrary 'fabrications' of successful schools (Ball 2004).

Professional burnout and implications for an inclusive education reform agenda

Concerns about precipitating and sustaining an inclusive education reform agenda should also concentrate on exploring the extent to which and also the ways in which teachers experience 'professional burnout', in their attempts to respond to their increasingly demanding professional roles in the light of this agenda. In so doing, it is important to identify possible gaps in inclusive education policy and provision; such as the lack of support networks, and inadequate teacher training and development programmes, which contribute towards creating and exacerbating teacher burnout. Understanding the ways in which burnout is 'lived' by teachers can elucidate the ways in which the notion of inclusion is understood and acted upon in particular contexts with a view to re-evaluating and repositioning existing policies, procedures and practices that are allegedly intended to promote inclusive education reforms.

The notion of burnout has varied and nuanced conceptualizations that are commonly related to accumulative effects of stress, which have negative physical, psychological and mental effects on a person's professional life and practice. The term was coined by Freudenberger (1974), who defined burnout as a state of physical and mental exhaustion (cited in Byrne 1999). He identified as one of the primary contributing factors to burnout the need to meet unrealistic expectations that put excessive demands on a professional's energy, endurance and strength. These demands give rise to negative self-perceptions and dissatisfaction, and undermine emotional and physical well-being. Kelchtermans (1999) equates burnout with the negative feelings and connotations associated with advanced symptoms of stress.

Although acknowledging that sometimes a moderate level of stress can have positive effects, as it can provide incentives for professional growth and improvement, the accumulative effects of stress contribute towards burnout that is manifested in 'emotional exhaustion', 'depersonalization' and 'reduced personal accomplishment' (Maslach et al. 2001). Lens and Jesus (1999) refer to additional consequences of burnout such as absenteeism, low professional involvement and a desire to leave the profession. Moreover, burnout might also result in enhanced use of alcohol and drugs, increased family and marital conflicts (Schwab 1983), as well as serious depression (Zwerling et al. 2002).

Based on systematic research evidence, Schwab (1983:21) pointed to the fact that burnout is a more prominent phenomenon amongst people who are 'in prolonged, constant, intensive interaction with people in an emotionally charged atmosphere'. These considerations are particularly true for teachers, whose professional effectiveness and fulfilment are highly contingent upon 'the quality and cognitive power of the classroom interaction they orchestrate' (Alexander 2009:4), as well as on the degree to which they build up a positive relationship with their students (Cornwall 1997).

There has been a significant body of research concerned with teachers' burnout that can be attributed to a number of factors related to professional contexts, relations, requirements and policy frameworks, which put excessive or contradictory demands on teachers, and undermine their professional integrity and well-being. A considerable volume of this work concentrates on the ways in which neoliberal policy imperatives have a negative impact on teachers' professional and personal lives. It is suggested that the ascendancy of neoliberal policy imperatives has put additional pressure on teachers, as they have been increasingly rendered accountable to meet preordained 'standards' and 'performance indicators' (Beck 1999; Ball 2003). These demands constitute an external 'locus of control' (Schwab 1983; Kelchtermans 1999) for teachers, as they are called upon to align concerns for equity and social justice with neoliberal constructions of educational excellence (Taylor 2004). Winzer and Mazurek (2011:8), for instance, while discussing the ways in which teachers were called upon to promote inclusion on top of a string of other requirements concerned with raising standards and implementing new curricula in the Canadian context, point to the fact that: 'Many teachers felt under siege and unprepared to comply with the broad array of requirements. They interpreted inclusion as requiring change to accustomed practice, felt that it increased their workload and stress levels, and demanded time they did not have.'

At the same time, considerable research evidence, drawing on teachers perspectives and voices, suggests that teachers' feelings of aversion towards inclusion can be attributed to the lack of funding, resources, and operational support, and any framework of support (e.g. extra personnel, planning time and class-size reduction). Winzer and Mazurek (2011) refer to a survey commissioned by a teaching association in Canada, which points to the fact that the lack of adequate learning resources was a source of stress for 85 per cent of teachers in both primary and secondary education. Additional surveys identified the lack of classroom support for students designated as having SEN/D as one of the most important contributing factors to teacher burnout alongside increased bureaucracy in order to determine students' eligibility for additional special education funding and support, as well as lack of professional training for inclusion.

Apart from the personal ways in which burnout is experienced, teacher burnout has dire implications for students' learning and identities. This is because teachers who experience burnout exhibit low teaching performance, negative attitudes towards their students, low expectations of students, deteriorating teaching performance, diminished involvement in teaching and little concern for their students (Schwab 1983; Talmor et al. 2005). Thus, even though one of the factors that has been identified as being related to teacher burnout within the context of inclusion is negative attitudes towards inclusion (Talmor et al. 2005), this has a reciprocal effect, in the sense that teacher burnout frequently results in diminished interest in teaching and students. This phenomenon gives rise to a negative stance towards including students with SEN/D in mainstream classrooms. This is related to what Maslach (1999) has identified as the 'depersonalization' syndrome of burnout, whereby teachers develop negative attitudes, and become cynical and condescending towards their students.

Given the above considerations and bearing in mind research evidence suggesting that teacher quality has a prodigious impact on students' learning (DfES 2010), it was very appositely suggested that the 'amelioration of teacher burnout is set to become one of the most important areas of global educational policy interest in the future' (Goddard and Goddard 2006:62). It should be noted, however, that teacher burnout cannot be addressed unless the problem is also located at the policy and institutional level (e.g. the existence of contradictory education policies). As Schwab put it, as early as 1983, 'The point has passed where we can continue to blame the individual teacher for developing feelings that anyone could develop if placed in a similar situation' (Schwab 1983:24).

Changing understandings, cultures and educational practices

Apart from the critical dimensions of the process of change, attention should also be given to a number of whole-school considerations that can leverage inclusive education reforms. Transformative change necessitates localized struggles that take into consideration contextual and demographic idiosyncrasies and micro-political exigencies. These '[m]ore context-specific, differentiated approaches to improvement are undoubtedly required for schools in the most challenging circumstances' (Harris 2010:70), for 'it is in these contextualized struggles over the values and purposes of education that hope lies' (Armstrong et al. 2010:135). These contextualized struggles and interventions can have positive effects on school performance and students' achievement, especially in schools with the most challenging circumstances, as they have greater potential to break the link between social disadvantage and underachievement.

Fullan (2006:4) suggests that some theories of change, albeit commendable, are incomplete and unsustainable because their remote implementation will lead only to superficial and short-term changes. For instance, reform initiatives that do not focus on changing school or district culture are short-sighted and ineffective. The notion of culture is given a pre-eminent position and, as Fullan (2006) suggests, one key question to ask in the process of change is 'How do we change cultures?' This refers to both school and socio-political cultures.

The Index for Inclusion (Booth and Ainscow 2002) exemplifies three conceptual and practice-oriented axes against which an inclusive education reform agenda should be predicated. The first one is concerned with creating inclusive cultures, while the two others concentrate on the necessity to formulate inclusive policies and foster evolving inclusive practices. Concerns about human rights should be firmly embedded in school policy and practice intended to promote an ethos that respects and valorizes difference and diversity. Arguably, these concerns can have a wider appeal in creating and cementing social cohesion by nurturing responsible and mindful citizens, who are not only well aware of their rights but are also aware of their fellow citizens' rights in a democratic and participatory society.

In parallel with attempts to promote an inclusive education reform agenda, there are a number of other policy initiatives aimed at introducing citizenship education in school curricula with a view to advancing a 'rights respecting' ethos (e.g. UNICEF UK 2013). These initiatives concentrate on eradicating discrimination and fostering non-discriminatory regimes and equitable social relations across schools as a means of promoting community cohesion. For instance, in the USA, the School Wide Integrated Framework for Transformation (SWIFT) Center's initiative has as its overarching aim to 'assist schools and their districts to create equity of access and opportunity for all members of their communities' (Stonemeier et al. 2013:2).

Teachers and school leaders are expected to understand and act upon the role of schools in 'addressing fractures in the communities which they serve, and the impact that such fractures and other obstacles have on the life chances of students' (Rowe et al. 2011:4). In so doing, educational professionals, according to Hursh (2007:515), 'would not merely employ the curriculum, pedagogy, and assessment as determined by others but would become educative leaders engaged in deliberation with the community'. Such an engagement, however, is significantly hampered by the standards agenda and its unfettered quest for meeting exam-driven effectiveness indicators, which undermine teachers' and school leaders' attempts to promote a school ethos that celebrates learner diversity as a way to foster cohesive and democratic communities for all (Rowe et al. 2011).

At the same time, mobilizing 'socially just change' (Hattam et al. 2009:304) in school cultures, policies and practices also entails questioning and subverting the dualistic logic between special and regular education. Special education needs to be seen from a broader perspective and to be firmly embedded in wider attempts to create quality forms of learning support, which do not stigmatize and marginalize students (Caldwell 2014). For instance, as already discussed, this wider perspective is manifested in the Finnish educational system, where learning support is provided on a proactive rather than a reactive basis, and is not limited to a designated group of students who are labelled as 'special'. This kind of learning support is available to all students, who might encounter difficulties in their learning at some point of their schooling.

By adopting this wider perspective on providing a co-ordinated learning support provision that extends to include all students, the additional learning support ceases to be considered as 'special', while the achievement gap between low- and high-achieving students can be narrowed. Moreover, in addition to adopting a proactive approach to providing learning support, the Finnish educational system adopts an early detection and intervention programme by means of providing periodic individualized students' assessment. These assessments are carried out by teachers, with the aim of identifying struggling students and providing relevant support at an early stage. To that end, it is crucial that professional practice is informed by a robust knowledge base of current research into learning, and fed into the continuous development and refinement of assessment instruments for early identification and intervention, through collaborative professional practice. The latter constitutes an important dimension of attempts to provide non-stigmatizing and effective forms of provision (Sabelk et al. 2010 cited in Caldwell 2014).

Along similar lines, the recent introduction of certain special and educational laws in the USA (the Individuals with Disabilities Education Act (IDEA) and the Elementary and Secondary Education Act (ESEA) mandate fundamental changes in K-12 education. For instance, schools must adopt high-quality instruction, implement research-based practices and introduce assessment procedures, as well as intervention strategies so as to ensure that students, including those students designated as having learning difficulties, make meaningful progress. To this end, educational professionals are expected to be able to use research-based strategies and interventions taking into consideration students' personal and biographical histories as well as social, cultural, linguistic and socio-emotional factors that impact upon students' lives and educational trajectories (National Joint Committee on Learning Disabilities 2011).

In particular, the IDEA (US Department of Education 2004) has introduced the multi-tiered Response to Intervention (RTI) or, as otherwise referred to, Response to Instruction, with a view to reducing special educational referrals for students whose learning difficulties can be attributed to 'poor' or 'inadequate' instruction. RTI is an approach that eschews categorization and special education interventions, and focuses on providing appropriate, high-quality and effective teaching for all students, including students with disabilities. This approach subscribes to an early intervention approach, rather than a 'wait to fail' model (Brown and Doolittle 2008). The first 'tier' of response concentrates on providing high-quality and evidence-based instruction for all children in general classrooms. Early intervention is applied through universal screening assessments so as to single out students at risk in terms of reading and behaviour.

Based on the above considerations, the SWIFT Center in the USA, in collaboration with states, districts and schools, has been commissioned by the US Department of Education to mobilize 'meaningful change in how schooling in the USA is organized to deliver equity of educational opportunity' (Stonemeier et al. 2013:3). The SWIFT initiative is informed by an equity and civil rights framework and endorses an 'equity driven change for all students', while it is anticipated that over a five-year period (2012–2017) this collaborative reform initiative will facilitate the implementation of the envisaged model, to proceed to an impact evaluation on educational practice and student outcome and to devise a plan for the sustainability and scale up of the reform (Stonemeier et al. 2013). In particular, the professed aim of the SWIFT initiative is articulated as follows:

> The SWIFT framework moves schools toward operating as a fully integrated organization that discourages the formulation of 'silos' (i.e., separate categorical systems for discrete populations within a school) and facilitates collaborative teaching at all grades and levels of intervention. SWIFT considers inclusive education as part of a theory of change guiding school reform (Burrello, Kleinhammer-Tramill, Sailor, 2013) as well as an organizational framework that enables teachers and schools to teach all students, including those with significant disabilities, within the physical spaces, routines, social interactions and schedules that are offered and expected for all other students. When a multi-tiered system of supports (MTSS) is used, and more intensive interventions are designed for either academic or behavioral needs, students receive them in addition to participating in the general education instruction offered to everyone else. The key is the fluidity and flexibility of grouping students based on individual need without restriction or qualification based on disability label or type. The SWIFT framework not only combines academic and behavioral support systems, but also guides change in policy, finance and leadership structures to ensure that no organizational barriers impede the delivery of evidence-based practices for all students.
>
> (Stonemeier et al. 2013:3)

A similar model of multi-tiered intervention strategies has also been introduced in the Finnish educational system. The aim of the new special education strategy (SPES), which was introduced in Finland by the Ministry of Education in 2007 (Thuneberg et al. 2011), aimed at introducing a three-tier support system that is informed by a pedagogical rather than a psychological and medical paradigm. The first tier of providing high-quality basic education and general support for every child is followed by a new phase, namely, intensified support before proceeding to the provision of special support. The SPES framework necessitates establishing collaborative practice, encouraging flexible student grouping and cultivating an informed awareness of differentiated and innovative educational interventions (Thuneberg et al. 2014).

The implementation of research-based strategies and interventions as a means of meeting students' special educational needs is also stipulated in the revised UK SEN Code of Practice (DFE and DOH 2014). It is expected that early-years settings, schools and colleges provide evidence-based interventions as part of a graduated approach, which includes a review of the progress made by students designated as having SEN/D with a view to providing adaptations to existing support as required. The support is reviewed and monitored by the class or subject teacher in close collaboration with parents, the SENCO and students. The quality and effectiveness of the provision along with its impact on children and young people designated as having SEN/D should be regularly reviewed and monitored. This is a positive step forward that holds teachers and schools accountable for the progress made by this group of students. Simultaneously, a more pronounced emphasis is placed on the importance of teachers' pedagogical expertise and ability to be engaged in collaborative professional practice so as to address learner diversity in effective and socially just ways.

A case study based on a whole-school framework for transformative action

The previous section highlighted a number of key issues and considerations that should inform the process of whole-school reforms. This section provides a whole-school case study in order to document the ways in which the process of whole-school change can be mobilized and sustained throughout the school. Theoharis and Causton (2014) concretize the varied dimensions and theoretical underpinnings of an inclusive education reform agenda by providing a comprehensive and practice-oriented account of the ways in which inclusive reforms for students with SEN/D can be navigated and implemented.

It should be noted that this practice-oriented account of a school reform process presupposes the existence of a particular value system, as well as related actions and evidence-based practices that should inform the various stages of a whole-school reform process towards inclusion. Florian (2014) presents a comprehensive framework in order to document inclusive pedagogical practice and to enhance knowledge about inclusive education. This theoretically informed conceptual framework can provide the basis of understanding the ways in which teachers make sense of and enact inclusive pedagogies, while taking into consideration the highly contextual nature of the process of change. The inclusive pedagogical approach in action (IPAA) framework embodies a number of value-based considerations, theoretical perspectives and evidence-based considerations that are presented and discussed throughout this book. One of the parameters referred to by Florian (2014) is concerned with the necessity to valorize learner diversity and nurture the 'whole child', an issue that is frequently downplayed by the propagation of narrow views of learning and attainment abetted by neoliberal ideologies as discussed in Chapter 1.

Theoharis and Causton's (2014) action plan provides a whole-school approach to mobilizing the process of inclusive education reforms. The analytical edge is concerned with the ways in which value-based considerations and the associated concepts and actions pertaining to inclusion are enacted in schools' organizational structures, working procedures and relations so as to precipitate the process of change. Their proposed plan for transformative change has been driven by the belief that:

When students are removed from the general education classroom for any type of service, there is a trade-off and cost to that. Students miss important content and fall further behind ... The focus is on seamlessly providing students the services and support that they need within the context of general education in order for all students to reach their social and academic potential through developing a school culture in which school staff members embrace a collective ethos that all students are their students and work together to know and respond to students.

(Theoharis and Causton 2014:97)

To this end, the authors outline a seven-part process along with a set of tools in order to create, as they write: ' authentically inclusive schools' (p. 82) aimed at fostering a 'climate of belonging' (p. 87) and developing a culture in which staff members nurture a collective ethos that valorizes learner diversity. Their proposed seven-part process necessitates collaborative practice and a collective problem-solving approach embodied in the constitution of a leadership team that consists of school administrators, special teachers and other staff members. Family involvement is also central to fostering a collaborative framework of reform planning and implementation.

A first step to the process of transformative change towards inclusion is to set a school vision for reform. The visionary strategy consists of three interrelated areas, which focus on students' placement in classrooms and on co-ordinating and overseeing meetings for staff to discuss inclusion. The second area focuses on setting school climate goals concerned with planning, supporting and implementing inclusion across grade levels, devising a coherent plan for consistent and continuous communication, developing professional learning communities, and fostering a welcoming and engaging learning environment. The third area focuses on creating child-centred, differentiated and evidence-based instruction for learner diversity through collaborative practice and professional development. Steps two and three are concerned with a transitional process aimed at creating a new service delivery map. This means that the utilization of human and material resources is geared towards serving all students inclusively. Hitherto, the parallel systems of educating disabled students in pull-out programmes, with the use of paraprofessionals and special teachers, have created a segregated system characterized by disparate and fragmented forms of special educational provision, which alienated disabled students from mainstream classrooms and the general education curriculum (Liasidou 2012a).

The new service delivery map of step three aims to make better use of the staff in alignment with the principles of inclusion. This is what Theoharis and Causton (2014) call an 'inclusive service delivery plan' aimed at redeploying staff members in order to work towards enhancing participation and belonging in heterogeneous inclusive classrooms. This can be achieved by creating inclusive teams to collaboratively design and deliver differentiated instruction for all students in inclusive classrooms. For instance, these teams consist of a special education teacher and two to three classroom teachers, who are paired in order to plan and implement inclusive pedagogical designs in general classrooms, so as to accommodate the needs of all students including students with SEN/D.

In the succeeding step the staff deployment reconfiguration plan is further developed and refined with a view to creating a balanced distribution of disabled students in general classrooms. This is followed by step five that aims at providing professional development opportunities to teaching teams with a pronounced emphasis on collaborative practice, co-teaching, educational differentiation, evidence-based instruction, behaviour management and English language learners (ELL), for example, bilingual special education (see e.g. Liasidou 2013b). Apart from professional development opportunities, school leaders are also expected to provide feedback to teaching teams, after observing their collaborative and co-teaching practices in general classrooms, so as to further enable them to improve their educational practice within the context of an inclusive education reform agenda. This process is facilitated by providing feedback through various 'feedback forms' that concentrate on separate aspects of teaching teams, professional practice and working relations. For instance, the co-teaching feedback form is used in order to provide feedback to teams where a special education teacher works alongside a mainstream teacher in the same classroom as a means of exchanging views on how to improve their co-teaching practices. Additional feedback forms focus on the classroom environment and behaviour so as to set out a conceptual framework against which to evaluate and address key parameters of creating effective inclusive classrooms.

The two final steps describe a recursive process of ongoing monitoring and reviewing of the reform plan by taking into consideration feedback from all staff members, students and families, while exhibiting unwavering commitment to implementing the inclusive reform plan, notwithstanding instances of resistance and dissension. The plan is consistently reviewed and adjusted while progress is acknowledged and celebrated; the aim being to reinforce efforts and reward achievement. The final step concentrates on enhancing the feeling of belonging amongst students and staff. This two-pronged process intends, on the one hand, to involve all staff members in the design and implementation of an authentic inclusive education reform agenda and, on the other, to valorize difference and diversity, to build collaborative classroom and school communities, and to enhance the active participation and involvement of students, staff members and families in the school development process (Theoharis and Causton 2014).

Social and emotional aspects of learning and whole-school considerations

In addition to creating inclusive pedagogical designs and strategies to meet learner diversity, inclusive schools are also expected to become more effective in meeting students' socio-emotional needs, for there is a direct and reciprocal relation between emotions and learning. Hence, apart from the placement of all students designated as having SEN/D in mainstream educational settings, inclusion is also concerned with students' well-being and ability to flourish and unleash their potential in effective and participatory learning communities. Without denouncing the ways in which individual attributes interact with the educational and wider societal context, inclusion gives particular prominence to the latter in order to advance new theorizations of human identities and behaviours, taking into considerations concerns about human rights and social justice.

By no means should it be assumed that students who are plagued by numerous 'socially toxic' conditions (Watts and Erevelles 2004:290) are always ready to comprehend academic material. Consequently, schools should nurture the necessary social and emotional skills to enable students to achieve personal well-being inside and outside of school (Elbertson et al. 2010). The importance of emotions in the process of learning is also documented by empirical evidence from brain research. For instance, it is suggested that emotions can facilitate the process of recalling information from the long-term memory and enhance learning (Muijs 2010). Moreover, empirical evidence from various school-based interventions suggest that social and emotional learning (SEL) – a term that was first coined in the Fetzer Institute conference of 1994 – is crucial for students' development, physical and mental health, self-esteem, moral judgement, academic achievement, citizenship and motivation. SEL has also been shown to have positive effects on minimizing truancy, improving classroom behaviour and facilitating academic engagement (Elbertson et al. 2010; Jones 2014).

The process of creating emotionally literate schools can be facilitated by a legislative framework aimed at promoting educational practices that concentrate on the social and emotional aspects of learning. For instance, notwithstanding the fact that many state governments in the USA have not yet embraced the SEL agenda, Elbertson et al. (2010) cite the example of the state of Illinois, which has a robust legal framework that stipulates the significance of social and emotional development for enhancing academic attainment and success. Schools are mandated to incorporate SEL into their regional educational programmes, while it is expected that other states will also mandate schools to implement SEL by formulating relevant policies.

In a similar vein, the SEAL (Social and Emotional Aspects of Learning) agenda in the UK was a government-funded project that was introduced in order to foster 'a comprehensive, whole school approach to promoting the social and emotional skills that are thought to underpin effective learning, positive behaviour, regular attendance and emotional wellbeing' (DfES 2007 cited in Boddington et al. 2014:86). The aim of the project was to supplement PSHE (personal, social, health and economic education) in schools and concentrated on developing students' self-awareness, empathy, social skills, motivation and ability to manage feelings while also equipping students with the social and emotional skills to understand and deal with the impact of their behaviour on their learning and social relations.

The overall evaluation of the SEAL project was positive. Amongst other things, the evaluation highlighted the positive impact of the project on improving professional practice in dealing with students' emotions and behaviour. The latter point is related to the ways in which teachers managed to make sense of the underlying causes of problem behaviour, which often result from the emotional or social needs of the student (Boddington et al. 2014). A pronounced emphasis on SEL brings to the fore the ways in which problem behaviour is linked to students' social and emotional needs, while recognizing the contextual nature of social emotional and behaviour difficulties (SEBD), thereby inferring the significant role of schools and educational professionals in enhancing students' 'resilience', so as to resist possible threats to their emotional and mental health (Blake et al. 2007:24).

This perspective is occasionally silenced, while students' SEBD are routinely addressed through a mono-dimensional approach focused on specific conditions or syndromes that give rise to individual deficit assumptions and practices. Educational professionals are presented with this perspective, which downplays or even ignores contextual and situational considerations that contribute towards creating or exacerbating SEBD. By excluding this significant dimension of SEBD, the role of schools and educational professionals in addressing these issues is trivialized on the grounds of a deficit-oriented and 'blame-the-victim' perspective.

Tracing the aetiologies and exploring the nature of SEBD, involves critically evaluating the cumulative effects of society, schooling, teachers and teaching styles on shaping students' behaviour and learning profiles. The rhetoric about the necessity to foster a systemic and proactive approach to dealing with socio-emotional and behavioural issues needs to be adequately rationalized and analysed in alignment with recent policy developments and theoretical frameworks that acknowledge the social dimension of 'problem behaviour'. It is suggested that biological and hereditary predispositions rarely are responsible for the emergence and development of psychopathology (Scarlet et al. 2009); hence, issues of SEBD should be addressed through the lens of social and organizational pathology that adversely affects students' emotional stability and educational ability. Stripped from their contextual and values-based consideration, SEBD are routinely addressed through a mono-dimensional and uncritical approach focused on specific conditions or syndromes that give rise to individual deficit assumptions and practices. In spite of the fact that some policy developments recognize the contextual nature of SEBD and emphasize the significant role of a whole-school approach to addressing issues of 'problem behaviour', other policy frameworks, such as zero-tolerance policies (Kennedy-Lewis 2014), act in antithetical ways and undermine attempts to shift the focus from an individual pathology perspective to one of social/organizational pathology.

A whole-school approach to managing social, emotional and behavioural difficulties

In trying to challenge certain conceptualizations of inclusion, it is important to analyse the ways in which the notion of difference has been constructed as learning and behaviour problems in schools and has been mobilized as a legitimate mechanism of managing and containing certain groups of children by providing alternative placements like pupil referral units and special schools (Armstrong et al. 2010). Arguably, these 'alternative placements' are nothing but a legitimate mechanism of managing potentially 'troublesome' individuals, who, allegedly, have nothing to contribute to the utilitarian ethos of modern schooling.

Morrison (2001) cites research evidence suggesting that 8 per cent of students who are placed in these alternative forms of provision, exhibit gifted and talented behaviours, an issue that needs careful consideration in the light of current debates on the arbitrary and highly subjective nature of identification and assessment procedures pertaining to SEBD. Different kinds of human 'deviance' have been devised and gauged against arbitrarily construed notions of normality with a view to protecting the normal functioning of mainstream schooling (Tomlinson 2013).

The necessity of introducing and institutionalizing holistic and critical whole-school approaches to understanding and dealing with various manifestations of 'problem behaviour' have long been recognized as a valid alternative to deficit-oriented and insular approaches to behaviour management (Blake et al. 2007; Rogers 2009). Theoretical insights drawn from the bio-psychosocial model of disability (Norwich 2010) provide a comprehensive understanding of the complex and contested nature of SEBD, while also exploring some of the ways in which this model can be applied in professional practice, while taking into consideration the social dimension of SEBD (Scarlet et al. 2009). Thus, a comprehensive understanding of SEBD involves looking at and understanding the presenting characteristics of individuals within their social context. The 'behaviour-in-context' approach necessitates taking a perspective of behaviour as a response to environmental and individual needs. Consequently, risk factors in the child need to be understood and examined in parallel with risk factors in the child's family and community.

Some authors also draw on post-modern and post-structural sociological frameworks in order to define and address issues of 'problem behaviour' (e.g. Graham 2005, 2006; Pihlaja 2007). Within this context, the emphasis is given to the role of linguistic constructs and discursive practices in creating and attributing negative labels related to SEBD. Gallagher (1997), for instance, refers to the use of destructive D's and the negative subjectivities imputed to students with SEBD. The destructive D's metaphor is used to describe the negative and pejorative ways in which certain behaviours are characterized, namely, dysfunctional, difficult, deviant, disordered, disturbed, disappointing, disruptive, delinquent, drop out. Attention is also given to the arbitrary ways in which labels and subjugating linguistic constructs are frequently construed, attributed and sustained through institutionalized practices and discriminatory regimes (Pihlaja 2007).

An important angle of this kind of analysis entails the exploration of the ways in which children with SEBD are perceived and dealt with in mainstream schools. The category of SEBD is conceived of as a discursive construct, and current schooling as a site of unequal power relations that gives rise to the formation of 'disrupting' and 'deviant' student-subjects (Graham 2005, 2008; Harwood 2008). For instance, reference is made to attention deficit hyperactivity disorder (ADHD), whose biological bases and the medication prescriptions associated with it have been widely questioned and problematized during the last few years. Graham (2006:2) characterizes the contemporary phenomenon of ADHD as a 'symptom of the pathologies of schooling', while court cases in the USA have addressed 'questions about whether certain groups of children (behaviorally disordered...learning disabled) are being appropriately identified' (Rothstein and Johnson 2010:90).

Simultaneously, the analytical perspective extends to include intersectional understandings of disability and 'problem behaviour' (see Chapter 8 for a more focused analysis of intersectionality) in order to supplement and reinforce the significance attributed to the role of the wider cultural and societal context in giving rise to and exacerbating SEBD. Such a perspective also rationalizes the necessity of adopting a social justice and human rights framework in addressing issues of SEBD. This analysis aims to delve into the culturally and socially mediating processes and dynamics that impact upon students' behaviour and socio-emotional well-being. Issues of culture, race/ethnicity and poverty are also examined in relation to the emergence and identification of SEBD. That said, it is no coincidence that the Supreme Court in Canada, for instance, encourages the adoption of an intersectional analysis in understanding issues of discrimination and marginalization of particular groups of students and, in particular, students designated as having SEBD (Cassidy and Jackson 2005). This kind of approach can foster critical awareness of the reciprocal and complex relation of a host of exogenous dynamics with students' cognitive and socio-emotional 'identities', which facilitate the emergence and propagation of 'problem behaviour', while also highlighting issues of human rights and social justice in education policy and practice (Liasidou 2013a).

Hence, in order to develop an informed understanding of the aetiologies and the nature of challenging behaviour of children and young people, it is crucial to critically evaluate the cumulative effect of society, community, home, schooling, teachers and teaching styles on shaping students' behaviour and learning profiles. This perspective goes beyond systemic approaches to dealing with SEBD and advances an 'intersectional' approach to understanding and analysing SEBD. An intersectional perspective takes a broader and more comprehensive approach to analysing the ways in which issues of culture, ethnicity, social class and other sources of social disadvantage as well as educational inequalities (Kennedy-Lewis 2014) affect children's socio-emotional stability, development and well-being; this is an issue that should be considered seriously in addressing students' social and emotional difficulties.

Arguably, adopting an 'intersectional approach' to policy and provision with regard to SEBD opens up new perspectives and strategies in addressing the complexity of the issues at hand, which cannot be reduced to the mere description and manipulation of certain 'syndromes' allegedly endemic to a person's psychological and emotional make up. Apart from providing a rationale for adopting 'joined up' policies (Ball 2009) and promoting inter-agency collaborative practice in managing SEBD, an intersectional approach, as already discussed, advances a rights-based and social justice approach to schooling and behaviour management.

These rights-based and social justice considerations can be better understood when we bear in mind the complex ways in which discrimination can undermine a child's ability to experience inclusive values and practices. For example, the nature of SEBD needs to be examined in relation to the controversial nature of non-normative categories of SEN/D (Tomlinson 1982, 2014), so as to understand the complexity and ambiguity of assessment and identification procedures, along with the variegated social and educational dynamics impinging upon the construction of SEBD. To this end, it is important to understand the ways in which non-normative categories of special education are construed and sustained within current schooling. Moreover, this perspective makes more salient the issues of prejudice and discrimination linked to ethnicity, social class and other sources of social disadvantage that impact upon the process of SEN/D identification and assessment (Cassidy and Jackson 2005).

Dyson and Kozleski (2008) point to the ways in which the identification of non-normative categories of disability, including SEBD, is contingent on professional judgement which is occasionally skewed by prejudice and discrimination. It is, for instance, empirically suggested that males of colour from low-income family backgrounds are disproportionately identified as being in need of disciplinary services. This kind of discriminatory treatment is inexorably linked with neoliberal imperatives and zero-tolerance policies that promote a deficit and 'blame-the-victim' view of students' behaviour.

Kennedy-Lewis (2014) provides an insightful account of the ways in which zero-tolerance policies promote a narrow role for schools and distinguishes two discourses: the discourse of safety and the discourse of equity, in order to describe dominant understandings in relation to the role of education and schooling in addressing student diversity. The former discourse aligns with neoliberal constructions of the 'ideal students' who must be protected and empowered to pursue their niche positioning in the competitive market place of a globalized economy. Students' future positioning is solely regarded as the result of their individual skills, effort and achievement, while it is maintained that students who achieve should be 'protected' from those who fail to achieve or misbehave. Within this context, schools tend to adopt punitive forms of provision for those students who deviate from dominant conceptualizations of the 'ideal student', while the common belief is that 'comprehensive schools' are 'only responsible for educating the majority of students who meet certain criteria or behave in particular ways' (Kennedy-Lewis 2014:173).

In contrast, the discourse of equity, promotes a different role of schooling that is premised on the assumption that social dynamics and contextual toxic conditions are accountable for creating uneven starting points for students and assigning hierarchical future social positioning. In this respect, the most important mission of schooling concentrates on the necessity to nurture and develop the whole child while unconventional forms of students behaviour call for further investigations against the wider social and educational context within which students develop and learn. In consequence, schools are expected to support students who misbehave in order to unleash their full potential in high-quality, inclusive educational settings (Kennedy-Lewis 2014).

Changing social policies and socio-political cultures

Bearing in mind that educational policies are not formulated in a cultural vacuum (Fulcher 1999; Armstrong et al. 2000), but are dynamically linked with the wider socio-political system and its underlying ideological and institutional norms (Liasidou 2012a), it is crucially important to discuss the ways in which educational reform efforts are affected by and shaped within the prevailing political, social and cultural milieu. The school improvement movement has been criticized on the grounds of the insular and monolithic ways in which it has theorized and framed issues of school change and development (Harris 2010). The movement has ignored, according to Harris (2010:696), 'the socio-economic influences that impact upon schools and for offering naïve and sometimes simplistic solutions to complex social problems'.

Grace (1991) gives particular emphasis to the wider picture of educational policymaking within which the 'struggles for inclusion' (Vlachou 1997) are taking place. This perspective highlights the necessity to recognize the reciprocal relationship between the educational system and society. Educational reform efforts are not disassociated from wider societal reforms and social policy initiatives; hence the focus of analysis should extend to include the 'wider picture of educational policymaking'. It is, therefore, equally important to interrogate the social edifice and the multiplicity of the ideological and structural dynamic impinging upon it. In so doing, it will be possible to disentangle the multidimensional and intricately complicated contextual framework within which inclusion is conceptualized, contested and implemented. As it has been suggested:

> Education policy is part of wider social policy and the welfare state in general. Consequently, education policy is interlinked and develops in parallel with other initiatives in social policy

(Oliver, 1988). By implication, inclusive education policymaking should be viewed in relation to wider economic and social interests of a developing society (Barton and Armstrong, 2001) that determine the ways in which disability and special educational needs are conceptualized and defined.

(Liasidou 2012a:75)

Thus, in order to understand and explain, for example, the impressive developments in the processes and outcomes of educational change in Finland, which reflect the country's 'journey from the educational periphery to international limelight', it is important to place an equal focus on understanding the 'contextual factors – especially sociocultural aspects and other public sector policies' (Sahlberg 2010:324) that have impacted upon the process of educational change. The features underpinning the educational reform efforts in the country have been closely aligned with those supporting the 'social and economic transformation of Finland into a welfare state and a knowledge society' (Sahlberg 2010:330).

The Finnish example documents the contention that improved learning outcomes cannot be achieved unless students have adequate material and moral support within their community in terms of health, safety, social welfare services and so on. In particular, Hargreaves and Shirley (2009) discuss the beneficial effects of the welfare system, which makes public investments on housing, medical care and community development as a means to effect positive changes in all aspects of educational and social domains. As Sahlberg (2010:338) writes with regard to the role of the welfare state in introducing socially just educational reforms in the Finnish socio-political and educational context:

> ... basic social services, including education, became public services for all citizens, particularly for those most in need of support and help. This increased the level of social capital, so did national government policies that affected children's broader social environment and improved the opportunities and willingness to learn.

The dominant socio-political features of the country have also contributed to attempts to create a more equitable educational system by abolishing the two parallel systems of education, which had sustained social division and provided unequal opportunities for students to access quality education. In an effort to provide more equitable educational opportunities to all students regardless of their corporeal, class, cultural, racial, linguistic and other characteristics, they have introduced a state-funded nine-year comprehensive school that, apart from providing equal opportunities for learning, also offers other social services for the holistic development and well-being of all students. These extended services include, amongst others, healthcare and dental care, special educational support, free meals and transportation.

The provision of extended school services can play an instrumental role in ensuring students' optimal socio-emotional and cognitive development in order to mitigate adverse social conditions and to enable students to reach their learning potential. In terms of the intersection of disability and social class/poverty, considerable research evidence suggests that malnutrition, inadequate child-care and healthcare can adversely affect neurological development (Bass and Gerstl-Pepin 2011:924) and cause disabilities (Elwan 1999; Mittler 1999; Department for Children, Schools and Families (DCSF) 2009). The reciprocal relationship amongst poverty, cultural diversity and disability has been characterized by Van Kampen et al. (2008:19) as a 'vicious circle' in order to denote the ways in which some groups of students are entangled in multiple and mutually reinforcing forms of social disadvantage. Similarly, Turnbull (2009:7) exemplifies the close link between the healthcare system and special education, and suggests that 'children who are not born healthy, raised in healthy homes, nourished well, and who do not have effective early intervention and robust medical treatment become special education students'.

Moreover, apart from the impact of a robust social welfare service system on education, the Finnish example of achieving an equitable educational system in a relatively short time can be attributed to culturally ingrained characteristics such as law-abiding citizenship, high levels of state legitimacy, a consensus-building orientation, a patriotic spirit and a widely accepted system of social values that is largely non-existent in other more individualistic and inequitable societies. In terms of other endemic characteristics that are more closely related to the educational system, Finland honours the autonomy of schools and valorizes the professionalism of teachers and head teachers, which leads them to undertake risks and to experiment in encouraging and nurturing creativity, as well as introducing innovations in terms of teaching and learning (Hargreaves and Shirley 2009; Sahlberg 2010).

Nevertheless, despite the praiseworthy role of social services in Nordic countries, and most notably in Finland, these systems are not without their critics in terms of the ways in which they deal with the issue of disability. Barnes (2012) notes that the Nordic states' welfare and educational policies are still informed by medical and psychological perspectives. Research is characterized as being

> top down, apolitical and often concerned with defining and measuring impairment with reference to impairment specific groups such as those with 'learning disabilities', for example, rather than oppression or discrimination.
>
> (Barnes 2012:20–21)

Along similar lines, Campbell (2005:109), while discussing the disabling nature of certain legislative frameworks, points to the ways in which individual pathology conceptualizations of disability underpin 'most of the claims of disability discrimination that are juridically sanctioned within the welfare state and is imbricated in compensatory initiatives and the compulsion towards therapeutic intervention'. The legally sanctioned authoring of disability as being 'ontologically intolerable, that is, inherently negative' (ibid.) legitimizes the implementation of assimilationist and remedial practices so as to enable the disabled 'Other' to approximate dominant conceptualizations of ontological normalcy.

In stark contrast to the culturally grounded considerations above that have been conducive to creating an equitable and effective schooling in Finland, it might be useful to provide a counter example from an entirely different European socio-political and educational context so as to highlight the impact of social, historical and cultural dynamics on education policy formulation and implementation. The following case study is not intended to provide a comprehensive comparative analysis of these two distinct and unrelated socio-political contexts. Rather, this is a tentative attempt to provide some insights into their endemic dominant socio-cultural dynamics, conditions and circumstances, which impact on the process of challenging the educational status quo and mobilizing socially just policy reforms.

The Republic of Cyprus constitutes a counter example because its socio-political and educational system differs enormously from that in Finland. Notwithstanding the fact that the recent introduction of the New National Curriculum (NNC) (MOEC 2010a) has marked a rhetorical 'turnaround' in terms of the pedagogical and ideological underpinnings of current schooling, there is no evidence that laudable rhetoric is to be transformed into educational reality. Even though the principle presented in official rhetoric is to create a 'humane and democratic school' so as to maximize the learning potential of every individual child by 'remov[ing] any adverse consequence that frequently affects children with disabilities, with difficult family backgrounds, with financial hardship and different cultural backgrounds' (MOEC 2008:4), the state continues to honour educational inertia. It is still the case that Cyprus continues to maintain a 'closed, ethnocentric and nationalistic' (Angelides et al. 2003:64) educational system that lacks a democratic and inclusive ethos. These considerations impact upon the ways in which the education system addresses issues of diversity, social exclusion and human rights. The facile official rhetoric articulated in the NNC is also an example of the ways in which language is skilfully used to disguise exclusionary regimes that systematically disempower and marginalize groups of students within the Cypriot educational context, especially students with disabilities in terms of education policy (see Liasidou 2008, 2011, 2014), curriculum (see Symeonidou and Mavrou 2013) and educational practice (see Liasidou 2007; Liasidou and Antoniou 2013).

The characteristics of the educational system mirror wider socio-cultural conditions and exigencies that account for the failure of Cyprus to establish a fully fledged democratic tradition and to prioritize issues of human rights and equality. Owing to its historical and colonial past, Cyprus is characterized by nationalism and cultural conservatism, something that is mirrored in the ways in which the society and the educational system address, for example, matters of social exclusion, sexism and racism. Phtiaka (2003:143) writes about the absence of a democratic tradition and the undeveloped public sphere of the island, which, by implication, lacks the potential to beget 'a broader democratic discourse where debates can be held on such rights issues as equal opportunities, or access to education in terms of race, class, gender or disability...'. As a result, the socio-political system of Cyprus is largely characterized by underdeveloped citizenship, political favouritism and a lack of pluralism (Mavratsas 2003), which has wider implications for the ways in which issues of human rights and equality of opportunity are understood and acted upon in the educational context (see Liasidou 2007, 2008b; Symeonidou 2009 for a more detailed analysis).

Conclusions

The chapter has been concerned with a number of socio-political and historical dynamics that need to be addressed in order to foster professional and institutional 'dynamos' to mobilize the process of change. The vestiges of the status quo in special education are deeply ingrained in the social and educational edifice; hence, their elimination calls for a multilayered and multidirectional transformative change, at the institutional, political and individual level.

Inclusion cannot be achieved unless there is a 'synergetic relation between institutional and ideological dynamics, between pragmatic and critical approaches to teaching...' (Liasidou 2012a:16). This perspective also applies to whole-school considerations aimed at precipitating inclusive educational reforms. Top-down policy reforms geared towards the realization of an inclusive discourse are inappropriate unless complemented by localized struggles that take into consideration contextual dynamics and idiomorphic socio-cultural exigencies and demographic conditions that impact upon the process of policy formulation and enactment.

5
Inclusive Classrooms and the Issue of Change

Introduction

The aim of this chapter is to explore the ways in which the notion of pedagogy constitutes a crucial element in the process of transformative change. Teachers' pedagogy is at the core of teaching and learning and, hence, at the core of an inclusive education reform agenda aimed at valorizing diversity and providing for learners' differing needs and abilities. Inclusive classrooms presuppose new pedagogical approaches that place learners at the centre of the educative process and facilitate the process of learning so as to enable all students to flourish and reach the maximum of their potential. To that end, existing classroom practice should be problematized and radically reconceptualized so as to be aligned with emergent theories of teaching and learning.

The chapter signifies the importance of classroom pedagogy while offering an overview of the varied ways in which teaching and learning have been conceptualized, and highlighting some implications for inclusive pedagogies. Moving away from a deficit-oriented and categorical approach, which still pervades to a significant extent in dominant pedagogical discourse, necessitates an informed understanding of alternative perspectives and evidence-based pedagogical insights that rationalize a socio-political approach to framing and accommodating disability-related needs. Mono-disciplinary analyses are less convincing than a cross-disciplinary analysis aimed at bringing together research and scholarship from diverse fields of study in order to rationalize the imperative to provide quality and effective learning environments for all, through inclusive pedagogical designs that draw on emerging theories of teaching and learning.

There is occasionally a misconception that inclusion relates to specific analyses of pedagogical discourse primarily focused on specialist educational practices and interventions for distinct groups of students. This chapter thus provides a more generic pedagogical perspective with a view to highlighting the ways in which the quest for inclusion is primarily a quest for reconceptualizing teaching and learning as contextually mediated processes aimed at creating inquisitive, independent, reflective and life-long learners, who are well aware of their strengths and weaknesses, as well as their preferred ways and modalities of learning.

Students with SEN/D should thus be primarily viewed as 'learners' who are part of a diverse learning community with varied capabilities and needs, and who are entitled to quality, interactive and engaging instructional environments. The needs of this group of students do not essentially differ from other students but, nevertheless, they might occasionally need more intensive, direct or sometimes more specialized pedagogical practices in order to create the optimal learning environment for them, without stigmatizing or segregating them on the basis of their additional or different learning needs and abilities, however. These pedagogical practices should be viewed as being part of adopting a diverse repertoire of teaching approaches and strategies (Norwich 2008b) in order to maximize students' learning by providing varied modalities of learning.

Teaching and learning in inclusive classrooms

Empirical evidence from school effectiveness research has shown that approximately twice as much discrepancy in student learning outcomes can be explained with reference to the classroom rather than to the school. Similarly, proximity theory, which provides information on key aspects that affect students' learning, points to the ways in which classroom-level, rather than school-level factors have a more substantial impact on students' learning. Hence, classroom-based interventions in teaching and learning can potentially improve the educational outcomes of students to a greater extent in comparison with other interventions across the school (Muijs 2010; Muijs and Reynolds 2010).

Nevertheless, notwithstanding the crucial role of teaching and learning, research evidence suggests that, despite prolonged research on educational reforms (Hargreaves and Goodson 2006), these reforms had minimal impact on the ways in which teachers teach and learners learn. Fullan (2006) draws on a number of case studies to suggest that the importance of instructional quality is frequently not taken into consideration when discussing 'theories of action' pertaining to the process of educational change. While trying to disentangle the key ingredients of theories of change, so as to identify their strengths and weaknesses in achieving effective and sustainable school reforms, Fullan (2006) concludes that teaching and learning are frequently discussed with reference to student outcomes and achievement rather than in relation to the quality of teaching, as well as in relation to the extent to which the instructional environment is conducive to students' learning. According to Fullan (2006:5), what is thus frequently missing from theories of change is 'the black box of instructional practice in the classroom'.

The 'black box of instructional practice' consists of a number of elements, some of which are central and others peripheral in addressing the issue of quality teaching and learning for learner diversity. All these elements can be extrapolated against the notion of classroom pedagogy that is both theoretically informed and action oriented, and plays a crucial role in attempting to mobilize large-scale and sustainable educational reforms. As Levin and Fullan (2008:291) write:

> Large-scale, sustained improvement in student outcomes requires a sustained effort to change school and classroom practices, not just structures such as governance and accountability. The heart of improvement lies in changing teaching and learning practices in thousands and thousands of classrooms, and this requires focused and sustained effort by all parts of the education system and its partners.

Consequently, the process of transformative change towards the realization of an inclusive discourse necessitates advancing new understandings of classroom pedagogy (Florian and Black-Hawkins 2011) that constitutes an integral aspect of a whole-school approach to initiating inclusive education reforms, while addressing a number of classroom-based factors that can contribute to the process of change. Amongst other considerations, it is also important to bear in mind the resilience of certain pedagogical practices, which perpetuate passive forms of learning and are still deeply ingrained in dominant professional practice and classroom routines. It is thus axiomatic that during the process of transformative change '[n]ew concepts have to struggle against a tendency favoring previous concepts and rigid forms of traditional teaching practices' (Thuneberg et al. 2014:38), something that further compounds the process of change.

The following section provides an overview of neoliberal understandings of pedagogical discourse that have given rise to reductionist forms of teaching and learning. The final section concentrates on providing some insights into the ways in which radical pedagogical reforms should embed inclusive pedagogies in a school's mission and professional practice. Particular emphasis is given to socio-cultural theories of learning and their impact on inclusive education.

Neoliberal forms of pedagogical discourse

Theoretical contestations in the field of inclusive education are not limited to concerns about the varied interpretations of a human rights and social justice discourse in education but, as Kershner (2009:56) points out, 'it seems to be useful to see that disagreements may rest as much on different ways of understanding learning'. In view of the ascendancy of market-driven imperatives, education has largely become a transactional process of conveying sterile knowledge that is devoid of critical and inquisitive content (Giroux 2012). Within such a market-driven educational context, the dynamic nature of teaching and learning is reduced to a mechanical process of imparting a predefined body of knowledge that is expected to be applied in known and predictable situations, thereby ignoring the evanescent and ever-changing nature of modern knowledge. As Giroux (2012:40) writes with regard to the economistic model applied to current forms of pedagogy: 'an emphasis on practice substitutes for the hard work of learning how to think; standardization replaces creativity; and efforts to deskill teachers all but destroy the economic, social, and pedagogical conditions for teachers to combine thinking and implementation in the service of the public good'. In consequence, the process of teaching and learning is characterized by teaching routines and standardized rote-learning techniques that lead to knowledge reproduction rather than knowledge (re)construction (Hursh 2009).

Market-driven schools in Western-centric educational contexts focus on the operational aspects of organizational development and improvement, while the experience of teaching and learning is limited to a mechanical process of 'teaching to the test'. The rigidity and standardization of school curricula establish pedagogical rituals that are commensurate with exam-oriented rote-learning regimes, thereby losing sight of the necessity to develop learners' capabilities to become adept at learning how to learn, as a means of becoming life-long learners in an ever-changing and turbulent social world (Kershner 2009). In this respect, education policy and practice concentrate on the products of learning rather than the process of learning, with the former solely measured against exam results (Ball 2004).

Hursh (2007), for instance, writes that schools in the USA allocate the bulk of their curriculum budget to test preparation material rather than other sophisticated learning resources that students need. In consequence, according to Hursh and Henderson (2011:181): 'Instead of learning to raise questions and engage with research, students are focusing on preparing for standardized exams.' Standardized testing has become the dominant educational emblem that provides both a ' "quality indicator" to the consumer and "objective assessments" of student learning within education markets' (Hursh 2007:500).

In consequence, teachers are inclined to teach the skills and knowledge that are expected to be tested, while ignoring other dimensions of their pedagogical role in nurturing rounded, critical and autonomous students in an increasingly complex social world. As Giroux (2012:88–89) writes with reference to the corporate-led education reforms of recent years, '...pedagogy has been reduced to a managerial and disciplinary process largely driven by market values, a crude empiricism, and the ideology of casino capitalism with its relentless prioritization of economic interests over human needs'.

As already discussed in Chapter 1, students who are expected to pass exams are valorized by the system, while those who need additional help and alternative ways of teaching are unobtrusively relegated to the margins of education. Gaming strategies are also linked to particular 'teaching to test' procedures that are meticulously designed to meet the demands of high-stakes testing. This kind of system favours the privileged groups of students who can have access to the $4.5 billion test-prep industry (*The Economist*, 9 February 2013), while teachers systematically ignore subjects that are not tested and concentrate on drilling exercises that emulate standardized tests. As a result, '(r)ather than for example, teaching students to write well, teachers taught students to write the five-paragraph essay with five sentences in each paragraph that would receive passing grades on the standardized tests' (Hursh 2007:507). Instead of enabling students to become life-long learners in an ever-changing and turbulent social world, the emphasis is placed on the products of learning so as to meet short-term educational goals and exam-driven effectiveness indicators (Claxton 2004).

Given the overarching effects of neoliberal pedagogical discourses, Gibson (2009) discusses the ways in which these discourses valorize forms of knowledge that subvert difference and frame it in negative terms, while suggesting that empowering 'children labeled with disability' can 'challenge and turn back the tide of neo-liberalism' (Gibson 2009:12). In order to achieve this, however, knowledge should be reconceptualized 'as an enabling force to secure a society where freedom and justice are not mere words but complete and meaningful practices' (ibid. 18).

Pedagogical considerations and the issue of change

One fundamental element that needs a thorough reconsideration is the notion of learning that underpins dominant conceptualizations of pedagogical discourse. This is an issue that has increasingly attracted the attention of educational reformers. The demands and conditions of modern society call for the abandonment of the 'banking model of education' (Freire 1970), whereby knowledge is thought to be conveyed and utilized in a linear and unwavering fashion. Such a conceptualization of knowledge is obsolete and ignores the dynamic, omnipresent and culturally bounded character of modern knowledge.

Hitherto, traditional conceptualizations of knowledge have constructed learning as a technical and mechanical process of knowledge reproduction that can be triggered by particular environmental stimuli within the classroom context. In this respect, learning has been understood in very insular and static ways, while the learner has been externally situated and positioned as a passive recipient of predetermined chunks of knowledge, which could be mastered through constant drilling and revision. Students' prior knowledge, mental processes and socio-emotional circumstances have not been regarded as being important in this process. The whole process has thus largely failed to incorporate more advanced understandings of learning linked to critical analysis, problem-solving processes, synthesis, etc. In consequence, learners have been solely expected to recall facts in order to deal with similar situations by means of knowledge transfer, without being encouraged to interrogate and reflect upon knowledge with a view to constantly questioning and updating aspects of knowledge that seem obsolete or inadequate in dealing with current situations (Ertmer and Newby 1993).

Predetermined and quintessential understanding of knowledge are questioned and substituted by more dialogical, mutable and fluid ways of knowledge production (Kershner 2009). Knowledge is redefined as a temporal–spatial and culturally mediated phenomenon that needs to be constantly interrogated and modified in the light of emerging perspectives and changing insights. The aim is to enable learners to move beyond knowledge acquisition to foster communities of learning characterized by higher order cognitive, thinking and problem-solving skills so as to critically analyse, converge, synthesize, update, diversify and modify current knowledge, in the light of the emerging demands of an increasingly complex social world (Claxton 2004). The convergence of diverse and seemingly unconnected chunks of knowledge and resources constitutes a cognitive prerequisite in order to enrich and diversify the learning process while developing the 'learning power [of students], so that they can feel a growing sense of achievement, not just in passing tests, but in becoming steadily more resilient, resourceful and reflective in the face of real difficulties' (Claxton 2004:4).

Given the above perspectives, the emphasis shifts from knowledge reproduction to knowledge interpretation and reconceptualization. To this end, the role of the teacher is transformed into that of an architect of learning in order to mobilize and orchestrate an autonomous, innovative, creative and inquisitive process of critical inquiry, negotiation and discovery, so as to produce aspects of knowledge that seem most appropriate to deal with novel situations in a particular spatial and chronological context. In this way, learners are enabled to become adept at learning and, by implication, to assume an active and life-long approach to their learning (Kershner 2009). Thus, learning becomes a perennial process of knowledge production rather than reproduction, where students are expected to relate disparate chunks of information and synthesize new knowledge within the context of certain socio-political situations and exigencies (Claxton 2004; Muijs 2010). Simultaneously, students' prior knowledge and biographical experiences are used as a means to infiltrate, compare and differentiate new knowledge, while learners' attitudes and predispositions are given prominent attention as they are believed to influence the quality of the learning process (Claxton and Carr 2004; Kershner 2009). The latter perspective brings to the fore the importance of personal experience and reflection in framing meanings and constructing knowledge.

The considerations raised in this section are directly linked to the theoretical underpinnings of an inclusive pedagogical approach to teaching and learning (Florian and Spratt 2013; Florian 2014). Florian (2014), for instance, presents an inclusive pedagogical approach in an action framework, which is based on a number of assumptions and associated concepts/actions that need to be cultivated and acted upon for transformative change. One important dimension of this pedagogical approach concentrates on 'replacing deterministic views of ability with those that view learning as open ended' as well as 'providing opportunities for children to co-construct knowledge' while adopting a 'flexible approach driven by needs of learners rather than a "coverage" of material' (Florian 2014:290–294).

Research perspectives on difference and diversity and implications for inclusive pedagogies

Inclusive pedagogies embrace new conceptualizations of learning and intelligence, which highlight all students' innate potential to learn by expanding their learning power (Kershner 2009; Florian and Spratt 2013). From this perspective, it is acknowledged that learning is learnable (Claxton 2004; Black et al. 2006) and, as a result, the aim should not only be to provide students with ample and diverse opportunities to learn, but also to amplify their learning and intellectual capabilities. The capacity to learn is seen as changeable and that 'teachers can and do make a difference to what and how children learn' (Florian and Spratt 2013:122) by creating pedagogical 'affordances' so as to enable students to be actively and creatively engaged in the learning process (Kershner 2009:58).

While it was traditionally assumed that the cognitive and psychological development of children followed normative and biologically determined sequential patterns, these assumptions have been problematized and gradually substituted by evidence-based understandings of biological and cultural diversity. Intelligence has thus been reconceptualized

> as a process of people in action rather than an individual capacity for learning, i.e. it is 'accomplished rather than possessed' This involves calling on the resources in the environment to help with tasks like remembering, reasoning, problem-solving and creating.
> (Pea 1996 cited in Kershner 2009:59)

Nevertheless, despite notable progress in understanding the mutable nature of intelligence and valorizing learner diversity, it is still the case that '[b]ell-curve thinking' and notions of fixed ability still underpin the structure of schooling' and pose significant challenges to promoting an inclusive pedagogical approach to current schooling (Florian 2014:290). The pernicious presumption of pre-existent normative cognitive developmental patterns have pathologized certain students on the basis of their non-middle class and non-dominant cultural origins (Artiles and Kozleski 2007; Artiles et al. 2007), as well as other students whose developmental trajectories differed from normative developmental milestones (Kugelmass 2010), thereby leading to the uncritical categorization of a large proportion of the student population on the grounds of their perceived 'differences' and 'deviations' from arbitrary notions of 'normalcy'.

In view of the above considerations, McPhillips et al. (2010:214) discuss the ways in which the category of 'literacy difficulties' should no longer be viewed through a deficit-oriented lens, but it should be reconceptualized as an endemic aspect of 'neurodiversity in the classroom'. Rather than labelling students with a 'learning difficulty' characterization, the aim should be to respond to 'individualised learner profiles' (McPhillips et al. 2010) and accommodate a wide range of abilities and needs (Burgstahler and Cory 2008). This can be achieved by understanding the impact of the theory of multiple intelligences (Gardner 1983) on literacy acquisition and development. While drawing on each student's idiosyncratic cognitive and learning profile, teachers can encourage and develop students' metacognitive skills which, in turn, can empower students to maximize their individual strengths and learning abilities (Armstrong 2009). Nurture is thus prioritized over nature while arbitrary and mono-dimensional understandings of human intelligence are denounced and reconceptualized in terms of the 'transformability of learning capacity' (Hart et al. 2004:192) in order to enhance learning.

Research on memory and its role in learning provides significant evidence to suggest that sensory systems and memory can be improved through appropriate training and learning (Mitchell 2008; Muijs 2010). Memorization and making connections are crucial aspects of learning; hence, these strategies need to be incorporated in attempts to create effective and stimulating learning environments. Mitchell (2008), for instance, provides research evidence to suggest that mnemonics and other memory strategies are instrumental in improving the learning potential of all students, especially students designated as having SEN/D. Along similar lines, Muijs (2010) draws on research evidence on differential brain functioning to suggest that learners differ in terms of the ways in which they learn, as they deploy different strategies to make conceptual connections in their brain so as to facilitate the process of learning. This kind of research opens up new opportunities for providing individualized interventions for problems such as ADHD by means of studying the extent to which individuals are susceptible to certain forms of training (e.g. attention training) (Muijs 2010).

Understanding and dealing with learner diversity in pedagogically informed ways involves bringing together research from diverse disciplines such as neuroscience, psychology and education so as to incorporate brain-based research in pedagogical thinking and practice with a view to improving teaching and learning. As Tokuhama-Espinosa (2012:4) writes:

> Education has never had so many tools at its disposal to improve the teaching and learning processes. These are exciting times for everyone in the discipline. Neuroscience and psychology nurture

our understanding of how the brain learns and help us identify the best teaching practices possible.

(Tokuhama-Espinosa 2012:4)

Socio-cultural views of learning and implications for inclusive pedagogies

Given the above considerations, the role of pedagogy acquires a key position in creating organizational conditions that can unleash and maximize students' potential to learn (Black et al. 2006). Drawing insights, for instance, from socio-cultural views of learning and in particular the work of Vygotsky, socio-cultural perspectives on learning challenge deficit-oriented understandings of pedagogical discourse that traditionally held sway over the field of special education.

As an antidote to the hegemony of the individual pathology perspectives that have created inferior and marginal student subjects, the process of learning has been radically reconceptualized and redefined by giving prominent attention to the crucial role of the socio-cultural milieu within which a child develops and interacts. Children's developmental trajectories are not biologically predetermined; rather they are constituted within and affected by immediate socio-cultural and educational contexts. Vygotsky's theorizations have impacted the field of special education in significant ways, while providing a theoretical and action-oriented platform against which to design and implement inclusive learning environments for learner diversity on the grounds of disability (e.g. Daniels 2009; Kugelmass 2010; Valenzuela 2010).

Socio-cultural perspectives sought to address the issue of disabled students' historical isolation and marginalization from mainstream communities. According to Vygotsky, segregated settings were designed to accommodate disenfranchised populations, thereby resulting in their social isolation and devaluation (Daniels 2009). His experiences with institutionalized children provided robust evidence of the ways in which the social isolation of disabled children accounted for the limited development of their higher cognitive skills and mental functioning. This was especially true for children with physical and sensory impairments and/or social and emotional problems (Kugelmass 2010). Along similar lines,

Cosier (2010) examined a national database to suggest that there is a positive correlation between every additional hour students with disabilities spend in general education and the level of achievement across all disability categories (cited in Theoharis and Causton 2014). Hence, one fundamental aspect of the socio-cultural perspective on learning is the necessity to transcend pre-occupations with children's presumed deficits and acknowledge their learning potential as well as their ability to develop and achieve. This perspective necessitates focusing on students' strengths and abilities upon which to build compensatory skills to facilitate developing culturally responsive capabilities for maximizing learning.

In addition to denoting the importance of dialogical encounters with others to enhance learning, socio-cultural perspectives foreground the significance of providing 'psychological tools' to facilitate the process of learning (Daniels 2009; Kugelmas 2010). It is frequently the case that students with multiple and pervasive needs are deprived of essential 'psychological tools' in order to enhance their learning. These tools include the use of their home language as a means of providing scaffolding activities to enhance learning with reference to bilingual special education provision and support (Liasidou 2013b). Other tools include augmentative and alternative ways of communication so as to provide a stimulating environment of social interactions with their non-disabled peers. Paradoxically, rather than being afforded these opportunities, students with multiple and pervasive needs are frequently segregated from their peers and are thereby deprived of the positive and empowering effects of social interaction in terms of their cognitive and emotional development (Kugelmas 2010).

To be successful, some children may also need more direct instruction than others as well as requiring external guidance from adults, while others may need more time and space to explore and reflect upon their learning on their own. Whatever the case, educators must first acknowledge that learning difficulties reflect a mismatch between the child and expectations emanating from the social context of the classroom. By emphasizing the significance of the context of learning, socio-cultural theories of learning work in synergy with inclusive pedagogies to valorize diversity and to promote welcoming and effective learning communities for all. As Kugelmass (2010:277) writes, on the pedagogical implications of socio-cultural theories of leaning:

> At its core, social constructivism proposes that no single answer is appropriate for every student, in any given context. Rather, teachers must understand that all learning and problem solving involves meaning-making for both themselves and their students, and that instructional decisions need to be the outcome of their reciprocal negotiations.

At the same time, however, it should be noted that, given the idiosyncratic nature of disability experience, it is important that inclusive forms of pedagogical discourse should take into consideration students' disability-related differences that call for more specialized forms of pedagogy for meeting students' disability-related needs (Norwich and Lewis 2007; Mitchell 2008; Norwich 2008b). Vygotsky was interested in 'creating "disability-specific" approaches' as he was 'critical of both "unlawful segregation" of the disabled and "mindless mainstreaming" ' that ignored students disability-related needs (Daniels 2009:35).

In close alignment with the above problematizations, considerable research evidence highlights the fact that, although there is no separate/distinct pedagogy for teaching students with SEN/D, there are some specific/specialist pedagogical approaches that need to be utilized in order to improve the learning outcomes of some students (Norwich and Lewis 2001; Davies and Florian 2004; Norwich 2008b). Teachers should adopt a diverse repertoire of teaching strategies and pedagogical approaches so as to provide differentiated learning and accessible learning environments for all students, irrespective of their biological, cognitive, developmental, cultural, racial/ethnic and other characteristics. It might often be necessary to adopt some specific educational interventions and strategies; this presupposes additional knowledge and expertise as well as collaborative professional practice in order to devise and implement intervention strategies (Mitchell 2008).

While alluding to the fact that there is no distinct/separate pedagogy for teaching students designated as having SEN/D, Norwich (2008b) suggests that the common and individual rather than the disability-related needs of children are more significant in devising and implementing pedagogical interventions. In this respect, teachers need to work across 'a continuum of pedagogical approaches' so as to provide clearer, directed and more intensive ways of teaching children with learning difficulties, however, without these pedagogical ways being qualitatively different from those used for all children. Nevertheless, the intensification of teaching methods along the continuum of pedagogical approaches infers the ways in which the different methods of instruction are no longer a matter of 'degree' or 'intensity', but perhaps of kind, something that requires more specialist knowledge in terms of educational differentiation (Norwich and Lewis 2007; Norwich 2008a, 2008b). Thus, the utilization of more specialist pedagogical approaches might be necessary for meeting the needs of some students (Mitchell 2008).

These specialist teaching approaches constitute part of educational differentiation, by means of adopting varied teaching methods and strategies in order to enhance learning. For instance, applied behavioural analysis (ABA) can contribute to developing precision teaching approaches for students on the autistic spectrum (Long et al. 2011). Likewise, the instructional strategy TEACCH (Treatment and Education of Autistic and other Communication Handicapped Children) can enhance educational accessibility for this group of students (Mesibov and Howley 2003). As part of providing information on the pedagogical approaches that work within the context of special and inclusive education, Mitchell (2008) has distilled a number of evidence-based strategies that can potentially foster effective learning communities for students designated as having SEN/D. In particular, he explicates 24 evidence-based strategies that can enhance the quality of teaching and learning in inclusive classrooms. These strategies are explored and rationalized, as well as contextualized with reference to the age of learners involved, their special educational needs, the nature of the interventions adopted and the behavioural outcomes achieved. Some of the evidence-based strategies related to classroom pedagogy are concerned with classroom climate, cognitive strategy instruction, self-regulated learning, reciprocal teaching, mnemonics and other memory strategies, phonological awareness and phonological processing, direct instruction, and augmentative and alternative communication.

The process of learning can also be facilitated by assessment procedures that transcend quantifiable measures of educational effectiveness (Ainscow et al. 2010), and embrace 'assessment for learning' procedures (Black et al. 2006), as well as criterion-referenced forms of assessment as a means to optimize the process of learning (Mitchell 2008). Current theories of learning and assessment, such as assessment for learning, bring to the fore new understandings of pedagogy that emphasize the process of learning and the ways in which this process can be optimized. Mitchell (2008) cites formative assessment and feedback as an effective evidence-based strategy to enhance learning.

Formative assessment is defined 'as a process of evaluating "learners" progress during a course or module so that they have opportunities to improve. It is as much assessment for learning as assessment of learning' (Mitchell 2008:202). Effective teaching cannot be achieved unless there is an informed understanding of students' current attainment levels, along with their underlying difficulties, so as to devise and implement relevant teaching plans and interventions. This is what McPhillips et al. (2010:217) call 'diagnostic teaching', which is based on a reflective evaluation of the process of learning in accordance with learners' needs and strengths. For instance, in terms of language difficulties, there are some effective methods and strategies in the teaching of reading that can be used as a means of providing diagnostic teaching. Even though these methods are not new, they are, nevertheless, sparingly used by educational professionals and, therefore, need to be reconsidered and become more firmly embedded in pedagogical discourse (McPhillips et al. 2010).

Simultaneously, it requires noting that inclusive classrooms should also be characterized by culturally and linguistically informed instruction (Garcia and Ortiz 2006). This is particularly true for bilingual students (e.g. ELLs), with or without SEN/D. Hence, in addition to adopting evidence-based teaching strategies and 'assessment for learning' practices, teachers need 'to provide culturally and linguistically informed learning opportunities for ELLs, and to distinguish second language learning difficulties from actual learning disabilities, or at least to have easy access to professionals who are able to do so' (Liasidou 2013b:14). To this end, it is important that issues of culture and language should be firmly embedded in discussions about teaching and learning in inclusive classrooms, with a view to meeting the intersectional needs of culturally and linguistically diverse students with special educational needs in effective and socially just ways.

Conclusions

The notion of pedagogy is central to the process of precipitating inclusive education reforms. Emerging theories of learning, such as social constructivist theory, which is predominantly embodied in the work of Vygotsky, have revolutionized dominant understandings of learning and development, while bringing to the fore the crucial role of socio-cultural and educational contexts in facilitating students' learning. Classroom practice is considered as being a key element for educational improvement, for it can have the greatest impact on pupils' lives and educational trajectories. Classroom-based organizational conditions concentrate on the role of teachers, and their pedagogical actions and behaviours that affect students' learning. Teachers' effectiveness is contingent on factors such as the quality of teaching and classroom and pupil management; this is especially true when teachers work with disenfranchised groups of students, including students designated as having SEN/D.

Effective classroom practice is also contingent on a whole-school approach to ensuring consistency of good pedagogical practice across the school. It is interesting to note that the difference between effective and ineffective schools lies at the variance that exists in terms of teachers' effectiveness (Furlong 2008; Muijs 2010); hence, the issue of pedagogy is not limited to classroom-based considerations but extends to include issues of pedagogical effectiveness across the school (Ekins and Grimes 2009). Even though ineffective schools provide some evidence of the existence of effective teachers' practices, this evidence is sporadic and inconsistent. The aim should be to achieve consistency of practice across the school through collaborative and supportive networks of facilitating an effective pedagogical practice for learner diversity.

6
Sustainable Inclusive Education Reforms

Introduction

The chapter explores the notion of sustainability, and uses insights from relevant theory and research (e.g. Hargreaves and Goodson 2006; Sindelar et al. 2006), in order to exemplify the factors that can facilitate or undermine sustainable inclusive education reforms. The notion of sustainability is important in order to advance debates on the perennial character of the process of change within the context of inclusion. It is well rehearsed by now that inclusive education should be regarded as a process rather than an end (Booth and Ainscow 2002); hence, the process of change and development should become a perennial organizational, pedagogical and ethical concern.

The need for sustainable school development is inferred in the Index for Inclusion, which provides a comprehensive guidance and a self-assessment resource for schools in order to facilitate change in school cultures, policies and practices to promote inclusion (Booth and Ainscow 2002). Fostering greater inclusive policies and practices necessitates a cyclical process of school development consisting of reciprocally related stages of action, evaluation, reflection and further action. A participatory action research process (PAR) (Polat and Kisanji 2009), for instance, draws on the Index for Inclusion in order to develop and implement a never-ending process of school change and development towards inclusion and social justice.

Sustainable inclusive education reforms

'Theories of action' intended to precipitate reforms cannot be effective unless they include, according to Fullan (2006:4), the harder question: 'Under what conditions will continuous improvement happen?' The notion of change is not a static concept that, once applied, can have a perennial effect on an organization. At the same time, when the notion of 'change' is seen through the narrow lenses of 'innovation', the transformative process is reduced to superficial and surface changes with limited effect and force (McIntosh et al. 2009). By no means should inclusive education be seen as an innovation or a contemporary policy trend that can be jettisoned once new innovative practices or ideas emerge. As McIntosh et al. (2009:328) write: 'In practical, school level terms, sustainability is the creation of a social norm, the point at which a practice ceases to be a project or initiative and becomes institutionalized.' Consequently, it is imperative that the notion of sustainability underpins discussions about transformative change within the context of inclusion.

Although there are many successful examples of introducing educational change due to effective leadership and systemic support, seldom are these changes institutionalized so as to become an entrenched and durable aspect of pedagogical discourse. According to Sindelar et al. (2006), the bulk of the research on educational change concentrates on the short-term effects of the process of change without considering or monitoring its long-term effects. Thus, even though there has been significant work on school reform and inclusive education practices, researchers have so far provided very little information about the sustainability of these innovative programmes, along with the factors that could have a positive effect on them.

The identification of the key components of the process of change is also immensely influenced by socio-historical dynamics that need to be thoroughly explored through longitudinal studies. The latter can explain the sustainability of educational change and advance discussion about the factors that facilitate or undermine the process of sustainable educational reforms (Hargreaves and Goodson 2006). At the same time, it should be noted that the sustainability of a reform initiative is largely contingent on its scope and the demands placed on educational practitioners. Small-scale and relatively easy to implement innovations have more possibilities to be realized and sustained. In contrast, complicated, large-scale and difficult to understand reforms, which pose exceeding demands on teachers and the system as a whole, are generally difficult to enact and maintain. Admittedly, inclusion falls into the second category of reform initiatives, as it is occasionally perceived as being a difficult and complicated pursuit, for it is not clearly understood and not adequately supported by school administrators (Sindelar et al. 2006).

Capacity building and sustainable school development within the context of an inclusive education reform agenda

The notion of sustainability necessitates constant capacity building (Levin and Fullan 2008) in order to ensure the continuation of improvement and development of a system or organization. Fullan (2006:9) points to the fact that 'Most theories of change are weak on capacity building and that is one of the key reasons why they fall short'. One important dimension of effective change is, therefore, to increase individual and collective capacity of all social agents, who are expected to initiate and sustain positive changes. According to Fullan (2005:ix), this process entails enhancing the capacity of a system 'to engage in the complexities of continuous improvement consistent with deep values of human purpose'.

Capacity building has many angles and can be applied to different aspects of a system in order to achieve sustainable results. Levin and Fullan (2008:295) define capacity building as:

> any strategy that increases the collective effectiveness of a group to raise the bar and close the gap of student learning. For us it involves helping to develop individual and collective (1) knowledge and competencies, (2) resources and (3) motivation. These capacities are specifically about getting results (raise the bar, close the gap).

The initial response to failing attempts to create inclusive learning communities is 'to test the capacity-building hypothesis' (Fullan 2010:127), with a view to developing relevant knowledge and skills to energize and sustain the process of transformative change. Schools, especially those hastily labelled as 'failing schools', need to be supported so as to enhance their capacity-building potential. For Fullan (2010), a crucial leverage of change is to provide these schools with specific capacity help in order to implement positive changes.

As part of a capacity-building network of support, it is imperative for each school to have a 'school improvement team', which utilizes a 'school effectiveness framework' to support, co-ordinate and monitor the process of school improvement; for instance, in terms of identifying educational interventions for struggling students and maximizing their learning outcomes. Simultaneously, this team should devise 'a school improvement plan' so as to strategically design future actions in order to facilitate and sustain the process of school development (Fullan 2010). Sustainability also has more possibilities to be achieved when there are manifold capacity-building strategies (Theoharis and Causton 2014).

Even in cases where these strategies are in place, sustainable change cannot be achieved unless educational professionals are actively and consciously involved in the process of change. A recent study on the impact of mandated, top-down changes on teachers suggests the ways in which the former have a negative impact on teachers' morale and professional identities in bringing about sustainable educational reforms in their contexts of practice (Clement 2014). What is suggested, therefore, is a more bottom-up approach, whereby educational practitioners and researchers work collaboratively on introducing and testing evidence-based interventions.

Capacity building is also concerned with professional development issues, which are intended to empower educational professionals to become more effective in adopting evidence-based practices for school improvement and development (Mitchell 2008). Hargreaves and Shirley (2009) cite the example of Ontario, Canada, whereby teachers' unions were allocated 5 million dollars, as part of a capacity-building process, to spend on professional development, which included sharing successful practice across schools. As part of a non-punitive culture, failing schools could seek advice and support from government teams and higher achieving peers.

The role of educational professionals within the context of inclusion is increasingly exemplified in relation to their ability to become researchers in their context of practice and get actively involved in action research projects, so as to constantly review, monitor and improve their professional practice in the light of inclusion (Armstrong and Moore 2004). In view of these considerations, it is suggested that schools should forge constructive links with research institutions so as to carry out small-scale research activities with a view to developing effective school practice through a cyclical process of reviewing and testing (Muijs 2010). This is in alignment with concerns about introducing collaborative action research agendas as a means to fostering greater inclusive policies and practices (Howes et al. 2009). At the same time, Ainscow et al. (2008:7) recognize the importance of embedding 'a critical dimension into a collaborative action research project' in order to enable educational practitioners to incorporate issues of social justice in shaping their sustained transformative action.

The notion of capacity building is inexorably linked with the ability of an organization to become self-transforming. According to Caldwell (2014:1), the process of transformative change cannot be achieved 'unless schools build a capacity for self-transformation. The most important role for the system is to build the capacity of schools to be self-transforming'. Schools' capacity for self-transformation is closely related to concerns about enabling schools to become learning organizations so as to 'develop innovative structures and processes that enable them to develop the professional capacity to learn in, and respond quickly and flexibly to their unpredictable and changing environments' (Giles and Hargreaves 2006:126). Learning organizations are human-centred and community-oriented organizations that draw upon the collective strengths and shared expectations of their human resources so as to insure a perennial process of improvement and development.

Based on a large-scale project, Caldwell (2014) identifies 'four kinds of resources or forms of capital that are required for transformation'. The first form of capital is intellectual capital, which refers to the importance of instilling relevant knowledge and skills in those who work in or for the school. Social capital refers to the establishment of collaborative formal and informal networks or partnerships involving the school and all professionals, agencies, organizations and institutions. Moral capital refers to the existence of moral purpose concerned with ethical and values-based considerations shared by professionals of the school and the community, while financial capital refers to the level of the allocated funding to support the school.

Apart from the positive strategies articulated for capacity building, the process of achieving sustainable school reforms also necessitates a concomitant emphasis on identifying and challenging potential 'distractors' that can undermine the process of change. What is crucially needed is capacity in 'proactively addressing the "distractors"' (Fullan 2006:10), so as to ensure a seamless and continuous process of transformative change towards inclusion. These potential 'distractors' can be identified at the classroom, school, district and state-wide level. Giles and Hargreaves (2006) identify some factors that contribute to the 'attrition of change'. These factors include: 'Changing leadership, the gradual loss and replacement of key faculty, changes in the size or composition of the student body, and shifts in policy or the district's attention to other priorities.' In terms of district state policies, these should be favourably predisposed towards inclusive education reform initiatives so as to ensure their success and sustainability. The existence of contradictory policies around inclusion pose difficult challenges for schools, and bear profound consequences for students designated as having SEN/D caught within the practice of these policies at school level.

It is frequently the case that the legislative shift towards more inclusive education policies has been fragmented and contradictory (Liasidou 2008a). The textual hybridity of ostensibly more inclusive policy documents undermines the process of transformative change towards a human rights approach to difference and diversity. The uncritical adoption of hybrid discourses of inclusion has inevitably led to the emergence of a contradictory inclusive education policy landscape and, as a result, the process of change is seriously undermined. The discursively hybrid nature of the current inclusive education 'policyscape' (Ball 1998) has had profound repercussions for educational practice. As the leading agents of policy enforcement, educational practitioners have been expected to juggle and compromise contradictory policy agendas within their context of practice (Day 2005), and have reportedly experienced 'confusion, frustration, guilt and exhaustion' (Allan 2008:9). Even though it is suggested that the high-stakes culture and its associated accountability measures can bring about some instant improvements, nevertheless, they are frequently unsustainable (Harris 2010), while hindering attempts to effect sustainable changes for the realization of an inclusive discourse. These are major issues that need to be considered in order to mobilize transformative and sustained changes in alignment with the theoretical and pedagogical underpinnings of inclusion.

Sustainable school reform within the context of inclusion: A case study

Sindelar et al.'s (2006) ethnographic study on the sustainability of inclusive education reforms in a large middle school, located in a large urban and suburban US district, sheds light on a number of aspects of the educational system, along with the macro/micropolitics of education that impact upon the process of achieving sustainable inclusive educational reforms. This ethnographic study is extensively cited and used as an example of discussing the various parameters of sustainable reforms in the context of inclusion. Through a co-ordinated effort and a close collaboration between the school and university-based researchers, the project concentrated on facilitating the design, implementation and sustainability of an inclusive education reform agenda in the school. Two years after the initial successful implementation of the anticipated reforms, in terms of creating school culture, and developing organization and teachers' pedagogies commensurate with the principles of inclusion, researchers returned to the schools in order to identify the extent to which these reforms were sustained. The project was named SIR, an acronym for sustained inclusive reforms.

The study reports on a number of factors and parameters that impacted the sustainability of these reforms. While reporting on a school's development 'from traditional to a teacher-developed inclusion programme', the authors suggest that innovations cannot be sustained, unless the district policy, leadership and classroom/teaching are favourable. Their analysis focuses on the ways in which changes in these factors have had a negative impact on the sustainability of the reforms.

It has been suggested that changes in district priorities promoting high-stakes accountability regimes and establishing certain attainment and progress thresholds in reading, mathematics and writing, shifted the focus from an inclusive orientation to improving test scores and school grades. To this end, the curricula were 'keyed to the standards and scripts teaching methods for each subject and grade level' (Sindelar et al. 2006:322). Disabled students were exempted from these exam-based attainment thresholds and school assessment criteria. Thus, the enhanced emphasis on high-stakes accountability regimes, along with the advancement of mono-dimensional conceptualizations of success gauged against academic test performance indicators, undermined the sustainability of inclusive education reforms. Notwithstanding some evidence suggesting that performance indicators can potentially enhance students' attainment, Smith and Douglas (2014:443) point out that it is crucially important to strike 'a balance between accountability measures which measure performance in traditional attainment-focused tests and other relevant assessments which are meaningful to the given students and/or SEND subgroup'. By no means are exam-driven accountability regimes a panacea to maximize the process of learning; rather, as already discussed, these kinds of regimes are detrimental to students' learning and teachers' professional identity, while inadvertently giving rise to exclusionary practices for those students whose 'performative worth' is not valorized by a utilitarian and exam-driven educational system. This is an issue that needs to be carefully considered and further explored in light of the necessity to promote and sustain effective learning communities for all.

Another unanticipated change was the transfer of the head teacher. This was the second time that the head teacher changed in this particular school. Owing to the fact that the first new head teacher adhered to her predecessor's commitment to inclusion, she succeeded in encouraging teachers to continue working towards inclusion. However, this was not the case with the second head teacher of the school. Unlike her predecessors, the new head teacher was not familiar with, and committed to the tenets of an inclusive discourse. At the same time, she had no experience of working in a secondary school context and, therefore, she experienced difficulties in adjusting to the culture of the school and dealing with an opinionated faculty. Moreover, this new head teacher adopted managerial and transactional forms of leadership. In stark contrast to her predecessors, she also put pressure on teachers to comply with even the most inconsequential, top-down, 'red-tape' district requirements at the expense of adopting more flexible, inquisitive and problem-solving collaborative compliance procedures, which were not inimical to the aims and scope of an inclusive education reform framework.

An additional significant 'distractor', or what McIntosh et al. (2009) call an element that undermines the 'fidelity of implementation' so as to ensure sustainability of novel practices, can be attributed to the increase of student numbers and the recruitment of new faculty, who were neither aware of and committed to the principles of inclusion nor had any previous experience in working in inclusive education settings. These new recruitments took place during the tenure of the third head teacher and, as a result, teachers were recruited without putting due emphasis on their knowledge of and commitment to the tenets of inclusion and its associated pedagogical practices (e.g. co-teaching). This phenomenon, along with the fact that some other teachers who participated in the design and development of the school's inclusive education reform programme left the school, increased the adversarial conditions that undermined the sustainability of the reforms. Thus, even though the number of staff increased, the 'enforcers' of inclusion decreased considerably, thereby undermining the sustainability of changes. Another important observation relates to the fact that some teachers did not fully capture the real meaning of inclusion, as their perceptions, understandings and related practices were clearly more aligned with a special education rather than an inclusive orientation. A possible response to these kinds of 'distractors' is to devise and implement 'a strategic, long term vision of sustainability' which aims to make explicit to new staff that inclusive practice is an endemic aspect of school staff culture, while providing relevant training to ensure 'a basic level of skill' in understanding and adopting the practice, in addition to ensuring the existence of 'core personnel with key skills' to disseminate, model and sustain this practice (McIntosh et al. 2009:338).

In addition to the above considerations, teachers also reported diminished levels of collaborative working relations in the school, as well as a lack of district and school-based support in order to sustain inclusive practice. In terms of collaborative practice, not only did the numbers of co-teachers decrease in the schools, but also their role changed. Thus, apart from their usual role in collaborating with mainstream teachers and other professionals to facilitate inclusion by differentiating assessments and curricula, as well as offering individualized and small-group support and completing individual educational plans for students designated as having special educational needs and disabilities, co-teachers were asked to do substitute teaching as well. Simultaneously, they were asked to support certain students so as to improve their test performance, as well as to provide learning support to other low-performing students, who were not necessarily students with SEN/D. This group of students was also allocated extra resources which were hitherto intended for enhancing inclusion.

The above examples denote the importance of inclusive leadership in ensuring the sustainability of reform efforts (Liasidou and Svensson 2011). The notion of inclusive leadership is embodied in the role of both head teachers and teachers. Lack of leadership as a means to initiating and sustaining educational reforms is well recognized and theorized in educational leadership literature (Chapter 8). The sustainability of an inclusive reform agenda presupposes forms of leadership whereby leaders envisage creating inclusive school communities as well as devising and communicating a strategic plan to this end. As Hargreaves and Shirley (2009:95) aptly put it: 'change without leadership has no chance of being sustainable'. That said, the authors place particular emphasis on 'developing leadership capacity' so as to create 'agents of change' through distributed and critical forms of leadership (e.g. leadership for social justice) (Hargreaves and Shirley 2009:98). Some of the seven principles of sustainable leadership are summarized as follows:

Depth of purpose in developing student learning that is meaningful and is not limited to high stake testing considerations.

Breadth of purpose that is communicated to and shared with staff through establishing collective ownership and responsibility of it.

Endurance so that the process of change continues in a seamless and unwavering fashion notwithstanding changes in governmental priorities or changes in a school's headship, since there will be clear succession leadership plans prior to a head teacher's possible transfer to another school or retirement.

Justice as a means to attending to all students' needs and achievement potential with a view to closing the gap between advantaged and disadvantaged students through collaborative schools networks of support and exchange of good practice.

Diversity of curriculum and pedagogy through collective inquiry and reflection.

(Hargreaves and Shirley 2009:98–99)

Conclusions

The chapter has been given over to exploring the notion of sustainability and its crucial role in the process of change. This is particularly true in the context of an inclusive education reform agenda, whereby the process of change necessitates a perennial engagement with a host of ideological and structural barriers that undermine attempts to pursue transformative change. Given the complexity of the issues at hand, the quest for inclusion has been defined as a process and not an end (Booth and Ainscow 2002; Barton 2008), for it constantly entails challenging exclusionary practices and discriminatory regimes that continuously arise and are skilfully disguised under the rhetorical facade of inclusion.

The occasionally inconspicuous nature of the variegated impediments to the process of change makes even more imperative the necessity to pursue sustainable attitudinal and systemic reforms. Without ensuring its sustainability, the process of change becomes a meaningless and superficial endeavour without real purpose and political intent. At the same time, there is the danger that narrow and short-sighted reform efforts might cultivate an illusory complacency and catastrophic abdication from the perennial need to be 'cultural vigilantes' (Corbett and Slee 2000:134) in challenging covert forms of power inequities, which engender exclusionary practices and deficit-oriented regimes. This is a significant issue that needs to more seriously inform debates on the sustainability of inclusive education reforms (see chapters 6, 7 and 8).

7
Disability Studies at the Crossroads of Critical, Feminist, Anti-racist Theories and the Issue of Change

Introduction

The chapter aims to highlight the critical character of the process of transformative change by focusing on the ways in which theoretical insights from critical, feminist and anti-racist theories are related to or can inform attempts to precipitate inclusive education reforms. The cross-fertilization of these diverse perspectives can contribute to highlighting the overtly political character of disability experience, with a view to encouraging a paradigm shift from a reductionist epistemology to a trans-disciplinary approach to addressing the ways in which disability is inexorably related with other axes of difference linked to race/ethnicity, social class gender and sexuality. This kind of analysis is fundamental in envisaging alternative pedagogical discourses and modes of thinking predicated on liberatory theorizations of difference and diversity. As Slee (2010:168) so appositely puts it: 'Inclusive education asks us to jettison linearity in our thinking, to invite new coalitions to the table to establish new parameters of the issues we are dealing with and directions for educational reconstructions.' The politics of difference and diversity call for theoretical pluralism and conceptual openness so as to utilize a number of trans-disciplinary analytical tools to delineate the complexity and fluidity of social identities.

The following sections provide an eclectic overview of the ways in which the abovementioned disciplinary camps can inform and facilitate the process of socially just change towards the realization of an inclusive discourse. The chapter focuses on highlighting the theoretical affinities of critical, feminist, anti-racist theories with disability studies, with the aim of extrapolating the ways in which these trans-disciplinary insights can reinforce/supplement theorizations about the political and socially mediated nature of disability experience. Theoretical intersections can provide fertile ground for analysing the social embedment of disability and the complex ways in which it is constituted, understood and experienced across diverse contexts and disciplinary frameworks (Liasidou 2013a, 2013b). This theoretical openness marks a paradigm shift from a reductionist approach to a pluralistic epistemology in theorizing disability experience. Pluralistic analyses of disability eschew mono-dimensional considerations and subscribe to a comprehensive analytical framework to explicate the complex nature of disability experience. The adoption of a pluralistic analytical framework brings together black, feminist and class perspectives in order to explore the gender, racial and class dimensions of disability experience (Goodley 2011).

The analytical emphasis on disciplinary intersections and theoretical affinities is a key theme in the emerging field of critical disability studies (CDS), which seeks to explore theoretical convergence and divergence amongst diverse disciplinary fields whereby disability is the epicentre of the trans-disciplinary analytical edge. As Goodley (2011:157) writes, even though CDS 'might start with disability, they never end with it, remaining ever vigilant of political, ontological and theoretical complexity'.

Theoretical complexity does not only infer the necessity of adopting a trans-disciplinary perspective on identifying points of convergence, but also infers the ways in which disability experience might differ from other markers of difference; something that necessitates maintaining a distinct focus on the idiosyncratic nature of disability experience. In this respect, 'theoretical convergence' does not equate with 'theoretical conflation', a proposition that alerts us to the importance for CDS to further develop and theorize the idiomorphic and distinct nature of disability experience (Liasidou 2013b): an issue that has significant implications for the process of mobilizing an inclusive education reform agenda (see the final section of this chapter).

Critical theory and transformative change

Schools have been routinely blamed for wider social ills, while educational professionals in the UK, for instance, have been demoralized on the basis of their alleged inability/unwillingness to tackle issues related to students' underachievement (Manguire and Ball 1994). Improving schools, however, should not be regarded as an isolated phenomenon that can be dealt with in remote and straightforward ways. Schools are embedded in societies and affected by a number of exogenous dynamics that occasionally leave educational professionals powerless to assume an active and effective role in improving schooling and providing effective and socially just forms of education.

Thus, changing schools involves mobilizing wider changes to create more democratic, non-discriminatory and egalitarian societies (see Chapter 1). This wider-reform quest, however, may be a bit too ambitious and not readily/easily feasible (Bringhouse 2010). Hence, the role of schools as critical sites of challenging the status quo should be acknowledged and theorized. Schools are a microcosm of society and, therefore, can play a crucial role in encouraging localized struggles to effect wider social changes. Large-scale social reforms towards more democratic and socially just communities need contextualized struggles to challenge the status quo and mobilize the process of transformative change (Benjamin 2002; Vlachou 2007).

Within the context of inclusion, the role of schools is redefined in terms of their potential to instigate wider social changes to redress inequalities of power that marginalize disenfranchised groups of people. As already discussed in Chapter 1, the quest for inclusive education should be seen as a precursor for creating an inclusive society within which 'all citizens experience full participation including the maximum development of their abilities' (Barton 2001:8). To this end, schools are expected to be transformed into critical sites for alleviating rather than reproducing social disadvantage on the basis of the accumulative effects of social and educational injustices (Giroux 1992; Freire 1998; McLaren 1998; Barbules and Berk 1999). Although these considerations are well rehearsed in educational debates on social justice they have reignited a renewed interest in the context of inclusion (Dyson 2001; Mittler 2001; Artiles et al. 2006).

Critical theories of education have long recognized the transformative role of schooling and pedagogy towards creating equitable, non-discriminatory and participatory schools and communities for disenfranchised and vulnerable groups of students. These theorizations can provide liberatory insights into the field of disability studies by supplementing the epistemological credentials of the social model of disability (Oliver 1996) to address the ways in which issues of power and culture (Freire 1985) are related to the constitution of human identities. Moving beyond individual perspectives, the aim is to uncover the contextual social and cultural factors that collude towards essentializing difference and creating social hierarchies. These processes are routinely reproduced and perpetuated in current schooling by creating subordinated student subjects in need of targeted interventions and assimilationist practices that inadvertently lead to their stigmatization and marginalization (Liasidou 2012b).

Slee (2008:108) articulates the ways in which the dominance of special education imperatives engenders 'reductive acts from which policy cannot recover'. These reductive acts undermine attempts to conjure up inclusion as a matter of radical educational and social reform. As already discussed, challenging deficit-oriented orthodoxies that have traditionally held sway over dominant understandings of disability (Erevelles 2000; Gabel 2002; Goodley 2007) necessitates questioning insular conceptualizations of students' identities, which fail to acknowledge the ways in which these identities consist of a complex and interactive amalgam of individual, social and cultural dynamics, which cannot be disentangled and reduced to one constituent element (Nash 2008). The latter approach is both reductioning and limiting: reductioning in that it fails to acknowledge the complexity of human identities, and limiting because it forecloses possibilities of addressing a number of social and educational pathologies that plague the lives and educational opportunities of a sizeable percentage of the student population. For Slee (2008), such understanding is crucial in mobilizing the process of transformative change. As he writes:

It is a suggestion that constructing a reform agenda for schooling that is both inclusive and provides an *apprenticeship in democracy* (Knight 1985) invites us to step outside of regular patterns

of responding to policy issues to maintain the regularity and con-
stancy of institutional life. The interrogations of intersectionalities
of student identities as they collide with the architecture and
culture of schooling may be a first step.

(Slee 2008:112) (emphasis in the original)

This kind of reflective and questioning thinking opens up 'space for
critique and intervention' (Davies 2008:77), for it provides insights
into the contextual levers of action that need to be mobilized in order
to instigate real changes in the lives and educational experiences of
disabled people. The notion of 'intersectionality' conjured up and discussed against concerns derived from critical pedagogy, feminism and
critical race theory can become an analytical and action-oriented tool
in interrogating and deconstructing assimilationist and individual
pathology perspectives.

Critical pedagogy at the intersection of multiple axes of difference

This section focuses on critical pedagogy and exemplifies the ways
in which it can facilitate the process of educational change. Critical
pedagogy focuses on the necessity to precipitate social transformation by addressing issues of marginalization, power and justice.
Notwithstanding some criticisms (e.g. see Beckett 2013), critical
pedagogy provides a powerful political platform in order to theorize
and materialize the transformative potential of pedagogy in creating
equitable, empowering and non-discriminatory communities for all.

Inclusion has close theoretical affinities with critical pedagogy
(Liasidou 2012b) as both disciplinary camps are interested in unveil-
ing the ways in which social issues are intricately interrelated with
power interplays endemic to institutional and ideological dynamics (Burbules and Berk 1999). In this respect, the emphasis is placed
on deconstructing these dynamics, which are presented as natural-
ized and sacred. What lies behind the surface is a major concern for
critical analysts in both disciplinary fields, who seek to uncover the
ways in which power and domination are surreptitiously implicated
in the constitution of human subjectivities and dominant social
and institutional realities. From a critical analytical perspective, the
marginal identities imputed to certain groups of students are regarded

as being socially and culturally mediated constructs that need to be questioned and deconstructed through critical forms of pedagogical discourse. This process involves understanding and acting upon the ways in which wider socio-political conditions and exigencies are accountable for affording certain privileges to some individuals while engendering oppressive conditions for some others (Giroux 1992; McLaren 1998).

In order to challenge the process of hierarchical ontological and social positioning – by means of valorizing certain individuals while devaluing some others – it is crucial to take a critical view of the ways in which unequal power relations and discriminatory regimes are institutionalized, sustained and regenerated through educational practices and dominant social norms: an issue that brings to the fore the complex ways in which education is affected/embedded in wider social structures and dominant ideological orthodoxies (Liasidou 2012a). The pedagogical implication of this theoretical perspective lies in the imperative to abandon sustaining and reinforcing a sterile educational enterprise that is solely concerned with knowledge transfer and reproduction. As discussed in Chapter 1, this kind of education ignores the democratic role of schooling in challenging wider social inequities that have an adverse impact on the lives and educational trajectories of a sizeable percentage of the student population.

In contrast to traditional forms of schooling and pedagogy, critical pedagogy envisages creating democratic school communities within which historically disenfranchised groups of students are enabled to counteract and challenge the dominant discourse through liberatory forms of pedagogical action. These forms of pedagogical action aim to address issues of inequality and injustice by empowering oppressed groups of students to pursue justice and emancipation. For Freire (2000) the process of mobilizing socially just educational reforms entails focusing on enhancing students' 'conscientization' so as to be empowered to understand their role and position in the social 'filtering' and 'calibration' process of assigning superior or inferior social roles and constructing either privileged or oppressed subjectivities. This understanding can enable students' political agency in questioning the status quo, and precipitating socially just reforms that destabilize existing social hierarchies and discriminatory regimes. To this end, particular emphasis has been given to exploring the intertwined nature of multiple forms of oppression experienced by vulnerable groups of students (Freire 1998; McLaren 1998; Barbules and Berk 1999) on the grounds of their ethnic and social class identities, while the issue of disability has been fundamentally ignored.

Notwithstanding the fact that other sources of social disadvantage, such as race and gender, have received prominent attention in critical pedagogy's discussions on the necessity to empower marginalized groups of people, disability has been excluded from these analyses (Erevelles 2000). Even through issues of social inequality in relation to ethnicity, gender and social class had already been extensively explored and theorized, similar sociological analyses pertaining to disability emerged much later. This theoretical omission was the result of a deficit-oriented perspective that held sway over the field. The overwhelming influence of modern biomedicine has reduced disability to a form of 'illness' and 'individual pathology' (Barton and Oliver 1992), thereby leaving little room to articulate alternative theorizations and analytical perspectives on disability experience. In addition, the deficit-oriented ontological status attributed to the notion of disability has provided a justification for the systematic unequal and paternalistic treatment of disabled people.

The biomedical perspective has rationalized the unequal and discriminatory treatment experienced by disabled individuals, whose inferior ontological status has been rationalized by their alleged deviations from arbitrary conceptualizations of 'normality' (Campbell 2005). Any perceived deviations from arbitrarily constructed corporeal, social and cultural kinds of normalcy have been used as a pretext in order to justify unequal and discriminatory treatment. This has been especially true for disability-related differences that have been traditionally used as a justification for the abysmal injustices experienced by disabled individuals. Treating disabled people unequally has thus been rationalized on the grounds of their alleged deficient and inferior identities, while discriminating against women and minority groups has been legitimized by attributing disability to them (Baynton 2001). Suffice to say that the ascription of a disabled status has also provided a justification for the systemic inequities and immigration restrictions experienced by people from ethnic minorities on the grounds of their alleged propensity to intellectual and other disabilities (Baynton 2001).

At the same time, children educated in special schools and disabled people in general were not regarded as being 'politically significant' in contributing to the wider social reforms envisaged by the sociologists, so as to reinstate the human rights for disenfranchised and vulnerable groups of people (Barton and Oliver 1992). As Erevelles (2000:5) writes with regard to the exclusion of disability from the theoretical debates in critical pedagogy:

> This could be because, unlike the other social categories of race, class, gender, and sexuality, where it has been possible to demonstrate that the deviance associated with their difference is actually a social construction, a similar argument has been very difficult to support when applied to students with multiple to severe disabilities.

A trans-disciplinary approach, drawn from critical disability studies and critical pedagogy, can exert a complementary and synergetic role in interrogating notions of normality, embodied in Western-centric versions of the 'able-bodied order' (Campbell 2008, 2009), whereby conceptual constructs of the latter are used as a heuristic framework to identify the 'disabled Other'. Critical pedagogy's concerns about redressing power inequities and oppressive regimes on the basis of race and social class can provide significant insights into the emancipatory potentials of schooling and professional practice to mobilize inclusive education reforms (Nevin et al. 2008; Liasidou 2012b). Such an approach necessitates transcending deficit-oriented and blame-the-victim approaches in order to question whose values and vested interests contribute to the creation and sustenance of oppressive and discriminatory educational regimes for certain groups of students (McLaren 1998).

Feminist analyses and intersectional implications for an inclusive education reform agenda

The question of change requires an informed understanding of the ways in which disability is embedded and embodied in intersectional forms of social disadvantage, with a view to devising and implementing liberatory pedagogical practices that transcend deficit-oriented understandings of disability and special educational needs. These liberatory analytical lenses are related to American feminist theoretical frameworks, which sought to explore and challenge the multiple sources of social disadvantage experienced by African American women (Makkonen 2002; Davis 2008). The term 'intersectional sub-ordination' was coined by American feminist analysts in order to denote the varied and accumulative forms of discrimination experienced by African American women and were not experienced by African American men or women from white ethnic backgrounds (Makkonen 2002; Kirk and Okazawa-Rey 2007). These analyses have extended the theoretical and political scope of feminist analyses that have hitherto concentrated on white, heterosexual, middle-class women.

Critical race theorist, Kimberlie Crenshaw (1989) was the first scholar to provide liberatory insights into the intersecting ways in which sex, race and class contribute to the multifaceted and interlacing nature of oppression experienced by women, especially women of colour. This intersectional analytical framework was subsequently applied to exploring the multiple forms of oppression experienced by other individuals on the grounds of their ethnic, cultural, social religious, sexual and ability attributes (Makkonen 2002; Kirk and Okazawa-Rey 2007; Davis 2008; Knudsen 2009).

In disability studies, 'disabled identities' were subsequently explored in relation to their gendered dimension, an issue that was hitherto not taken into consideration in understanding the complex experience of disability. Intersectional understandings of human experience have formed the basis of feminist analyses of disability, which sought to exemplify the simultaneous and overlapping forms of oppression and discrimination experienced by disabled women. This was especially true for women from ethnic minorities, who routinely experience what has been termed 'simultaneous discrimination' (Thomas 1999; Barnes and Mercer 2010).

As far as the subjectifying role of legislation is concerned, feminist legal scholars have used the term 'social injury' to reconceptualize and redefine 'once privatized injuries into collectivist raced, sexed, and disabilized domains' (Campbell 2005:114). These analyses have introduced new theorizations of the racial, class and age dimensions of disability experience and made transparent the necessity of going beyond reductionist understandings of human identities that concentrate on a single characteristic of a person's make up (e.g. disability).

Goodley and Runswick-Cole (2010) discuss the multifaceted dimensions of social exclusion whereby disablism constitutes only one aspect of an intricately interwoven network of power, marginalization and social disadvantage that converges towards creating marginal social and educational identities. Understanding 'need' as an individual pathology outcome is both pernicious and inadequate in meeting the needs of a great percentage of disabled individuals who are routinely relegated to the margins of mainstream social and educational spheres. Hence, achieving positive changes in the lives of disabled individuals necessitates an informed understanding of the wider socio-political and cultural contextual factors that converge towards creating subordinate subject positions as these are calibrated against conventional bodily, race and so forth norms.

To that end, an intersectional framework of intervention necessitates a broader approach to understanding the notion of 'needs' (Mittler 1999; Dyson 2001). The latter do not solely result from alleged individual pathologies; rather, they are the result of an interactive web of social and educational disadvantage that creates the various axes of difference against which human identities are constituted and hierarchically positioned. Human identities are not immutable and transcendental entities, but are formed and reformed according to the dominant socio-cultural and biographical conditions.

Intersectional feminist analyses of disability can supplement the role of the social model of disability as an emancipatory political tool in mobilizing positive changes for disabled individuals. Exposing the ways in which disability intersects with other sources of disadvantage linked to race, gender and social class can advance liberatory perspectives on challenging essentialist understanding of disabled identities, which foreclose possibilities for transformative action. While being a powerful political tool, intersectionality not only goes beyond rhetorical proclamations but extends to include forms of activism aimed at challenging the oppressive institutional and ideological regimes that pathologize social disadvantage (Davies 2008).

Intersectionality and implications for inclusive education policy and practice

As we have seen, intersectional understandings of disability foreground the ways in which disabled individuals experience multiple and intersecting forms of social and educational disadvantage on the basis of their, ethnic, racial, linguistic, social class and other characteristics. This approach seeks to effect changes on the contextual factors which engender and consolidate power inequities and social hierarchies that impact upon disabled individuals' lives and educational trajectories. What is needed, therefore, is an intersectional framework of intervention, which focuses on a number of educational and social injuries that adversely affect the lives and educational experiences of disabled individuals (Liasidou 2013a).

Given the above considerations, current debates on inclusive education should draw on the notion of 'intersectionality' with the aim of challenging reductionist and neoliberal discourses of inclusive education and bringing to the fore the ways in which educational structures and institutions create/perpetuate inequality. Addressing these inequalities, within the context of inclusion involves going beyond pedagogical interventions and accessibility measures at school level and involves a critical approach to understanding the socio-political origins and educational ramifications of these inequalities. For instance, introducing reading interventions, through experimental designs and devising universally designed environments (as discussed in Chapter 3), constitutes just one aspect of a broader approach of redressing the host of systemic injustices and power inequities experienced by disabled students. Students' reading difficulties, for example, might be the result of impoverished social environments and contextually toxic conditions that undermine students' ability to learn on an equal basis with their more advantaged peers. These difficulties might also stem from students' inadequate social capital that is the outcome of impoverished and disadvantaged family backgrounds (DCSF 2009b).

In this respect, the teaching process becomes a highly political act that is underpinned by cultural negotiations and power interplays related to issues of race, class and ethnicity (Race and Lander 2014). For instance, research evidence suggests the ways in which the effectiveness of science instruction can be undermined by cultural negotiations between students and teachers related to low academic expectations in impoverished rural school settings (Blase and Bjork 2010). In a similar vein, a number of studies attribute the creation of a 'learned learning disability' (Goldstein 1995:463) to factors related to inadequate learning opportunities in impoverished schools, where teachers are inadequately prepared and hold low expectations for students in overcrowded and under-resourced classrooms (Dyson and Kozleski 2008). Even though these negative contextual issues have long been discussed and theorized in education, they are frequently not taken into consideration when discussing 'school failure' or SEN/D.

It is well documented that disabilities and special educational needs are to a significant extent the result of mitigating social conditions and circumstances that impair children's cognitive development and socio-emotional well-being. Hargreaves and Shirley (2009:80) point to the ways in which '[m]alnutrition, untreated infant health concerns, hearing and sight problems, environmental pollutants that attack the brain, and fetal alcohol and drug-dependency difficulties all impair learning, sometimes for life'. Students' developmental trajectories and learning potential are affected by the wider social conditions within which students live, develop and are educated. Schools are expected to assume a compensatory role in empowering disenfranchised groups of students to overcome a vicious circle of social hardships and power asymmetries that undermine their process of learning and development. Therefore, schools should work alongside communities and society by investing in community and family development and introducing sustained 'efforts to end child poverty, integrate housing patterns by social class ... provide reasonably high quality and easily accessible health care for all children' (Bringhouse 2010:48).

An intersectional perspective privileges a systemic approach to aligning concerns about mobilizing an educational reform agenda with wider concerns over reducing poverty, social exclusion and other sources of social disadvantage. A systemic framework of intervention embodies what Bringhouse (2009:49) calls a 'broader and bolder' approach to targeting inequities and injustices. This approach seeks to facilitate changes on the social and cultural contextual factors which engender and consolidate power inequities and social hierarchies that impact upon students' lives and educational trajectories.

Schools are called upon to co-ordinate a multidisciplinary educational provision from health, counselling, nursing, social services, childcare and so on, in order to address students' needs in holistic and comprehensive ways. For instance, current policy initiatives in the UK are concerned with introducing a new education, health and care plan intended for children and young people from birth to 25, who have SEN/D. The statutory introduction of EHC is expected to radically change the way in which education, health and social care professionals work with families and young people, with the aim being to assess individuals' needs globally by looking at individuals' life circumstances and conditions beyond education (DfE and DOH 2014).

At the same time, the role of schools needs to be supplemented by a more systemic approach at the macro level that includes the wider social context both at the local and global level (Raffo et al. 2011). After years of school effectiveness research, it is still the case that differences in students' outcomes, by and large, can be attributed to factors outside the school (Hargreaves and Shirley 2009). Even though schools can make a huge difference to students' lives and educational trajectories, there are other exogenous dynamics that have an equal or even bigger impact.

Nevertheless, notwithstanding the above considerations, individual pathology perspectives continue to significantly dominate policy and school-based discussions, thereby undermining attempts to question a host of contextual factors that are responsible for creating disadvantaged and subordinated student identities across different social and educational domains. Even in terms of higher education provision, it is occasionally the case that discussions on enhancing accessibility in higher education on the basis of disability is limited to providing deficit-oriented measures of support to this group of students (Beauchamp-Pryor 2013:5). Notwithstanding significant progress in incorporating innovative programmes and assistive technology equipment to accommodate the needs of disabled students in higher education (Sachs and Schreuer 2011), there are also other equally significant issues that need to be addressed in order to implement a social justice reform agenda in higher education (Liasidou 2014b). For instance, it is suggested that the under-representation and high drop-out rates of disabled students in higher education (Barnes 2007; Gibson 2011; Sachs and Schreuer 2011; Beauchamp-Pryor 2013) need to be addressed from an intersectional perspective with to the aim of alleviating the accumulative effects of multiple sources of social disadvantage on the lives and educational trajectories of disabled and other disenfranchised groups of people.

Another important issue that requires attention is the way in which resources are disproportionately diverted to disabled individuals from high socio-economic backgrounds. This point also relates to the varied degrees of privilege afforded to certain disabled individuals in accessing disability-related support services. Riddell et al. (2005) point to the ways in which the latter usually benefit male, middle-class students with specific learning difficulties such as dyslexia. Moreover, it needs noting that, even though there are a number of policy initiatives intended to subvert ingrained inequalities, such as the British 'Schools for the Future' and the USA's full service schools, aimed at facilitating community development and com-bating racism (Hargreaves and Shirley 2009), these policies do not take an intersectional perspective on addressing issues of social dis-advantage. An intersectional perspective criticizes policies and anti-discrimination legislation that address separately issues of disability, ethnicity, socio-economic background and gender, while ignoring the ways in which certain individuals might experience intersectional forms of unequal and discriminatory treatment (Liasidou 2013a).

Critical race theory and disability studies: Theoretical convergence/divergence and implications for a social justice reform agenda

Despite their similar theoretical orientations, critical race theory (CRT) and disability studies (DS) have developed in distinct ways, something that prohibited the advancement of a joint and mutually reinforcing analytical framework (Ferri 2010) in making transparent the socio-political dynamics that are accountable for the creation of negative ontologies on the grounds of race and/or ability. Even though racial categorization has been explicated as the outcome of power interplays and socio-political exigencies, similar analyses related to disability have been untenable owing to the overarching influence of an individual pathology discourse that monopolized the field of special education (Erevelles 2000; Watts and Erevelles 2004). Insights from CRT can reinforce the field of DS (and the change possibilities afforded by the social model of disability) by advancing new theorizations of gender, race, class and other dimensions of dis-ability experience, thereby providing fertile ground for challenging individual pathology approaches to difference and diversity (Liasidou 2013b).

Critical race theory has concentrated on challenging forms of knowledge that privilege 'whiteness' by ascribing to it infinite value and supremacy. The bipolar nature of the whiteness/blackness continuum has legitimized social hierarchies and categorical ascriptions that determined non-white people's positioning and role within society. 'Whiteness' has been valorized as a property, which by default conveyed a number of social privileges to people who possessed it while ascribing subordinated ontological status to those who have not (Ladson-Billings 1998).

The critical dimensions of efforts towards change aim at questioning the legitimization and the sanctified status ascribed to certain kinds of knowledge at the expense of others. In terms of a social justice approach to difference and diversity, it is suggested that material socio-cultural inequalities stem from 'epistemological inequities', which privilege certain forms of being that are commensurate with dominant constructs of knowledge and accepted 'social orders' (Gale and Tranter 2011). For instance, 'eurocentric knowledge' engenders particular ways of viewing and understanding human identities. CRT has sought to explore and challenge the ways in which the predominance of eurocentric knowledge has created a hierarchical matrix against which the value of individuals has been calibrated and used as a backdrop against which to afford them certain privileges. In terms of processes of racial stratification, whiteness has been used as a heuristic to single out and ostracize those individuals whose skin colour differs from hegemonic norms and expectations (Ladson-Billings 1998; Gillborn 2008).

In analogous ways, the notion of 'normalcy' is portrayed as an ontological 'a priori' that pervades social understandings and attitudes in relation to the notion of disability. Normalcy is valorized by the 'able-bodied order' (Campbell 2008, 2009), while relegating any perceived deviation from it to the sphere of negative ontology. Campbell (2008, 2009) gives pre-eminent emphasis to the overarching influence of 'able bodied order' that pervades dominant understandings of disability. The notion of ableism or 'able-bodied order' is used as a heuristic when exploring disablism and its associated discriminatory regimes. The supremacy of the able-bodied order is accountable for the subordinate positioning of certain individuals on the basis of their perceived deviation from an arbitrarily fabricated intellectual, corporeal and emotional norm. The alleged deviance of some individuals from this socially mediated norm is accountable for their subjugated social positioning and marginal subjectivities (Watts and Erevelles 2004).

Owing to these dominant conceptualizations and symbolic representations, disability is portrayed as an aberrant condition that needs to be contained and eliminated. These kinds of depictions of disability undermine attempts to challenge fabricated notions of normality and problematize disabling conditions and attitudes that create marginal and subordinated human identities. At the same time, due to the predominance of the 'able-bodied order', the notion of disability, unlike other sources of disadvantage linked to gender, race and social class, has been regarded as an individual pathology and not a social justice issue. The process of abnormalization has exerted a prodigious influence in engendering negative connotations of 'difference' on the basis of corporeal forms of normalcy, which legitimized the discriminatory and unfair treatment of disabled people (Campbell 2008, 2009).

While acknowledging the immense contribution of CRT in highlighting the socio-political dimensions of disability experience, it is still crucially important to understand the idiomorphic nature of disability experience by addressing some points of theoretical divergence (Liasidou 2013b). It is, therefore, important that:

> Disability should not be subsumed and diluted within the wider remit of human diversity on the erroneous assumption that the latter constitutes a paradigm shift from a reductionist individual pathology epistemology. Addressing the needs of disabled individuals necessitates a nuanced analysis of the personalized, intersectional and contextually grounded nature of disability experience, as well as an informed understanding of the relationship between 'personal troubles' and 'public issues' (Mills 1961) in constituting hybridized social and educational identities.
>
> (Liasidou 2013b:12)

An uncritical 'theoretical conflation' of CRT and DS might fail to recognize the ways in which 'impairment effects' (Thomas 1999) can affect disabled people's lives and experiences. Apart from the reductionist and pernicious consequences of an individual pathology perspective, there is also the danger of uncritically and hastily ignoring certain disability-related needs that might need specialist interventions and support services. Paradoxically, apart from the overwhelming evidence documenting the over-representation of ethnic minority students with SEN/D in non-normative categories of disability due to prejudice and discrimination, there is parallel evidence suggesting the under-representation of this group of students in disability categories due to their placement in bilingual education, while ignoring their disability-related needs (Liasidou 2013c). The latter phenomenon is an under-investigated, yet equally problematic phenomenon that is accountable for the scarcity and inadequacy of disability support services experienced by this group of students (Artiles and Ortiz 2002; Hui-Michael and Garcia 2009).

In relation to the above considerations, Norwich (2002:493) very appositely points to the ways in which this kind of theoretical conflation might dissolve disability issues in education into a nebulous inclusive education bandwagon, which advances an indiscriminate approach to issues of diversity and difference. This approach embodies a tension between commonality and differentiation stances, whereby the notion of inclusion is based on a complex and, in some instances, mutually exclusive interrelation of the values of equality and common provision, and respect for individual differences (Norwich 2008a). This problematic approach engenders the 'dilemma of difference' that denotes the ways in which 'difference' can be understood and responded to. As discussed in a previous section, on the one hand, recognition of difference might run the risk of 'singling out' and 'stigmatizing' some students, while on the other hand, failure to recognize difference might run the danger of homogenizing individual 'differences', thereby failing to address and provide for individual needs (Norwich 2008a).

In terms to responding to disability-related needs, Kayess and French (2008) distinguish between a 'minority rights' approach that emphasizes difference and deviance from a conventional social norm and a 'universalist approach' that focuses on modifying the social norm with the aim of accommodating learner diversity. A universalist approach concentrates on creating universally designed environments that can be accessible to all people including those with disabilities. Nevertheless, even a universalist approach does not downplay the necessity of providing targeted or more specialized forms of support when necessary in order to enhance accessibility (Burgstahler and Cory 2008). It is occasionally the case that the process of responding to disability-related needs might necessitate more specialized forms of pedagogy for meeting students' needs (Norwich and Lewis 2007; Mitchell 2008; Norwich 2008) as discussed in Chapter 4.

Conclusions

The previous sections have discussed the ways in which the notion of disability should be explored through an interdisciplinary perspective in order to address the social and political nature of disability experience. Such an approach transcends disciplinary monologue and eclectically deploys distinct disciplinary insights to provide a comprehensive analysis of difference and disability while highlighting some implications for the process of transformative change.

The notion of intersectionality (Crenshaw 1989), which explores the relationship of disability with other sources of disadvantage, such as race and social class, can be used as a heuristic theoretical device and political tool in order to foreground the multiple and interlacing forms of disadvantage experienced by disabled people on the grounds of varied characteristics, such as ethnic, cultural and sexual identities (e.g. Bhopal and Preston 2011). The notion of intersectionality can thus be used as a theoretical and action-oriented means to challenge reductionist and neoliberal understandings of inclusion that perpetuate an individual pathology approach to disability and special educational needs. Understanding the intersections of multiple systems of oppression and challenging the profusion of factors that disable certain groups of people entail critiquing dominant ideologies, educational policies and institutional arrangements that maintain and perpetuate social and educational injustice (Liasidou 2013a).

At the same time, it should be noted that the advocacy for 'theoretical convergence' amongst distinct disciplinary camps exploring issues of difference and diversity does not preclude the importance of discussing 'theoretical divergence' in order to delineate some important aspects of the distinctive nature of disability experience, along with its implications for mobilizing inclusive education reforms. While trying to avoid any theoretical dogmatism, critical disability studies subscribe to 'eclecticism' (Goodley 2012) in order to explain points of convergence and divergence amongst various analytical frameworks that can be utilized in order to explain the socio-cultural dimensions of disability experience (Liasidou 2013b).

A comprehensive and nuanced analysis of disability experience, necessitates adopting 'a pluralistic theoretical and analytical framework predicated on the values of individual respect and equality, along with the need to converge some of their mutually exclusive dimensions in more "inclusive" ways enacted through appropriate policy reforms' (Norwich 2010 cited in Liasidou 2012a:55). Hence, as a response to the somatophobic tendencies of some analytical frameworks and their failure to acknowledge the occasional real-life effects of disability experience linked to pain, fatigue, discomfort and loss of functioning (Shakespeare and Watson 2001), a trans-disciplinary analytical approach seeks to explore points of convergence as well as divergence in order to theorize the distinct nature of disability experience and examine possible implications for inclusive education policy and practice (Liasidou 2013b, 2013c).

8
Educational Leadership and Socially Just Change

Introduction

The chapter concentrates on exploring the notion of educational leadership and the ways in which it is linked to attempts to initiate inclusive education reforms. The role of leadership has been recognized as being crucial in precipitating and maintaining inclusive education reforms (Mayrowetz and Weinstein 1999; Riehl 2000; Kugelmass 2003; Kugelmass and Ainscow 2004; Theoharis and Causton-Theoharis 2008). Drawing insights from theories of inclusive education and educational leadership, the chapter is given over to the ways in which research on educational leadership can be applied to inclusive education (Ryan 2006a, 2006b; Edmunds and Macmillan 2010).

Traditional understandings of leadership were framed against technical and managerial issues intended to ensure the smooth operation of the organization. Stripped from its political and transformative dimensions, leadership was solely perceived as being a technical and operational process aimed at maintaining preordained organizational structures and ideological regimes (Riehl 2001). At the same time, leadership was believed to reside within the role of a single individual (e.g. the head teacher), whose responsibilities included the monitoring and evaluation of teachers' efficacy, maintenance of the school building, and individual and organizational responsiveness to bureaucratic regimes and the containment of students' behaviour (Shepherd and Brody Hasazi 2010).

In recent years, dominant understandings of leadership have been radically reconceptualized and positioned in terms of its strategic, visionary and, hence, transformative potential (Liasidou and Svensson 2011). The managerial approach to school leadership has been deemed to be inadequate due to the increasingly complex nature of educational organizations that necessitates new forms of leadership (Wright 2001). As Shepherd and Brody Hasazi (2010:476) point out: 'issues such as growing diversity in the school population, recognition of the ways in which knowledge is socially constructed and the inherently political nature of school require a new vision for leadership'.

Leaders have been increasingly seen as the 'enforcers' of transformative change (Liasidou and Svensson 2011) through sustained efforts to question the operational and cultural realities of organizations, and to inspire and create communities of practice based on collaboration, strategic planning and vision. In this respect, leaders have been (re)positioned as significant agents of change, who are expected to mobilize a whole-school reform agenda with the aim of creating effective and participatory learning communities. Fullan (2010) identifies central leadership as being instrumental in ensuring improvement of learning, especially in relation to vulnerable groups of students, as well as in enabling peers to interact and to learn from each other in order to facilitate the process of transformative change. Instructional leadership, for instance, works towards enhancing schools' capacity to become 'learning organizations' in order to constantly adapt to the challenges posed and the possibilities ensued by the increasing diversification of student populations (Ryan 2006). However, apart from the operational and strategic dimensions of leadership, particular emphasis needs to be given to the 'emancipatory' dimensions of educational leadership (Riehl 2000), which are concerned with tackling social and educational injustices that give rise to segregating and discriminatory practices (Liasidou and Svensson 2013).

Riehl (2000:55) is especially concerned with the critical dimension of leadership that 'is rooted in values of equity and social justice', and entails cultivating new understandings of learner diversity and promoting a value-based approach to redressing the asymmetrical power interplays that stigmatize and marginalize vulnerable groups of students. To this end, it is imperative that: 'school leaders must increase their awareness of various explicit and implicit forms of oppression, develop an intent to subvert the dominant paradigm, and finally act as a committed advocate for educational change' (Jean-Marie et al. 2009:4).

The chapter concentrates on the ways in which leadership for social justice can strengthen educational professionals' role in redressing inequalities of power, and social hierarchies that create abnormal and inferior 'student-subjects' (Yuddel 2006). This role can be best portrayed and exemplified against wider concerns about leadership for social justice (Shields 2004; Cambron-McCabe and McCarthy 2005; Bates 2006; Blackmore 2006; Theoharis 2007). This kind of leadership should inform educational professionals' preparation and development programmes (Cambron-McCabe and McCarthy 2005; Ryan 2006; Theoharis and Causton-Theoharis 2008), so as to enable them to ' "act as an equalizing force" in disrupting rather than reproducing privilege and disadvantage' (Gerwirtz and Cribb 2009:36). To this end, leaders need to acquire a reflective and reflexive understanding of their own role in contributing to the emergence and perpetuation of social and educational inequalities that impact upon students' lives and educational trajectories.

Leadership for social justice

In recent years, there has been an increased interest in highlighting the necessity to promote a social justice discourse in school reforms aimed at providing more equitable forms of education for learner diversity (Brown 2004; Shields et al. 2008; Theoharis 2008; Jean-Marie et al. 2009). A social justice discourse in educational leadership is crucial in fostering greater inclusive policies and practices for students who come from disenfranchised populations, on the grounds of disability and other sources of social disadvantage such as race and socio-economic status (Riehl 2000; Shields 2004; Cambron-McCabe and McCarthy 2005).

Scholarly work on leadership for social justice has advanced and elaborated discussion about the ways in which school leaders can be prepared in order to be in a position to bring about transformative changes geared towards more socially just forms of teaching and learning (Guyton 2000; Hackman 2005; Mullen and Jones 2008). The notion of leadership is not only embodied in the role of head teachers but extends to include distributed forms of educational leadership (NCSL 2004; Harris 2008; Harris and Spillane 2008), which place teachers at the centre of attempts to promote more socially just ways of thinking and acting in dealing with learner diversity. This (re)educative process entails cultivating new kinds of professional knowledge, praxis and ethos commensurate with the values of equity and social justice that are at the heart of an inclusive education reform agenda (Slee 2001; Artiles et al. 2006; Lingard and Mills 2007).

Leadership for social justice epitomizes educational professionals' commitment to redressing power imbalances and hierarchical social relations that create inferior and subjugated 'student subjects' on the basis of varied bodily, psychological and cognitive differences. This commitment entails, according to Shepherd and Brody Hasazi (2007:476), leaders' understandings of related concepts, as well as critical awareness of forms of leadership which can contribute to adopting a social justice approach to fostering inclusive learning communities. For instance, leaders must understand the role of moral leadership, multicultural education, instructional leadership, democratic discourse, community engagement, and a variety of strategies for building consensus about inclusive school cultures.

Leadership for social justice is essential in mobilizing transformative pedagogical action, with a view to improving the learning experiences and educational chances of all students irrespective of their personal attributes, developmental trajectories and lived experiences. Leadership implies potential for agency and institutional empowerment in precipitating a 'deliberate intervention that requires the moral use of power' (Bogotch 2000:2 cited in Shields 2004:110), in order to subvert discrimination and injustice. Socially just pedagogies entail an informed awareness of the ways in which schools valorize certain student identities while devaluing others (Graham 2005; Youdell 2006; Harwood and Humphrey 2008), thereby acting as sites of reproducing and perpetuating social and educational disadvantage. This kind of awareness presupposes establishing a clear definition of social justice, along with the ways through which it can be promoted and acted upon in educational contexts.

The next section is given over to providing a definition of social justice so as to forge and exemplify links with inclusive education in the succeeding section. This is followed by a discussion of the ways in which teacher leadership should be reconceptualized and redefined in the light of a social justice reform agenda, while the final section concentrates on the ways in which the notion of social justice is currently conceptualized and enacted in market-based educational systems and undermines the process of inclusive education reforms.

Understanding social justice in education

The notion of social justice is characterized by semantic plurality as it is understood and interpreted in varied and occasionally contradictory ways. This plurality has implications for the ways in which a social justice discourse can be enacted in current schooling (Johnson 2008). Hence, a definitional clarification and specification is needed in order to discuss the ways in which the notion is or should be understood and implemented within the context of an inclusive education reform agenda (Ainscow 2005; Slee 2006).

Notwithstanding the multiple understandings of the notion of social justice as well as the multiplicity of its practical implications and the ensuing conflicting views with regard to the sources of social and educational disadvantage, there is consensus about the magnitude of the extent to which a sizeable number of students experience systemic inequities at a number of levels (Brown 2004; Hattam et al. 2009). This is particularly true for disabled students who have been historically devalued and systematically denied access to education.

Concerns about equity and social justice should primarily concentrate on the 'challenging and changing of structural and systemic injustice in which certain groups are singled out for less favourable treatment and others are privileged' (Choules 2007:463). Social justice is about ensuring a fair distribution of and accessibility to educational resources for all students irrespective of their personal attributes and their material, socio-political and cultural conditions. In this sense, Carlisle et al. (2006:57) define social justice 'as the conscious and reflexive blend of content and process intended to enhance equity across multiple social identity groups (for example race, class, gender, sexual orientation, ability), foster critical perspectives, and promote social action'.

The notion of social action implies potential for political agency in promoting transformative change (Mullen and Jones 2008). Therefore, a firm commitment to social justice necessitates that concerns about social justice 'move beyond being buzzwords and instead become part of the lived practice in the classroom'

(Hackman 2005:103). This entails mobilizing political agency, in order to challenge the status quo and initiate transformative changes towards more equitable and just forms of educational provision for learner diversity (Choules 2007; Evans 2007). As Mullen and Jones (2008:331) write: A firm commitment to a social justice discourse involves 'activism of a more political nature' so as to challenge power inequities and discriminatory regimes. Acting upon a social justice agenda necessitates educational professionals' agency in generating and adopting pedagogical practices that:

> take into account and are responsive to students' disparate lived experiences, their unequal material and social realities, and their diverse needs – and that, ideally, shape the curriculum, edu-cational strategies, relationships among members of the school community, and create an inclusive learning environment.
>
> (Shields and Mohan 2008:290)

Schools need to be radically transformed so as to become sites for alle-viating wider social and educational inequalities by devising action plans and adopting long-term strategies to create policies, cultures and practices which valorize learner diversity and envisage creating socially just and inclusive learning communities for all. To this end, educational professionals need to become 'democratically account-able leaders' (Mullen and Jones 2008:329) so as act as agents of transformative change for social justice and inclusion.

A social justice discourse in inclusive education policy and practice

International policy imperatives geared towards promoting inclusion advocate more socially just ways of thinking and acting in order to embrace and build upon learner diversity to improve teaching and learning in mainstream schools (Slee 2001; Artiles et al. 2006; Armstrong and Barton 2007). The struggles for inclusive education (Vlachou 1997) presuppose radical changes in educational thinking, practice, roles and working relations. A crucial aspect of this process is to exemplify and forge closer links between education and social justice (Shields and Mohan 2008).

As already discussed, inclusive education denotes a perennial process of school improvement and development (Booth and

Ainscow 2002; Ekins and Grimes 2009) with a view to enabling disabled students to reach the maximum of their potential and to have a meaningful and active participation in educational and social domains. Hence, the notion of social justice is at the core of an inclusive education reform agenda aimed at reinstating disabled learners' rights and entitlements to receive socially just and equitable forms of educational provision (Lipsky and Gartner 1996; Sapon-Shevin 2003; Artiles et al. 2006). As Armstrong and Barton (2007:6) have put it poignantly, inclusive education is 'fundamentally about issues of human rights, equity, social justice and the struggle for a non-discriminatory society. These principles are at the heart of inclusive educational policy and practice'.

Notwithstanding the inexorable relationship between inclusion and social justice, Capper and Young (2014) draw on a meta-analysis of educational leadership for social justice to suggest that educational leadership for social justice has mainly concentrated on specific characteristics of student groups, such as race and social class, while ignoring disability issues. At the same time, the authors suggest that the notion of inclusion is peripheral to the educational leadership for social justice discourse. In this discourse, inclusion has been marginalized and remained 'ill defined, and undebated' (Capper and Young 2014:159); this is an issue that needs to be seriously considered in the light of international legal mandates and policies promoting the realization of inclusion on the basis of a human rights and social justice approach to difference and disability.

A crucial step towards embedding a social justice discourse in inclusive education policy and practice involves transcending deficit-oriented and blame-the-victim approaches that ostracize certain students on the basis of arbitrary and mono-dimensional constructions of ability (Liasidou 2013a). At the same time, another significant issue raised by Capper and Young (2014:160) relates to the ways in which social justice leadership practice is frequently limited to meeting the 'needs of particular student differences or the implications of specific student identities for social justice leadership practice'. This perspective needs to extend to include the

> thinking across differences and their intersecting identities... In sum leaders for social justice must consider how and to what extent promising practices in one area of diversity/difference

might address the full range of student differences and their intersections.

(Capper and Young 2014:160)

Essentialist understandings of students' identities that have historically legitimized and corroborated deficit-oriented and individual pathology perspectives need to be substituted by alternative understandings of the fluctuating and complex nature of these identities (Nash 2008; Cole 2009). Students designated as having SEN/D have been considered to be burdened by their own pathology without paying due attention to the intersections of various vectors of power that produce the negative dimensions of their identities. In view of these considerations, a school's mission and ethos should be characterized by a firm commitment to the belief that all students can learn and achieve (Florian 2014), provided that the system recognizes their diverse needs and is responsive to their differing learning styles and interests, which might not be served by the educational status quo. Within the context of a social justice pedagogical discourse, which valorizes students' intersecting identities that span across various markers of difference, it is understood that schools need to be reorganized and restructured in order to enhance achievement and participation of all students, including those students designated as having SEN/D. Within such a system, leaders need to be acquainted with effective curricula and instructional modifications as well as assessment processes in order to create more inclusive learning communities (see chapters 4 and 5).

Simultaneously, apart from the need for instructional and organizational restructuring, a social justice perspective also privileges an intersectional approach to aligning concerns over mobilizing an educational reform agenda with wider concerns over reducing poverty, social exclusion and other sources of social disadvantage, as discussed in Chapter 6. It is understood that the notion of leadership for social justice is embedded within a wider context that impacts upon the transformative potential of schooling. However, in order to reconceptualize and redefine the role of schools in minimizing rather than reproducing social disadvantage, leaders also need institutional empowerment, through relevant education policy and legislation, to become 'enforcers' of 'socially just change' (Hattam et al. 2009:304). As Blackmore (2006:196) puts it: 'To promote equity locally, school leaders require systemic and systematic support through a policy frame focusing on equity.'

While acknowledging the need for institutional empowerment, it is crucially important that there should be a more pronounced emphasis on 'intersectional thinking in both policy and research' (Wilkinson 2003:32), with a view to formulating and implementing policies to simultaneously address multiple sources of disadvantage that engender and multiply disabling conditions and attitudes. In recent years in the UK, there has been a raft of policies (e.g. DfES 2004; DCSF 2009), as well as related practices (e.g. extended schools, Sure Start, Every Child a Talker), which recognize the social and educational inequalities that impact upon students' lives and identities (Shields et al. 2008; Bass and Gerstl-Pepin 2011). Bass and Gerstl-Pepin (2011) draw upon Ladson-Billings' (2006) work in order to discuss the ways in which we need to acknowledge and repay the 'educational debt' owned to many students, who experience the accumulative and intersecting effects of multiple forms of educational and social disadvantage. This can only be achieved by 'valuing and supporting children and their families through educational policy that supports equity' (Bass and Gerstl-Pepin 2011:908). Educational professionals are expected to become the 'enforcers' of these equity-centred policies as their role is pivotal in alleviating social injustice by rejecting 'forms of schooling that marginalize pupils who are poor, black and least advantaged' (Giroux 2003:10).

Teacher leadership for social justice

While discussing the factors that affect large-scale reform initiative, Levin and Fullan (2008) highlight that reform programmes should be concerned with building teacher leadership at the school level. Teacher leadership denotes teachers' agency in taking a more active and critical approach to educational practice, thereby transforming instructional routines into alternative, more liberating pedagogies that are committed to progressive social change. 'Empowering teachers as leaders' (Sindelar et al. 2006:318) can transform teachers into agents of change in order to facilitate school improvement and development at a number of levels. Towards this end, head teachers should strive to enhance teachers' leadership role, so as to transform them into 'social justice workers committed to citizenship, ethics, and diversity' (Mullen and Jones 2008:330).

Webb et al. (2004:254) discuss the importance of teachers seeing themselves as 'leaders', for they are in a unique position to have an insightful and comprehensive knowledge of 'local school conditions – knowledge that policymakers and curriculum developers rarely have – to facilitate successful reform attempts'. Critical leadership aims to raise a collective awareness and responsibility of the ways in which a school's vision can be materialized (Webb et al. 2004; Blackmore 2006). This model of educational leadership is in alignment with 'emancipatory' (Ryan 2006b:9) and 'moral' (Riehl 2000:55) dimensions of leadership aimed at addressing issues of power, privilege and oppression that are endemic to current schooling, and have a significant impact on students' lives and educational trajectories. At the core of this process is the importance of critical dialogue (Webb et al. 2004) or moral dialogue (Shields 2004) in identifying discriminatory practices and inequities in schools and the community, so as to proceed to devising a joint plan to '*emancipate the organization from dominating structures*' (Webb et al. 2004:260) (emphasis in the original). Moreover, the scope of influence should also go beyond schools in order to influence wider social changes so as to empower disadvantaged individuals to be afforded educational and social opportunities tantamount to the ones experienced by their advantaged peers (Jean-Marie 2008; Jean-Marie et al. 2009; Bass and Gerstl-Pepin 2011).

Jean-Marie et al. (2009) discuss the crucial role that critical pedagogy (Giroux 1992; McLaren 1998) can play in raising leaders' critical consciousness with regard to the emancipatory potential of their pedagogy (see Chapter 7). This is a relatively neglected dimension in educational leadership preparation programmes, which needs to be advanced (Theoharis and Causton-Theoharis 2008) and made more salient in order to create opportunities for 'critical reflection, leadership praxis, critical discourse, and develop critical pedagogy related to issues of ethics, inclusion, democratic schooling, and social justice' (Jean-Marie et al. 2009:20). Towards this end, it is crucially important that educational leadership preparation programmes for justice and equity engage participants in 'substantive discussions concerning the dynamics of difference' (Brown 2004:80). This will enable teacher leaders to overcome their 'pathologizing silences' that focus on 'a single characteristic or factor as a way of labelling and consequently of essentializing others' (Shields 2004:117). As Shields and Mohan (2008:295) suggest:

> Deficit thinking too often takes over, and misplaced assumptions about the less advantaged children's abilities often influence their future opportunities [....] When such assumptions are made repeatedly over time, children soon receive the message that they do not really belong in school.

Lloyd (2008) discusses the ways in which barriers to learning and participation are often uncritically presented as being the sole result of individual and family pathology. This insular and essentializing perspective is manifested in the ascendancy and proliferation of remedial and compensatory measures of learning support that place the emphasis squarely on alleged individual 'deficits'. Such an approach is both limited and limiting. It is 'limited' because it ignores that a student's 'disabled identity' (Thomas 1999) is 'a complex amalgam, an often-messy matrix of human and social pathology' (Slee 2011:122), whilst it is 'limiting' because it forecloses possibilities for overturning injustice and hierarchical social relations.

Thus, 'leadership for the differently-abled' (Ryan 2006b:9) necessitates, amongst other things, a comprehensive understanding of the 'ways in which disabled childhoods are imbricated with other forms of exclusion' with a view to working 'with numerous forms of educational intervention that address the exclusion of disabled children' (Goodley and Runswick-Cole 2010:274). The notion of difference should be disassociated from individual pathology perspectives, which locate 'difference' within the sphere of abnormality that needs to be contained and remedied through expert intervention and remedy.

In this respect, disability needs to be viewed as being part of a complex web of interactive and overlapping sources of social disadvantage that give rise to and proliferate disabling conditions and identities (Garland-Thompson 2004). These perspectives can create liberatory conditions in order to subvert interlacing sources of inequity and devise strategies (e.g. instructional leadership) to touch upon learner diversity and create effective and socially just learning communities (Jean-Marie 2008). Professional praxis needs to be permeated by 'a social justice pedagogical lens' (Hackman 2005:103), and a vision for 'improving access and opportunity for children historically marginalized by mainstream public schooling' (Jean-Marie 2008:351–352).

It needs noting, however, that visionary and liberatory rhetoric alone are not a panacea to dismantle social injustice. Brown (2004) draws upon Freire's (1994) work and highlights the necessity to transcend critical reflection and liberatory thinking in order to mobilize transformative social action. Activism constitutes an important dimension of raising educational leaders' critical consciousness with regard to their emancipatory role in redressing inequalities of power and oppressive regimes. Pedagogical activism necessitates imparting relevant knowledge and cultivating specific skills for instigating transformative change. Capper et al. (2006) present three horizontal axes against which educational leaders' preparation programmes should be based. The first axis is concerned with enhancing participants' critical consciousness, whilst the two others are concerned with instilling specific knowledge and skills so as to provide practical tools for activism. While exemplifying the nature of knowledge and skills necessary for socially just political and pedagogical action, Capper et al. (2006:213) suggest that it is crucially important that school leaders are equipped with:

> evidence-based practices that can create an equitable school. For example, this knowledge would include understanding the positive and equitable effects of de-tracking and eliminating pull-out programs. It would include developing a specific knowledge base around language acquisition, disability, and current research on reading and mathematics curriculum and instruction.

Moreover, in terms of acquiring skills, educational professionals need, for example, 'to be able to establish a service delivery team to work toward eliminating pull out programs, use data to lead conversations about equity and school improvement, and hire and supervise staff to carry out these socially just ideas' (Capper et al. 2006:213). The imperative of professional development and practice is also portrayed in Guyton's (2000:110) discussion about the ways in which the notion of social justice should be conceptualized in teacher education. In addition to developing critical consciousness with regard to the emancipatory and transformative potential of their pedagogies, teacher leaders need to be equipped with relevant knowledge and skills in order to reflect upon their professional praxis and ask themselves the following questions, so as to take effective steps for political and pedagogical action:

- How is what I do in my classroom contributing to or detracting from social justice?
- How is my teaching ensuring that all pupils in my class can and do learn?

(Guyton 2000:112)

The aim is to create an accommodating and engaging instructional context so as to enable all students to flourish and develop their potential. This process entails fostering learning communities that offer ample opportunities to teacher leaders to be involved in a dialectical process of reflection, as well as individual and collective inquiry into the varied sources of social and educational disadvantage that create and perpetuate inequity and injustice.

Social justice in the globalized economy and teachers' leadership

As discussed in Chapter 1, globalization has instigated the necessity to ensure the development of a skilled and versatile workforce capable of contributing to a nation state's competitiveness and economic vitality. In consequence an achievement-based education system has emerged that prioritizes effectiveness and efficiency over values and principles (Dyson 2001, 2005; Roulstone and Prideaux 2008). Within this system, what matters most is the 'performative worth of individuals' (Ball 2009:42) that is gauged against a student's ability to succeed in high-stakes testing, whilst concerns about equality and social justice are marginalized (Welch 1998; Barton and Slee 1999; Bottery 2000).

The notions of equality and social change have been reconceptualized and redefined on the basis of a neoliberal and meritocratic perspective which privileges the view that it is fair that some people have more and others less, precisely because the disproportionate allocation of material resources simply reflects their individual contribution to society. From this perspective, 'equality is based on a narrowly defined and measurable set of abilities that contribute to the social and economic order.... This slips quickly into the argument that the economic and social distributions in society are a reflection of biological capacity' (Rioux 2010:113). Market-based educational imperatives are thus regarded as being more democratic than democracy itself (Barton 1996:3), for they are understood as being the 'most efficient mode of allocating resources and more responsive to individual needs' (Barton and Slee 1999:5). By implication, the notion of social justice, as we have seen in Chapter 1, is reduced to enhancing the entrepreneurial potential of individuals to pursue their own ends (Masschelein and Simons 2005), whilst disabled students are regarded as being an unbearable burden and a significant threat to a school's unfettered quest for mono-dimensional constructions of educational excellence (Ball 2008).

A direct consequence of this kind of instrumental approach to education policy and practice is 'the hollowing out and emptying of leadership and management of its moral, ethical and political vitality' (Smyth 2008:225). Karlsen (2000) exemplifies the ways in which educational systems in the Western world are characterized by 'decentralised centralism'. Decentralization has precipitated market-based educational imperatives of increased competition, efficiency and effectiveness, whilst centralization has given rise to stringent accountability regimes embodied in prescribed curricula, national standards and performance indicators that need to be diligently adhered to and monitored by educational professionals. Far from being empowered and called upon to act as leading agents in redressing power inequities and oppressive regimes (Freire 1998; McLaren 1998), teachers experience professional oppression within a system that imposes preordained standards and quantitative performance indicators (Ainscow 2005:119). It is suggested that teachers have also been victimized by the neoliberal discourse (Beck 1999; Karlsen 2000; Sleeter 2008), as they have been increasingly rendered accountable to meet certain 'standards' that are gauged against 'performativity' thresholds (Ball 2009). In this way, teachers have become 'professional accountants' rather than 'accountable professionals', whereby accountability is 'ill defined with regard to social justice' (Karpinski and Lugg 2006:285).

Conclusions

The chapter has been concerned with the relationship between leadership and social justice in order to discuss the ways in which the role of leaders needs to be reconfigured in alignment with the demands of a social justice reform agenda within the context of inclusion (Liasidou and Svensson 2013). The notion of leadership epitomizes the potential for transformative action, with a view to creating socially just ways of thinking and acting to ameliorate the intersectional forms of disadvantage experienced by disenfranchised groups of students. In particular, the emphasis has been placed on the ways in which disabled students experience systemic injustices on the basis of their varied bodily, mental and psychological differences (Liasidou 2013a). These differences have been uncritically and hastily relegated to the sphere of individual pathology without paying attention to the 'long term accumulations of societal and cultural inequities' (Bass and Gerstl-Pepin 2011:909) that collude towards creating 'disabled identities' (Thomas 1999:109). The ascendancy and proliferation of market-oriented policy imperatives have given rise to new understandings of social justice that are subsumed within wider concerns linked to economic ends and market-based considerations (Ball 2009). Given this perspective, the notion of leadership is eclipsed by managerial considerations and 'gaming', the system techniques (Ross and Berger 2009:470) that stifle teachers' autonomy and agency in challenging their 'disabling pedagogies' (Goodley 2007).

Striving for socially just schools entails an informed recognition of the ways in which schools can become sites of reproducing rather than eradicating social disadvantage, thereby compounding the forms of oppression and discrimination experienced by those students whose 'performative worth' (Ball 2009:42) is perceived as being minimal or non-existent. To that end, inclusive education necessitates questioning educational leaders' preparation programmes that subordinate the ethical and value-based dimensions of professional praxis (Allan 2005) and, simultaneously, entails questioning the nature and ramifications of predominant accountability regimes, which undermine attempts to promote an egalitarian and social justice discourse in education policy and practice (Shields 2004; Bringhouse 2010).

Notwithstanding its rhetorical appeal and immense professional standing, leadership for social justice runs the risk of becoming a cliché unless it is linked with wider policy and institutional reforms (Mittler 1990; Dyson 2001), with a view to establishing new account-ability measures to make schools and teachers redistribute and focus resources on groups of students, who are entangled in a complex web of social and educational disadvantage (Artiles et al. 2006; Bringhouse 2010). This is an arduous, but nevertheless an urgently needed pursuit. As Shields and Mohan (2008:298) write: 'if educa-tors or policymakers reject social justice as one of the foundations of an excellent educational system, we risk perpetuating inequality, dis-parity, and poor achievement on the part of those who are the least academically successful in our current systems and structures'.

9
Disability Studies and the Issue of Change: The Voices of Disabled People/Students

Introduction

Having identified the systemic dimensions of educational change within the context of inclusion, the aim of the chapter is to explore the ways in which the notion of change has been conceptualized within disability studies. These theorizations have played a pivotal role in highlighting the necessity to initiate radical social reforms for fostering just and non-discriminatory social and educational communities (e.g. Barton 1992; Barnes 1996). These accounts have provided a political and action-oriented platform for challenging discrimination and precipitating transformative changes through 'the engagement with issues of equality, politics, power and control, in which forms of discrimination will need to be identified, challenged and changed' (Barton 1997:32).

Goodley (2011:xi) defines disability studies as 'a broad area of theory, research and practice that are antagonistic to the popular view that disability equates with personal tragedy'. The social model of disability is at the heart of 'disability studies', while the term 'disablism', in parallel with racism and sexism (e.g. Goodley 2011, 2012), denotes the ways in which disability emanates from hegemonic conceptions of normality that are morphed in and affected by dominant socio-political conditions and circumstances. Disability studies are thus focused upon challenging individual pathology perspectives and advancing a social and cultural theory of disability experience (Barton and Oliver 1997; Goodley 2011).

A crucial aspect of transformative change is the notion of political agency manifested in individual and collective 'political action' to facilitate the process of change. The role of disabled people and their organizations has been crucial in exerting agency and mobilizing transformative change. As Oliver and Barton (2000:2) point out:

> In Britain at least and in our version of the story of the emergence of disability studies, disabled people have been absolutely crucial, providing the main ideas and shaping the academic agenda throughout.

Disabled people's enactments of political agency have been instigated by the social model of disability that epitomizes the struggles of disabled people to pursue transformative material and cultural changes. The advent of the social model of disability has sought to challenge the domination of the medical model of disability that relegated disability to the sphere of individual pathology, and created a culture of silence with regard to the negative authoring of disabled peoples' subjectivities and social positioning. The social model of disability constitutes an evolving set of ideas and a powerful political force in empowering disabled people to challenge their longstanding incarnation in institutions, hospitals and special schools, and to acclaim their rights and entitlements to live and be educated in humane, dignified and non-discriminatory ways.

The social model of disability and political agency for transformative change

Through the lens of the medical model of disability, disabled people have been historically portrayed as deficient and as a less-than-human species in need of rehabilitative and normalizing procedures to approximate conventional projections of corporeal, psycho-emotional and intellectual normalcy. Their incarceration in segregated settings and their abysmal exploitation have been skilfully disguised and presented as a humanitarian approach to allegedly protect them from the dangers and the complexities of the social world (Barton and Tomlinson 1981; Tomlinson 1982, 2014).

The less-than-human and negative ontological portrayals of disability have been internalized by disabled individuals, who fatalistically succumbed to the propagation of paternalistic forms of provision. The internalization of the negative ontological status with regard to the notion of disability has delayed disabled people's self-empowerment and political struggle to pursue their emancipation and to reclaim their rights and entitlements. Campbell (2008, 2009) discusses the ways in which conventional corporeal norms have been internalized by disabled people whose difference has been 'experienced' in negative and self-aberrant terms, thereby leading to feelings of 'internalized oppression'.

The process of normalization, linked to assimilationist and remedial processes of the predominance of an 'able-bodied order' has not only been externally imposed, but it has also been self-imposed in terms of the ways in which 'the marginalized person attempts to emulate hegemonic norms, whiteness or ableism, and assumes the legitimacy of a devalued identity imposed by the dominant group' (Campbell 2008:155), which does not apply to him/her. Reminders of this kind of internal oppression are still found in the ways in which disabled individuals are occasionally reluctant to disclose their disabilities and to claim their entitlements (Campbell 2008, 2009). For instance, empirical evidence suggests that students with invisible disabilities in higher education institutions are sometimes reluctant to disclose their disabilities and claim access to disability-related support services (Barnes 2007; Gibson 2012; Madriaga et al. 2011). While discussing the reasons as to why some disabled students fail in higher education, Madriaga et al. (2011:917) point out that 'their lack of achievement reflects the pervasiveness of normalcy within the institution, where disabled students who are considering take-up of support are placed in vulnerable positions to disclose their impairments'.

The sanctified status attributed to the medical model of disability, along with the paraphernalia of normalizing practices linked to it, has been challenged by sociologists in the field of disability studies (Barnes 1996; Oliver 1996), who have criticized the essentialist ways in which the notion of disability has been understood and theorized. Disability has been reconceptualized and redefined as a multifaceted form of social oppression on a par with racism, sexism and other sources of social disadvantage that needed to be tackled in socio-politically informed ways (Abberely 1987; Oliver 1990; Barnes et al. 1999).

The social model has acted as a powerful political tool in fostering 'a social world in which all people experience the realities of inclusive values and relationships' (Barton 2003:11). A social model view of disability prioritizes a human rights and social justice discourse in challenging the host of power inequities and discriminatory regimes that relegate disabled individuals to the margins of social and political life. These understandings have provided the impetus to introduce anti-discrimination and human rights legislation so as to safeguard disabled peoples' rights and entitlements (Gabel and Peters 2009). From this perspective, disability has been redefined as a highly political issue that needed socio-political interventions to eradicate the multiple forms of discrimination and oppression which have been endemic aspects of disabled people's lived experience. The emphasis has been subsequently shifted to the imperative of questioning and ultimately removing environmental and ideological disabling barriers that exclude and marginalize groups of people on the basis of varied bodily, emotional and intellectual differences (Oliver 1990; Shakespeare 1997; Thomas 1999). This perspective has brought to the fore the necessity to pursue fundamental social changes so as to foster equity and justice for disabled individuals.

Notwithstanding theoretical scepticism about the validity of particular standpoints and interpretations of the social model of disability (Thomas 2004), the latter has acted as a mobilizing force to unravel the highly political and culturally grounded nature of disability experience. Even though Oliver (2013:1025) is critical of the ways in which 'these criticisms have received more prominence than the social model itself', Barton (2000:4) considers that dissonant voices and theoretical tensions are a testament to 'the dialogue that is taking place within the disability movement and disability studies'. Theoretical contestations provide fertile ground for reflective and reflexive thinking with regard to the diverse ways in which disability has been perceived and experienced with a view to articulating new perspectives and navigating new forms of disability politics and transformative action.

The complex nature of disability experience calls for the cross-fertilization of diverse theories and analytical frameworks in delineating the ways in which disability is 'lived' in different socio-political conditions and is affected by idiosyncratic biographical experiences. Social constructionist and post-modern/post-structural analyses of disability experience bring to the fore the socially mediated character of disability, and unveil issues of power, privilege and oppression that are at play in the constitution of human identities and social hierarchies (Shakespeare 1997, 2006; Corker and French 1999; Thomas 2004). The former analyses concentrate on the socio-cultural construction of disability and special educational needs (Barton and Tomlinson 1981), while the latter focus on problematizing and deconstructing the discursive constitution and legitimization of dichotomous couplets (e.g. normality vs disability, whiteness vs blackness) that emanate from power inequities and discriminatory regimes. The valorization of one part of the couplet is premised upon or results in the devaluation of the other (Tremain 2005).

Feminist analyses, in parallel with post-modern analyses, have also been utilized in order to criticize the social model of disability for its mono-dimensional emphasis on the social dimension of disability and its failure to adequately explain the complexity of disability experience (Crow 1996; Morris 1996; Shakespeare 1997; Corker and French 1999). These criticisms have largely concentrated on the alleged failure of the social model of disability to take into consideration the notion of impairment (Thomas 1999, 2004), as well as the heterogeneity of disabled people in terms of their cultural, gender, class and sexual characteristics.

By shifting the gaze to the socio-political dimensions of disability experience, the predominance of social modellist thinking has fuelled disabled people's individual self-worth, collective identity and political orientation, and instigated the emergence and development of disability self-advocacy groups. Their aim has been for disabled people to empower themselves to become autonomous and self-determined citizens in an equitable and non-discriminatory society, while challenging power inequities and discriminatory regimes. As Oliver (2013:1024–1025) points out:

> Armed with the idea that we needed to identify and eradicate the disabling barriers we had in common, the disabled peoples' movement forced the media to change their images of us, transport providers to open up many of their services to us, public buildings to become much more accessible and the legal system changed to make it illegal to discriminate against us.

While reviewing the contribution of the social model of disability, Barnes (2012) points to the fact that all of the critics of the social model have eventually acknowledged the significance of adopting this form of analytical approach. For instance, notwithstanding her earlier criticisms about the dichotomous analytical perspective adopted by the social model in theorizing disability as opposed to impairment, Morris (2000), a disabled woman, activist and writer, acknowledged the political significance and revolutionary power of the social model of disability in bringing about socially just reforms.

> The social model of disability gives us the words to describe our inequality. It separates out (disabling barriers) from impairment (not being able to walk or see or having difficulty learning).... Because the social model separates out disabling barriers and impairments, it enables us to focus on exactly what it is which denies us our human and civil rights and what action needs to be taken.
>
> (Morris 2000:1–3 cited in Barnes 2012:19)

Without denouncing the experiential aspects of their impairment, disabled people have been empowered to recognize the socio-political dimensions of disability experience so as to pursue individual and collective emancipation. By shifting the focus from an individual pathology perspective to a social pathology one, the social model of disability has opened up infinite possibilities for disability activism in order to challenge discriminatory attitudes and oppressive regimes, which have historically led to the marginal and subordinate existence of disabled individuals.

Voice, participation and the quest for transformative change

Theorizations in disability studies have a stated aim: that of facilitating transformative change in the lives of disabled individuals. This quest necessitates giving priority to the voices of disabled individuals (Barton 2000) in articulating their own understanding and perspectives regarding their socio-culturally mediated experiential aspects of disability, as well as the barriers they come across in their daily lives. Barton (2005) was especially concerned about the necessity to assist in the empowerment of disabled people through emancipatory and participatory research agendas capable of giving voice to disabled people, and forging constructive partnerships between disabled and non-disabled researchers. Hitherto, research on disability has failed to provide useful information to the policymaking process and has marginally contributed to the improvement of the material life circumstances experienced by disabled people (Oliver 2002). It needs noting, however, that by alluding to the importance of improving the material conditions that affect disabled people's lives, it should not be assumed that the process of change is limited to attempts to compensate and care for disabled people. As Rioux (2001:38) puts it:

> Providing services, while important, is not the essence of the political struggle but a means towards empowerment.... The litmus test about the struggle for change is, therefore, how much progress there has been to end the political disenfranchisement, economic disempowerment and social inequality that are the reality for disabled people. Providing services and care do not lead to empowerment. It is the right to choose – the right to self determination that will lead to the societal transformation in which 'difference [will no longer be considered] disruptive (if not threatening) and community involvement a luxury at best and an intrusion at worst'....

Without ignoring the importance of providing appropriate forms of support for disabled people, the crucial point is to recognize that the issue of political agency and 'voice' are crucial elements in a socio-cultural context characterized by power inequities and social hierarchies, where disabled individuals are systematically placed in subordinated and passive positions. The latter observation also relates to their subordinated positioning or inexistent presence in disability-related organizations that are allegedly intended to represent and safeguard disabled people's 'best interests'.

Barnes and Mercer (2001) make the useful distinction between 'disability' and 'disabled people's' organizations. The former are usually run by non-disabled people while they adopt a deficit approach to disability. These organizations are mainly concerned with enhancing access to support services for certain groups of disabled people and their families. Their role is occasionally limited to offering paternalistic and charitable forms of support and provision without encouraging political action as a means of empowering disabled individuals to pursue the full range of their rights and entitlements. Drake (1996) is critical of the ways in which traditional charities subscribe to the medical model of disability and place disabled people in subordinate and dependent subject positions. Non-disabled people hold positions of power in these charities and adopt a helpers/helped perspective in order to rationalize the exclusion of disabled people from leadership positions in these organizations. Given their inferior and depended social positioning, disabled people have systematically sought to question the right of these charities and professional people to determine their lives and educational trajectories.

Dealing effectively with diversity on the basis of disability entails developing understanding and raising relevant questions with regard to ways in which disabled people wish to be educationally and socially positioned, the role they should play in the process of change and the nature of change they envisage (Barton 2003:5). According to Mercer (2002:233), 'The emancipatory mode is geared to praxis-oriented research that exposes social oppression and facilitates political action to transform society.' Central to an inclusive education reform agenda is the recognition of the importance of seriously listening to disabled students' voices (Barton 2008; DfE and DOH 2014) in order to pursue fundamental changes in professional relations, praxis and ethos, and foster a socially just pedagogical discourse (Lingard and Mills 2007).

The notion of 'voice', however, needs to be problematized in terms of the ways in which disabled individuals do not constitute a homogeneous group of people. The multiplicity of 'voice' calls for devising diverse agendas of disability research, in order to understand the varied, and occasionally contradictory, aspects of disability experience. As already alluded to, the issue of disability experience should not be seen in isolation from issues of racism, sexism and classism that constitute interdependent and reciprocally related systems of control and oppression (Artiles et al. 2007). In adopting this analytical perspective, it will be possible to highlight the ways in which disability is a socially dependent and culturally mediated construct that calls for political interventions at the individual and societal level. Simultaneously, the multiplicity of the notion of 'voice' needs to be understood in relation to the ways in which the differing nature of disabilities evokes different socio-cultural responses as well as different experiential embodiments of disability (Liasidou 2013b).

Goodley (2011:3) discusses the ways in which political activism, embodied in the Disabled People's Movement, 'has revolutionised a global understanding of disability' by highlighting the personal experience of disability and by recognizing disability as a social problem that can be dealt with by socio-political interventions. These interventions should be premised on nuanced understandings of the ways in which the dialectic of the global and the local create hybridized human identities that 'demand analysis of the complex glocal response to disablism' (Goodley 2011:170). At the same time, the notion of 'voice' should be explored in relation to the ways in which social hierarchies are not only enacted through the effect of disablism but also within it. Goodley (2000), for instance, applies the notion of self-advocacy to people with learning difficulties, who have been traditionally excluded from disability activism on the basis of their alleged intellectual limitations to assume an active and self-determined role in their lives and social relations. The same exclusionary regimes from grass roots activism have been applied to older disabled people and disabled individuals from ethnic minorities (Barnes and Mercer 2001).

The notion of 'voice' also needs to be taken into consideration in designing and providing disability-related services. The 'voices' of disabled people should inform policymakers, service providers and professionals' understandings of the experiential aspects of disability within the context of a human rights and social justice framework. These social agents are institutionally empowered to influence the decision-making processes that determine, through policymaking and institutional arrangements, the biographical and educational trajectories of disabled people. As part of the process of transformative change, disability-related decisions should not be arbitrarily and uncritically taken without consultation with disabled people. Simultaneously, it is imperative that these professionals are trained in order to better understand and reflect upon the theoretical underpinnings and value-based considerations associated with the importance attributed to the notion of 'voice' (self-advocacy) as a means of reinstating disabled people's human rights and entitlements, especially with reference to people with learning disabilities, who have been traditionally excluded from disability activism. As Goodley (2000:212–213) suggests, in relation to the role of self-advocacy groups in promoting participatory forms of decision-making processes intended to improve the material and social conditions of disabled people:

> Professional models of empowerment should be continuously appraised by a user-led perspective... self advocates have a clear idea about how services should be developed... People with learning difficulties are not just the users of services, but are effectively the unpaid employers. Professionals would benefit from training by these employers.

Rather than expanding and strengthening the liberatory and empowering role of the social model of disability in valorizing disabled people's voices and perspectives in framing their lives and determining their futures, Oliver (2013) discusses the role of the social model in the aftermath of the global financial crisis, and points to the ways in which the disabled people's movement has been weakened due to the criticisms levelled against the social model of disability. Government policies in the UK have drawn upon these criticisms in order to re-introduce impairment and difference into their economic and social policy, while ignoring the barriers faced by disabled people. According to Oliver:

> The disabled peoples' movement that was once united around the barriers we had in common now faces deep divisions and has all but disappeared, leaving disabled people at the mercy of an ideologically driven government with no-one to defend us except the big charities who are driven by self-interest. As a consequence of this, most of the political campaigning that has taken place in defence of our benefits and services have forced disabled people back into the role of tragic victims of our impairments and has involved others undertaking special pleading on our behalf. In fact it has taken us back more than 30 years to the time before the social model came into existence.
>
> (Oliver 2013:126)

Moreover, the consequences of the global financial crisis are expected to further enhance the role of non-governmental organizations (NGOs) in substituting the attenuated and even non-existent role of national governments 'to anticipate and respond to the vulnerabilities of excluded people.... This has led to disability organizations becoming business offering services to disabled people that have been lost through the rolling back of the State' (Goodley 2011:171). These considerations not only raise issues about the distinction between 'disability' and 'disabled people's' organizations, as discussed earlier, but also raise significant questions about the direction of disability activism will follow at the start of the 21st century (ibid.), along with its impact on understanding and framing the notions of 'voice' and 'participation' in disability politics.

Conclusions

The agenda of social change is firmly embedded in theoretical and action-oriented discussions and debates with a view to re-authoring disabled people's eroded ontological status and lived experiences (Campbell 2008, 2009). Such a transformative endeavour should actively involve disabled people, who have been hitherto excluded from decision-making procedures, research agendas and policymaking processes germane to their lives, social relations and educational trajectories. Undoubtedly this is the first critical step for transformative change: an issue that has been prioritized by theorists of disability studies, many of whom are disabled people themselves and have first-hand experience of the embodied experience of disability (Morris 1991, 1996; Oliver 1991, 1996; Corker and French 1999). The pleas for change emanate from disabled people's collective and individual experience to challenge the overarching influence of a suppressive 'able-bodied' order, which rationalized their systematic exclusion and marginalization from social, political and cultural domains.

Given the hostile and suppressive social milieu that valorizes certain ways of ontological existence and epistemological theorizing, 'finding a voice is an essential part of the struggle for freedom' (Barton 2005:31). Disability activism has provided the impetus to precipitate a bottom-up approach to the process of change by giving voice to disabled people to articulate their concerns about the ways in which they wish to be positioned in wider theoretical and action-oriented efforts to eradicate discriminatory and suppressive institutional and ideological regimes. At the same time, however, it should be noted that the notion of 'voice' in disability politics needs to be problematized in terms of the ways in which people with certain kinds of impairments or biographical conditions have been excluded from disability activism. Notwithstanding the immense impact of disability movements on the introduction of anti-discrimination and other legal mandates promoting the need to include disabled individuals in all aspects of social and political life, these developments have reportedly generally benefited white, middle-class and well-educated people with physical or sensory disabilities (Barnes and Mercer 2001). Similar observations apply to the introduction of anti-discrimination legislation and the provision of disability-related services in education (e.g. Riddel et al. 2005) and the community (Ali et al. 2001).

10
Conclusions

The process of educational change towards the realization of an inclusive discourse is a chaotic, unpredictable and multidimensional endeavour, as it is contingent on a plethora of factors and dynamics that are reciprocally related and affected. These factors and dynamics are embedded in moral, political, personal, social and institutional domains and formulated against a host of power inequities and social hierarchies (Artiles et al. 2007; Liasidou 2012a), which need to be concurrently addressed and transformed in order to mobilize a comprehensive reform agenda. The process of change is further compounded by the contentious and contested nature of inclusion; the notion is understood and acted upon in varied ways, thereby leaving little room to devise a uniform strategy for initiating effective changes towards this end.

Notwithstanding the relatively newly introduced notion of inclusion, it reflects long-standing debates about the role of schooling in societies and its contribution to exacerbating wider social inequalities (Moreau 2014). Inclusion has expanded and contextualized these debates by offering novel theoretical, policy and pedagogical frameworks in order to precipitate the process of educational change. At the same time, inclusion has reinforced and made transparent the socio-political nature of disability experience. Hitherto, unlike other sources of social disadvantage linked to race/ethnicity, gender, socioeconomic status and so on, the issue of disability has been silenced and excluded from educational debates. This omission mirrors the ingrained tendency to medicalize disability and to relegate it in the realm of individual deficit (Erevelles 2000; Gabel 2002; Goodley

2007; Liasidou 2012b): an issue that is still prevalent despite laudable 'rhetorical turnaround' in favour of socio-cultural approaches to understanding difference and diversity on the grounds of disability.

Nevertheless, in spite of the fact that one might have expected the quest for inclusion to have, in a way, concretized the theoretical and action-oriented elements of the change process towards the realization of socially just and democratic social and educational communities, paradoxically, this process has become an even more complex, demanding, contested and elusive pursuit. This can be partly attributed to the fact that inclusion has brought to the fore a hitherto neglected dimension of human diversity linked to corporeal, psychological and cognitive markers of difference, which have been historically thought to fall within the remit of medicine and psychology.

The emergent analytical focus on disability experience has created seismic changes to dominant ways of thinking about human diversity, while further compounding theoretical discussions about the aims and nature of transformative social and pedagogical agendas to empower disenfranchised groups of people to pursue individual and collective emancipation (Artiles et al. 2007). Inclusion, as a revolutionized conceptual and analytical framework of mobilizing socially just reforms, has thus evoked contradictory responses and has spurred both enthusiastic (Ainscow 1997; Stainback and Stainback 1998) and sceptical thinking and theorizing (Funch and Funch 1994; Low 1997) with regard to its ideological and pedagogical underpinnings, as well as its political orientations.

Inclusion can thus be better defined as being in the process of 'becoming' rather than 'being', for it is not a static phenomenon but an evolving and changing one, which is constantly contested, negotiated and redefined depending on dominant values-based considerations and changing socio-political dynamics and exigencies (Liasidou 2012a). As an evolving and mutable phenomenon, inclusion is in a perennial process of 'transition' towards radically new educational paradigms that can facilitate the process of fostering effective and socially just learning communities for learner diversity. This transition, however, is occasionally hampered by ideological, policy and systemic minefields, which contribute to 'inclusion backlash' moments (Dyson 2001). It is imperative that the origins and ramifications of these 'moments' are identified, critically understood and theorized, with a view to bringing about relevant changes at the political, social and individual level.

The notion of inclusion is concerned with a number of important pedagogical, epistemological and moral considerations, as well as a number of vexed dilemmas that pose huge challenges and raise significant questions in relation to attempts to provide a concise and concrete conceptual, theoretical and action-oriented framework for precipitating and sustaining an inclusive education reform agenda. The quest for inclusion embodies the complex process of understanding and accommodating learner diversity; this raises significant issues with regard to the varied dimensions of 'diversity' and the ways in which they interact with disability experience.

At the same time, inclusion is not only concerned with diversity but also embodies diversity, in terms of the ways in which it is conceptualized, contextualized, related, internationalized and enacted. As a result, the process of change within the context of inclusion becomes an even more demanding and multidimensional quest. The definitional pluralism, as well as the definitional polarities and dissensions pertaining to an inclusive education reform agenda, epitomize the sheer complexity of the issues at hand. Given the complexities, conceptual intricacies and multi-axial associations of inclusion, it is not surprising that the process of change becomes a rather challenging endeavour that cannot be presented and enacted in a piecemeal fashion. For instance, some current versions of inclusion, patently influenced by neoliberal imperatives, promote different understandings of social justice and individuality, thereby evoking and consolidating a neo-special perspective on formulating and implementing education policy reforms. By regenerating a neo-special education paradigm, the concept of inclusion is problematized, distorted or simply ignored and silenced on the grounds of its alleged utopian nature (Croll and Moses 2001) or perceived ineffectiveness (Kauffman and Badar 2014).

The sheer complexity of the change process for the realization of more inclusive forms of thinking and doing, calls for theoretical openness and convergence (Liasidou 2013b) in order to examine the multidimensional character of the attempts to bring about inclusive education reforms. Inclusion can be characterized, by default, as a multi-disciplinatory theoretical terrain, for it embraces theoretical pluralism as a means of exploring a number of theoretical, political and pedagogical issues related to the notion of disability experience. What is needed therefore, in addressing the complexity of the issues at hand, is a fertile cross-disciplinary and cross-cultural dialogue that can potentially instigate a reflective and critical approach to the possibilities and challenges of pursuing an inclusive educational reform agenda.

The cross-fertilization of diverse insights and perspectives can bring to the fore the theoretical affinities and political orientations that inclusion shares with other disciplinary fields, which seek to address similar issues and considerations, albeit in different contexts and through different theoretical lenses. These include such issues as school effectiveness, quality teaching and learning, social justice, empowerment, issues of discrimination and exclusion, learner diversity, professional development and community involvement to name but a few. Inclusion brings the different themes together by providing a comprehensive analytical perspective on viewing and discussing these themes, while paying particular attention to exploring points of convergence and divergence in dealing with issues of difference and diversity.

Given the diverse and contrasting understandings of inclusion, it is crucial, quoting Ball (2012:xii), to adopt 'a more cosmopolitan sociology of policy' within the context of inclusion. Inclusive education policymaking needs to be seen through the lens of 'a dialectical process' in which the similar and the dissimilar, the global and the local interact in reciprocal and complex ways (Green 2002). From this perspective, it is imperative to have a global discussion on disability and inclusive education so as to understand the culturally and socially bound nature of the struggles for inclusive education reforms. To this end, the role of cross-cultural research in inclusive education policy and practice needs to be further pursued and developed in order to delineate the ways in which socio-political and cultural dynamics impact upon dominant understandings of difference and diversity and shape idiomorphic inclusive education policy landscapes (Barton and Armstrong 2007).

Given the complexity and profundity of the issues at hand, the book has been a tentative attempt to address the issue of change within the context of inclusion by exploring the varied dimensions, contexts, theoretical perspectives, challenges and possibilities against which this process can be mobilized and acted upon. The epithet of 'tentative' infers the necessity to further explore the theoretical dynamics and the magnitude of the action-oriented possibilities that can arise from an informed understanding of the pluralistic and intricate nature of the process of change.

Thus, bearing in mind the contentious nature of inclusion and the complex nature of the process of change, this book – while applying Branson's (2010:125) words – has 'striven to create an impression rather than a blueprint' for theorizing educational change within the context of inclusion. This 'impression' has been primarily concerned with providing some insights into the multiple theoretical terrains within and against which the notion of inclusion is morphed, understood and contextualized. Each theoretical strand that relates to the varied aspects of the process of change discussed in this book represents a transformative possibility; this opportunity, when combined with others, can bring about sea changes to existing ideological, institutional, policy and pedagogical regimes that converge towards sustaining and regenerating special education imperatives. Central to any analytical framework is the necessity to focus on the workings of power in the constitution of 'disabled identities' without homogenizing the ways in which disability is experienced and reciprocally interrelated with other markers of difference (Artiles et al. 2007; Liasidou 2013a).

Bibliography

Abberley, P. (1987). 'The concept of oppression and the development of a social model of disability'. *Disability, Handicap & Society*, 2(1), 5–19.

Ainscow, M. (1997). 'Towards inclusive schooling'. *British Journal of Special Education*, 24(1), 3–6.

Ainscow, M. (2005a). 'Developing inclusive education systems: What are the levers for change?' *Journal of Educational Change*, 6(2), 109–124.

Ainscow, M. (2005b). 'The Next Big Challenge: Inclusive School Improvement' *Keynote Presentation at the Conference of School Effectiveness and Improvement*, Barcelona, January, 2005.

Ainscow, M. (2010). 'Achieving excellence and equity: Reflections on the development of practices in one local district over 10 years'. *School Effectiveness and School Improvement*, 21(10), 75–92.

Ainscow, M., Booth, T., Dyson, A., Farrell, P., Frankham, J., Gallannaugh, F., Howes, A. and Smith, R. (2006). *Improving Schools, Developing Inclusion*. London: Routledge.

Ainscow, M., Dyson, A., Goldrick, S. and Kerr, K. (2009). 'Using research to foster inclusion and equity within the context of new labour education reform'. In Chapman, C. and Gunter, H. (Eds) *Radical Reforms: Perspectives on an Era of Educational Change*. London: Routledge. 169–201.

Ainscow, M. and Miles, S. (2009). 'Developing inclusive education system: how can we move policies forward?' (Chapter prepared for a book in Spanish to be edited by Climent Gine et al. 2009). Retrieved from http://www.ibe.unesco.org/fileadmin/user_upload/COPs/News_documents/2009/0907Beirut/DevelopingInclusive_Education_Systems.pdf.

Alexander, R. (2009). 'The Cambridge primary review and its final report'. Royal Society of Arts, 19 October 2009. Retrieved from http://www.thersa.org/__data/assets/pdf_file/0004/248026/RSA-091019.pdf (accessed 3 December 2011).

Ali, Z., Fazil, Q., Bywaters, P., Wallace, L. and Singh, G. (2001). 'Disability, ethnicity and childhood: A critical review of research'. *Disability & Society*, 16(7), 949–967.

Allan, J. (2004). 'Deterritorializations: Putting postmodernism to work on teacher education and inclusion'. *Educational Philosophy and Theory*, 36(4), 417–432.

Allan, J. (2005). 'Inclusion as an ethical project'. In Tremain, S. (Ed.) *Foucault and the Government of Disability*. Michigan, IL: University of Michigan Press, 281–298.

Angelides, P., Stylianou, T. and Leigh, J. (2003). 'Forging a multicultural education ethos in Cyprus: Reflections on policy and practice'. *Intercultural Education*, 14(1), 57–66.

Archer, M. (1982). 'Morphogenesis versus structuration: On combining structure and action'. *The British Journal of Sociology*, 33(4), 455–483.

Armstrong, A.C., Armstrong, D. and Spandagou, I. (2010). *Inclusive Education: International Policy and Practice*. London: Sage.

Armstrong, F. (1999). 'Histories of inclusion: Perspectives on the history of special education'. In Barton, L. and Armstrong, F. (Eds) *Difference and Difficulty: Insights, Issues and Dilemmas*. Sheffield: University of Sheffield. 25–38.

Armstrong, F. and Barton, L. (2007). 'Policy, experience and change and the challenge of inclusive education: The case of England'. In Barton, L. and Armstrong, F. (Eds) *Policy, Experience and Change: Cross-Cultural Reflections on Inclusive Education*. Dordrecht: Springer, 5–18.

Armstrong, F. and Moore, M. (2004). 'Action research: Developing inclusive practice and transforming cultures'. In Armstrong, F. and Moore, M. (Eds) *Action Research for Inclusive Education: Changing Places, Changing Practices, Changing Minds*. London: RoutledgeFalmer. 1–16.

Armstrong, Th. (2009). *Multiple Intelligences in the Classroom*. Alexandria: ASCD.

Arnesen, A.L. (2011). 'International politics and national reforms: The dynamics between "competence" and the "inclusive school" in Norwegian education policies'. *Education Inquiry*, 2(2), 193–206.

Artiles, A.J., Harris-Murri, N. and Rostenberg, D. (2006). 'Inclusion as social justice: Critical notes on discourses, assumptions, and the road ahead'. *Theory into Practice*, 45(3), 260–268.

Artiles, A.J. and. Kozleski, E.B. (2007). 'Beyond convictions: Interrogating culture, history, and power in inclusive education'. *Language Arts*, 84(4), 351–358.

Artiles, A. and Ortiz, A.(2002). 'English language learners with special education needs: Contexts and possibilities'. In Artiles, A. and Ortiz, A. (Eds) *English Language Learners with Special Education Needs*. Washington, DC: Center for Applied Linguistics, 3–27.

Audit Commission (2002). *Special Educational Needs: A Mainstream Issue*. UK: Audit Commission.

Ball, S. (2003). 'The teacher's soul and the terrors of performativity'. *Journal of Education Policy*, 18(2), 215–218.

Ball, S. (2004). 'Performativities and fabrications in the education economy: Towards a performative society'. In Ball, S. (Ed.) *The RoutledgeFalmer Reader in the Sociology of Education*. London: RoutledgeFalmer, 143–155.

Ball, S. (2008). 'The legacy of ERA, privatization and the policy ratchet'. *Educational Management Administration and Leadership*, 36(2), 185–199.

Ball, S. (2009). *The Education Debate*. Bristol: Policy Press.

Ball, S. (2012). *Global Education Inc.: New Policy Networks and Neo-Liberal Imaginary*. London/New York: Routledge.

Barnes, C. (1996). 'Theories of disability and the origins of oppression of disabled people in Western society'. In Barton, L. (Ed.) *Disability and Society: Emerging Issues and Insights*. London: Longman, 43–60.

Barnes, C. (2007). 'Disability, higher education and the inclusive society'. *British Journal of Sociology of Education*, 28(1), 135–145.

Barnes, C. (2012). 'The social model of disability: Valuable or irrelevant?' In Watson, N., Roulstone, A. and Thomas, C. (Eds) *The Routledge Handbook of Disability Studies*. London: Routledge, 12–29.

Barnes, C. and Mercer, G. (2010). *Exploring Disability*. Cambridge: Polity.

Barton, L. (1993). 'The struggle for citizenship: The case of disabled people'. *Disability, Handicap and Society*, 8(3), 235–246.

Barton, L. (1997). 'Inclusive education: Romantic, subversive or realistic?'. *International Journal of Inclusive Education*, 1(3), 231–242.

Barton, L. (2000). *Disability studies and the quest for inclusivity: Some observations.* Retrieved from http://www.revistaeducacion.mec.es/re349/re349_07ing.pdf.

Barton, L. (2001). 'Disability, struggle and the politics of hope'. In Barton, L. (Ed.) *Disability, Politics and the Struggle for Change*. London: David Fulton, 1–10.

Barton, L. (2005). 'Emancipatory research and disabled people: Some observations and questions'. *Educational Review*, 57(3), 317–327.

Barton, L. (2008). 'Foreword'. In Gabel, S. and Danforth, S. (Eds) *Disability and the Politics of Education*. New York: Peter Lang. xvii–xx.

Barton, L. and Armstrong, F. (2007). *Policy, Experience and Change: Cross–Cultural Reflections on Inclusive Education*. Dordrecht: Springer.

Barton, L. and Oliver, M. (1997). *Disability Studies: Past, Present and Future*. Leeds: The Disability Press.

Barton, L. and Tomlinson, S. (Eds) (1981). *Special Education: Policies, Practices and Social Issues*. London: Harper and Row.

Bass, L. and Gerstl-Pepin, C. (2011). 'Declaring bankruptcy of educational inequality'. *Educational Policy*, 25(6), 908–934.

Bates, R. (2006). 'Educational administration and social justice'. *Education, Citizenship & Social Justice*, 1(2), 141–156.

Beauchamp-Pryor, K. (2013). *Disabled Students in Welsh Higher Education: A Framework for Equality and Inclusion*. Rotterdam: Sense Publications.

Beck, J. (1999). 'Makeover or takeover? The strange death of educational autonomy in neo-liberal England'. *British Journal of Sociology of Education*, 20(2), 223–238.

Beckett, A.E. (2013). 'Anti-oppressive pedagogy and disability: Possibilities and challenges'. *Scandinavian Journal of Disability Research*, 17(1), 1–19.

Benjamin, S. (2002). *The Micropolitics of Inclusive Education*. Buckingham: Open University Press.

Bereiter, C. and Scardamalia, M. (2010). 'Beyond Bloom's taxonomy: Rethinking knowledge for the knowledge age'. In Hargreaves, A., Lieberman, A., Fullan, M. and Hopkins, D. (Eds) *Second International Handbook of Educational Change*. Dordrecht: Kluwer. 675–692.

Berkhout, S. and Wielemas, W. (1999). 'Towards understanding educational policy: An integrative approach'. *Educational Policy*, 13, 402–420.

Best, R. (2008). 'Education, support and the development of the whole person'. *British Journal of Guidance and Counselling*, 36(4), 343–351.

Best, S. and Kellner, D. (2001). 'Dawns, twilights, and transitions: Postmodern theories, politics and challenges'. *Democracy and Nature*, 7(1), 101–117.

Black, P., McCormick, R., James, M. and Pedder, D. (2006). 'Learning how to learn and assessment for learning: A theoretical inquiry'. *Research Papers in Education*, 21(2), 119–132.

Blackmore, J. (2006). 'Social justice and the study and practice of leadership in education: A feminist history'. *Journal of Educational Administration and History*, 38(2), 185–200.

Blake, S., Bird, J. and Gerlach, L. (2007). *Promoting Emotional and Social Development in Schools. A Practical Guide*. London: Paul Chapman Publishing.

Blase, J. and Bjork, K.L. (2010). 'The micropolitics of educational change and reform: Cracking open the black box'. In Hargreaves, A., Lieberman, A., Fullan, M. and Hopkins, D. (Eds) *Second International Handbook of Educational Change*. London: Springer. 119–130.

Boddington, N., King, A. and McWhirter, J. (2014). *Understanding Personal, Social, Health and Economic Education in Primary Schools*. London: Sage.

Booth, T. and Ainscow, M. (2002). *The Index for Inclusion* (2nd edn). Bristol: Centre for Studies in Inclusive Education.

Bottery, M. (2000). *Education, Policy and Ethics*. London: Continuum.

Branson, C. (2010). *Leading Educational Change Wisely*. Rotterdam: Sense Publishers.

Brehony, K. (2005). 'Primary schooling under New Labour: The irresolvable contradiction of excellence and enjoyment'. *Oxford Review of Education*, 31(1), 29–46.

Bringhouse, H. (2010). 'Educational equality and school reform'. In Haydon, G. (Ed.) *Educational Equality*. London: Continuum, 15–68.

Brown, G. (2007). *Education speech*, 31 October 2007, University of Greenwich. Retrieved from http://www.ukpolitics.org.uk/node/154.

Brown, E.B. and Doolittle, J. (2008). 'A cultural, linguistic and ecological framework for response to intervention with English language learners'. *Teaching Exceptional Children*, 40(5), 66–72.

Brown, K.M. (2004). 'Leadership for social justice and equity: Weaving a transformative framework and pedagogy'. *Educational Administration Quarterly*, 40(1), 77–108.

Burbules, C.N. and Berk, R. (1999). 'Critical thinking and critical pedagogy: Relations, differences, and limits'. In Popkewitz, T.S. and Fendler, L. (Eds) *Critical Theories in Education*. New York: Routledge. 45–55.

Burgstahler, S. (2012). 'Universal Design of Instruction (UDI): Definition, principles, guidelines, and examples'. University of Washington College of Engineering. Retrieved from http://www.washington.edu/doit/Brochures/PDF/instruction.pdf.

Burgstahler, S. and Cory, R. (2008). 'Moving in from the margins: From accommodation to universal design'. In Gabel, S. and Danforth, S. (Eds) *Disability and the Politics of Education*. New York: Peter Lang, 561–581.

Burkitt, I. (2002). 'Technologies of the self: Habitus and capacities'. *Journal for the Theory of Social Behaviour*, 32(2), 219–237.

Byrne, B. (1999). 'The nomological network of teacher burnout: A literature review and empirically validated model'. In Vandenberghe, R. and Huberman, M. (Eds) *Understanding and Preventing Teacher Burnout*. Cambridge: Cambridge University Press, 15–37.

Byrne, B. (2012). 'Hidden contradictions and conditionality: Conceptualizations of inclusive education in international human rights law'. *Disability & Society*, 28(2), 232–244. DOI: 10.1080/09687599.2012.699282.

Caldwell, B. (2014). 'Re-imagining special education: A pre-requisite for the transformation of schools'. Keynote presentation at the *First Asia-Pacific Congress on Creating Inclusive Schools on the theme Reflect – Shift – Transform*, co-hosted by the Australian Special Education Principals Association (ASEPA) and the Australian Council for Educational Leaders (ACEL), Sydney, 2 May 2014.

Cambron-McCabe, N. and McCarthy, M. (2005). 'Educating school leaders for social justice'. *Educational Policy*, 19(1), 201–222.

Campbell, F.A.K. (2008). 'Exploring internalized ableism using critical race theory'. *Disability & Society*, 23(2), 151–162.

Campbell, F.K. (2005). 'Legislating disability. Negative ontologies and the government of legal identities'. In Tremain, S. (Ed.) *Foucault and the Government of Disability*. Ann Arbor, MI: University of Michigan Press, 170–204.

Campbell, F.K. (2009). *Contours of Ableism: The Production of Disability and Abledness*. Basingstoke: Palgrave MacMillan.

Capper, C. and Young, M. (2014). 'Ironies and limitations of educational leadership for social justice: A call to social justice educators'. *Theory into Practice*, 53, 153–164.

Capper, C.A., Theoharis, G. and Sebastian, J. (2006). 'Toward a framework for preparing leaders for social justice'. *Journal of Educational Administration*, 44(3), 209–224.

Carlisle, L.R., Jackson, B.W. and George, A. (2006). 'Principles of social justice education: The social justice education in schools project'. *Equity & Excellence in Education*, 39(1), 55–64.

Carrington, S. (1999). 'Inclusion needs a different school culture'. *International Journal of Inclusive Education*, 3(3), 257–268.

Cassidy, W. and Jackson, M. (2005). 'The need for equality in education: An intersectionality examination of labelling and zero tolerance policies'. *McGill Journal of Education* [Special Issue on Law and Education], 40(3), 445–466.

Choules, K. (2007). 'The shifting sands of social justice discourse: From situating the problem with "them" to situating it with "us"'. *Review of Education, Pedagogy & Cultural Studies*, 29, 461–481.

Cigman, R. (2006). *Included or Excluded?* London: Routledge.

Claxton, G. (2004). 'Learning is learnable (And we ought to teach it)'. In Cassel, J. (Ed.) *National Commission for Education Report, Ten Years On*. Retrieved from http://www.guyclaxton.com/documents/New/Learning%20Is%20Learnable.pdf (accessed 18 June 2013).

Claxton, G. and Carr, M. (2004). 'A framework for teaching learning: The dynamics of disposition'. *Early Years*, 24(1), 87–97.

Clement, J. (2014). 'Managing mandated educational change'. *School Leadership & Management: Formerly School Organisation*, 34(1), 39–51.

Corker, M. and French, S. (1999). 'Reclaiming discourse in disability studies'. In Corker, M. and French, S. (Eds) *Disability Discourse*. Buckingham: Open University Press, 192–210.

Cornwall, J. (1997). *Access to Learning for Pupils with Disabilities*. London: David Fulton.

Crenshaw, K. (1989). 'Demarginalizing the intersection of race and sex: A black feminist critique of antidiscrimination doctrine, feminist theory, and antiracist politics'. *University of Chicago Legal Forum*, 14, 538–554.

Croll, P. and Moses, D. (2003). 'Special educational needs across two decades: Survey evidence from English primary schools'. *British Educational Research Journal*, 29(5), 731–747.

Daniels, H. (2009). 'Vygotsky and inclusion'. In Hick, P., Kershner, R. and Farrell, P. (Eds) *Psychology for Inclusive Education. New Directions in Theory and Practice*. London: Routledge, 25–37.

Davis, K. (2008). 'Intersectionality as buzzword: A sociology of science perspective on what makes a feminist theory successful'. *Feminist Theory*, 9, 67–85.

Davis, P. and Florian, L. (2004). *Teaching strategies and approaches for pupils with Special Educational Needs: A Scoping Study*. Brief No. RB516. London: DfES. Retrieved from www.dfes.gov.uk/research/data/uploadfi les/RB516.doc.

Day, C. (2005). 'Sustaining success in challenging contexts: Leadership in English schools'. *Journal of Educational Administration*, 43(6), 573–583.

DCSF (Department for Children, Schools and Families) (2009a). *Independent Review of the Primary Curriculum: Final Report*. Annesley: DCSF.

DCSF (2009b). *Breaking the Link between Disadvantage and Low Attainment. Everyone's Business*. Annesley: DCSF.

DCSF (2009c). *Independent Review of the Primary Curriculum: Final Report*. Annesley: DCSF.

De Valenzuela, J.S. (2010). 'Sociocultural views of learning'. In Florian, L. (Ed.) *The Sage Handbook of Special Education*. London: Sage, 280–289.

Department for Social Inclusion of Persons with Disabilities/Ministry of Labour and Social Insurance (2013). *First Report of Cyprus for the Implementation of the UN Convention on the Rights of Persons with Disabilities*. Nicosia: Department for Social Inclusion of Persons with Disabilities/Ministry of Labour and Social Insurance.

DfE (Department for Education) (2010). *The Importance of Teaching*. London: The Stationery Office.

DfE and DOH (Department for Education and Department of Health) (2014). *Special Educational Needs and Disability* (SEN) Code of Practice: for 0 to 25. UK: Department for Education. Retrieved from https://www.gov .uk/government/publications/send-code-ofpractice-0-to-25 (accessed August 2014).

DfES (Department for Education and Skills) (2003). *Excellence and Enjoyment: A Strategy for Primary Schools*. London: DfES.

Douglas, A.S. (2014). *Student Teachers in School Practice: An Analysis of Learning Opportunities*. London: Palgrave Macmillan.

Doyle, C. and Robson, K. (2002). *Accessible Curricula. Good Practice for All*. Cardiff: UWIC Press. Retrieved from http://www.adcet.edu.au/StoredFile .aspx?id=1352&fn=accessible.pdf.

Drake, R.F. (1996). 'A critique of the role of the traditional charities'. In Barton, L. (Ed.) *Disability and Society: Emerging Issues and Insights*. London: Longman, 147–166.

Dudley-Marling, C. and Baker, D. (2012). 'The effects of market-based school reforms on students with disabilities'. *Disability Studies Quarterly*, 32(2), 1–19 (online version). Retrieved from http://dsq-sds.org/article/view/3187.

Dyson, A. (2001a). 'Special needs education as the way to equity: An alternative approach?' *Support for Learning*, 16(3), 99–104.

Dyson, A. (2001b). 'Special needs in the twenty-first century: Where we've been and where we're going'. *British Journal of Special Education*, 28(1), 24–29.

Dyson, A. (2005). 'Philosophy, politics and economics? The story of inclusive education in England'. In Mitchell, D. (Ed.) *Contextualising Inclusive Education: Evaluating Old and New International Perspectives*. London: Routledge, 63–88.

Dyson, A. and Kozleski, E.B. (2008). 'Disproportionality in special education: A transatlantic phenomenon'. In Florian, L. and McLaughlin, M. (Eds) *Dilemmas and Alternatives in the Classification of Children with Disabilities: New Perspectives*. Thousand Oaks, CA: Corwin Press, 170–190.

Edmunds, A.L. and Macmillan, R.B. (Eds) (2010). *Leadership for Inclusion, A Practical Guide*. Rotterdam: Sense Publishers.

Ekins, A. and Grimes, P. (2009). *Inclusion: Developing an Effective Whole School Approach*. Maidenhead: Open University Press.

Elbertson, N., Brackett, M. and Weissberg, R. (2010). 'School-based social and emotional learning (SEL) Programming: Current perspectives'. In Hargreaves, A., Lieberman, A., Fullan, M. and Hopkins, D. (Eds) *Second International Handbook of Educational Change*. London: Springer, 1017–1032.

Elwan, A. (1999). *Poverty and Disability: A Survey of Literature*. Washington, DC: Social Protection. Unit, Human Development Network, World Bank. Retrieved from http://siteresources.worldbank.org/DISABILITY/Resources/ 280658-1172608138489/PovertyDisabElwan.pdf

Erevelles, N. (2000). 'Educating unruly bodies: Critical pedagogy, disability studies, and the politics of schooling'. *Educational Theory*, 50(1), 25–47.

Ertmer, P. and Newby, T. (1993). 'Behaviourism, cognitivism, constructivism: Comparing critical features from an instructional design perspective'. *Performance Improvement Quarterly*, 6(4), 50–72.

Evans, A.E. (2007). 'Horton, Highlander, and leadership education: Lessons for preparing educational leaders for social justice'. *Journal of School Leadership*, 17, 250–275.

Farrell, M. (2009). *Foundations of Special Education*. Oxford: Blackwell.

Ferri, B.A. (2010). 'A dialogue we've yet to have: Race and disability studies'. In Dudley-Marling, C. and Gurn, A. (Eds) *The Myth of the Normal Curve*. New York: Peter Lang Publishers, 1–11. Retrieved from https://syr.academia.edu/BethFerri/Papers (accessed 2 December 2014).

Florian, L. (2014). 'What counts as evidence of inclusive education?' *European Journal of Special Needs Education*, 29(3), 286–294.

Florian, L. and Black-Hawkins, K. (2011). 'Exploring inclusive pedagogy'. *British Educational Research Journal*, 37(5), 813–828.

Florian, L. and Spratt, J. (2013). 'Enacting inclusion: A framework for interrogating inclusive practice'. *European Journal of Special Needs Education*, 28(2), 119–135.

Foster, J.B. (2011). 'Education and the structural crisis of capital: The US case'. *Monthly Review* (Education and Capitalism Series), 63(3), 6–37 (July–August). Retrieved from http://monthlyreview.org/2011/07/01/education-and-the-structural-crisis-of-capital/

Foucault, M. (1977). *Discipline and Punish: The Birth of the Prison*. New York: Pantheon Books.

Foucault, M. (1978). 'Politics and the study of discourse'. *Ideology and Consciousness*, 3, 7–26.

Foucault, M. (1979). *History of Sexuality*, Vol. 1. New York: Pantheon Books.

Foucault, M. (1980a). 'Truth and power'. In Gordon, C. (Ed.) *Power/knowledge; Selected Interviews and Other Writings, 1972–1977*. Brighton: Harvester Press, 109–134.

Foucault, M. (1980b). 'Discourse, power and knowledge'. In Sheridan, A. (Ed.) *The Will to Truth*. London: Tavistock Publications, 111–132.

Foucault, M. (1984). 'The order of discourse'. In Shapiro, M. (Ed.) *Language and Politics*. London: Blackwell, 108–138.

Francis, B. (2006). 'Heroes or zeros? The discursive positioning of "underachieving boys" in English neo-liberal education policy'. *Journal of Education Policy*, 21(2), 187–200.

Freire, P. (1970). *Pedagogy of the Oppressed*. New York: Continuum.

Freire, P. (1985). *The Politics of Education: Culture, Power and Liberation*. South Hadley, MA: Bergin and Garvey.

Fulcher, G. (1999). *Disabling Policies?: A Comparative Approach to Education Policy and Disability*. London: The Falmer Press.

Fullan, M. (2006). 'Change theory. A force for school improvement'. *Centre for Strategic Education*. Seminar Series Paper No. 157, November 2006.

Fullan, M. (2010). 'Positive pressure'. In Hargreaves, A., Lieberman, A., Fullan, M. and Hopkins, D. (Eds) *Second International Handbook of Educational Change*. London: Springer. 119–130.

Fullan, M.G. (1993). *Change Forces: Probing the Depth of Educational Reform*. London: Falmer Press. 19–41.

Fuchs, D. and Fuchs, L. (2004). 'Inclusive schools movement and the radicalization of special education reform'. *Exceptional Children*, 60(4), 294–309.

Furlong, J. (2008). 'Making teaching a 21st century profession: Tony Blair's big prize'. *Oxford Review of Education*, 34(6), 727–739.

Gabel, S. (2002). 'Some conceptual problems with critical pedagogy'. *Curriculum Inquiry*, 32(2), 177–201.

Gale, T. and Tranter, D. (2011). 'Social justice in Australian higher education policy: An historical and conceptual account of student participation'. *Critical Studies in Education*, 52(1), 29–46.

Garcia, S.B. and Ortiz, A. (2006). 'Preventing disproportionate representation: Culturally and linguistically responsive prereferral interventions'. *Teaching Exceptional Children*, 38(4), 64–68.

Gardner, H. (1983). *Frames of Mind: The Theory of Multiple Intelligences*. New York: Basic Books.

Garland-Thomson, R. (1997). *Extraordinary Bodies: Figuring Physical Disability in American Culture and Literature*. New York: Columbia University Press.

Garrett, P.M. (2009). *'Transforming' Children's Services: Social Work, Neoliberalism and the 'Modern' World*. Maidenhead: Open University Press.

Gewirtz, S. and Cribb, A. (2009). *Understanding Education: A Sociological Perspective*. Cambridge: Polity.

Gibson, S. (2009). 'Inclusion versus neoliberalism: Empowering the "Other"'. In Gibson, S. and Haynes, J. (Eds) *Perspectives on Participation and Inclusion. Engaging Education*. London: Continuum, 12–26.

Gibson, S. (2012). 'Narrative accounts of university education: Sociocultural perspectives of students with disabilities'. *Disability & Society*, 27(3), 353–369.

Gibson, S. and Haynes, J. (2009). 'Introduction'. In Gibson, S. and Haynes, J. (Eds) *Perspectives on Participation and Inclusion. Engaging Education*. London: Continuum, 1–8.

Giddens, A. (1986). *The Constitution of Society*. Berkley: University of California Press.

Giles, C. and Hargreaves, A. (2006). 'The sustainability of innovative schools as learning organizations and professional learning communities during standardized reform'. *Educational Administration Quarterly*, 42(1), 124–156.

Gillborn, D. (2008). 'Coincidence or conspiracy? Whiteness, policy and the persistence of the Black/White achievement gap'. *Educational Review*, 60(3), 229–248.

Giroux, H. (1992). *Border Crossings: Cultural Workers and the Politics of Education*. New York: Routledge.

Giroux, H. (2003). 'Public pedagogy and the politics of resistance: Notes on a critical theory of educational struggle'. *Educational Philosophy and Theory*, 35(1), 5–16.

Giroux, H. (2012). *Education and the Crisis of Public Values*. New York: Peter Lang.

Goddard, R. and Goddard, M. (2006). 'Beginning teacher burnout in Queensland schools: Associations with serious intentions to leave'. *The Australian Educational Researcher*, 33(2), 61–76.

Goldstein, B.S.C. (1995). 'Critical pedagogy in a bilingual special education classroom'. *Journal of Learning Disabilities*, 28(8), 463–475.

Goodley, D. (2000). Self-advocacy in the lives of people with learning difficulties. Buckingham: Open University Press.

Goodley, D. (2007). 'Towards socially just pedagogies: Deleuzoguattarian critical disability studies'. *International Journal of Inclusive Education*, 11(2), 317–334.

Goodley, D. (2011). *Disability Studies. An Interdisciplinary Introduction*. London: Sage.

Goodley, D. (2012). 'Dis/entangling critical disability studies'. *Disability and Society*, DOI: 10.1080/09687599.2012.717884.

Goodley, D. and Runswick-Cole, K. (2010). 'Len Barton, inclusion and critical disability studies: Theorising disabled childhoods'. *International Studies in Sociology of Education*, 20(4), 273–290.

Goodson, I.F (2010). 'Times of educational change: Towards an understanding of patterns of historical and cultural refraction'. *Journal of Education Policy*, 25(6), 767–775.

Goransson, K. and Nilholm, C. (2014). 'Conceptual diversities and empirical shortcoming – a critical analysis of research on inclusive education'. *European Journal of Special Needs Education*, 29(3), 265–280.

Gore, J.M. (1993). *The Struggle for Pedagogies: Critical and Feminist Discourses as Regimes of Truth*. New York: Routledge.

Grace, G. (1991). 'Welfare labourism versus the New Right: The struggle in New Zealand's education policy'. *International Studies in Sociology of Education*, 1, 25–42.

Graham, L. (2005). 'The incidental "Other": A Foucauldian interrogation of educational policy effects'. *Proceedings: American Educational Research Association*, Montreal.

Graham, L. (2006). 'The politics of ADHD'. Paper presented at *AARE*, November 2006, Adelaide. Retrieved from http://eprints.qut.edu.au/4806/1/4806.pdf (accessed 2 December 2014).

Graham, L. (2008). 'From ABCs to ADHD: The role of schooling in the construction of behaviour disorder and the production of disorderly objects'. *International Journal of Inclusive Education*, 12(1), 7–33.

Graham, L. and Jahnukainen, M. (2011). 'Wherefore art thou, inclusion?: Analyzing the development of inclusive education in New South Wales, Alberta and Finland'. *Journal of Education Policy*, 26(2), 263–288.

Graham, L. and Slee, R. (2008). 'Inclusion?' In Gabel, S.L. and Danforth, S. (Eds) *Disability and the Politics of Education: An International Reader*. New York: Peter Lang, 82–99.

Green, A. (2002). 'Education, globalisation and the role of comparative research'. Professorial Lecture, Institute of Education, University of London.

Guillaume, L. (2011). 'Critical race and disability framework: A new paradigm for understanding discrimination against people from non-English speaking backgrounds and indigenous people with disability'. *Critical Race and Whiteness Studies*, 7(6), 6–19.

Hargreaves, A. and Goodson, I. (2006). 'Educational change over time? The sustainability and nonsustainability of three decades of secondary school change and continuity'. *Educational Administration Quarterly*, 42(1), 3–41. DOI: 10.1177/0013161X05277975.

Hargreaves, A. and Shirley, D.L. (2009). The *Fourth Way. The Inspiring Future for Educational Change*. Thousand Oaks, CA: Corwin.

Hargreaves, A. and Shirley, D.L. (2012). *The Global Fourth Way. The Quest for Educational Excellence*. Thousand Oaks, CA: Corwin.

Harris, A. (2008). *Distributed School Leadership: Developing Tomorrow's Leaders*. Oxon: Routledge.

Harris, A. (2010). 'Improving schools in challenging contexts'. In Hargreaves, A. Lieberman, A., Fullan, M. and Hopkins, D. (Eds) *Second International Handbook of Educational Change*. London: Springer, 693–707.

Harris, A. and Spillane, J. (2008). 'Distributed leadership through the looking glass'. *Management in Education*, 22(1), 31–34.

Hartley, D. (2010). 'Rhetorics of regulation in education after the global economic crisis'. *Journal of Education Policy*, 25(6), 785–791.

Harwood, V. (2010). 'Mobile asylums: Psychopathologisation as a personal, portable psychiatric prison'. Special Issue, *Discourse: Studies in the Cultural Politics of Schooling*, 31(4), 437–451.

Harwood, V. and Humphrey, N. (2008). 'Taking exception: Discourses of exceptionality and the invocation of the "ideal" '. In Gabel, S. and Danforth, S. (Eds) *Disability and the Politics of Education*. New York: Peter Lang, 371–383.

Hattam, R., Brennan, M., Zipin, L. and Comber, B. (2009). 'Researching for social justice: Contextual, conceptual and methodological challenges'. *Discourse: Studies in the Cultural Politics of Education*, 30(3), 303–316.

Howes, A., Davies, S.M.B. and Fox, S. (2009). *Improving the Context for Inclusion: Personalising Teacher Development through Collaborative Action Research*. London: Routledge.

Hui-Michael, Y. and Garcia, S. (2009). 'General educators' perceptions and attributions about Asian-American students: Implications for special education referral'. *Multiple Voices for Ethnically Diverse Exceptional Learners*, 12(1), 21–37.

Hursh, D. (2007). 'Assessing no child left behind and the rise of neoliberal education policies'. *American Educational Research Journal*, 44(3), 493–518.

Hursh, D. (2009). 'No child left behind, really?' In Kassem, D. and Garrat, D. (Eds) *Exploring Key Issues in Education*. London: Continuum, 160–174.

Hursh, D. and Henderson, J.A. (2011). 'Contesting global neoliberalism and creating alternative futures'. *Discourse: Studies in the Cultural Politics of Education*, 32(2), 171–185.

Jean-Marie, G. (2008). 'Leadership for social justice: An agenda for 21st century schools'. *The Educational Forum*, 72(4), 340–354.

Jean-Marie, G., Normore, H.A. and Brooks, S.J. (2009). 'Leadership for social justice: Preparing 21st century school leaders for a new social order'. *Journal of Research on Leadership Education*, 4(1), 1–31.

Johnson, B.L. Jr. (2008). 'Exploring multiple meanings of social justice: Comparing modern, interpretive and post-modern perspectives'. *Teacher Development*, 12(4), 301–318.

Johnson, J.R. (2004). 'Universal instructional design and critical (communication) pedagogy: Strategies for voice, inclusion, and social justice/change'. *Equity & Excellence in Education*, 37, 145–153.

Jones, S., Bailey, R. and Jacob, R. (2014). 'Socio-emotional learning is essential to classroom management'. *Phi, Delta, Kappan*, 96(2), 19–24.

Kassah, B.L., and Kassah, A.K. (2013). 'Implementing inclusive education: a Commonwealth guide to implementing Article 2244 of the UN Convention on the Rights of Persons with Disabilities'. *Disability & Society*, 28(2), 291–293.

Karlsen, G.E. (2000). 'Decentralised centralism: Framework for a better understanding of governance in the field of education'. *Journal of Education Policy*, 15(5), 525–538.

Karpinski, C. and Lugg, C. (2006). 'Social justice and educational administration: Mutually exclusive social justice and educational administration: mutually exclusive?' *Journal of Educational Administration*, 44(3), 278–292.

Kauffman, J.M. and Badar, J. (2014). 'Instruction, not inclusion, should be the central issue in special education: An alternative view from the USA'. *Journal of International Special Needs Education*, 17(1), 13–20.

Kayess, R. and French, P. (2008). 'Out of darkness into light? Introducing the convention on the rights of persons with disabilities'. *Human Rights Law Review*, 8(1), 1–34. DOI: 10.1093/hrlr/ngm044.

Kelchtermans, G. (1999). 'Teaching career: Between burnout and fading away? Reflections from narrative and biographical perspectives'. In Vandenberghe, R. and Huberman, M. (Eds) *Understanding and Preventing Teacher Burnout*. Cambridge: Cambridge University Press, 167–176.

Kennedy-Lewis, B.L. (2014). 'Using critical policy analysis to examine competing discourses in zero tolerance legislation: Do we really want to leave no child behind?' *Journal of Education Policy*, 29(2), 165–194.

Kenworthy, J. and Whittaker, J. (2000). 'Anything to declare? The struggle for inclusive education and children's rights'. *Disability and Society*, 15(2), 219–231.

Kershner, R. (2009). 'Learning in inclusive classrooms'. In Hick, P., Kershner, R. and Farrell, P. (Eds) *Psychology for Inclusive Education. New Directions in Theory and Practice*. London: Routledge, 52–65.

Kirk, G. and Okezawa-Rey, M. (Eds). (2007). *Women's Lives: Multicultural Perspectives*. New York: McGraw-Hill.

Knoll, K. (2009). Feminist disability studies pedagogy. *Feminist Teacher*, 19(2), 122–133.

Knudsen, S.V. (2006). 'Intersectionality – A theoretical inspiration in the analysis of minority cultures and identities in textbooks'. In Bruillard, E., Aamotsbakken, B., Knudsen, S.V. and Horsley, M. (Eds) *Caught in the Web or Lost in the Textbook?* Caen: IARTEM, STEF, IUFM, 61–76.

Kugelmass, W.J. (2003). 'Inclusive leadership; Leadership for inclusion'. *National College for School Leadership* (Spring 2003), 1–21. Retrieved from www.ncsl.org.uk/researchassociates, http://dera.ioe.ac.uk/5081/1/kugelmass-inclusive-leadership-full.pdf (accessed 27 February 2015).

Kugelmass, W.J. (2010). 'Constructivist views of learning: Implications for inclusive education'. In Florian, L. (Ed.) *The Sage Handbook of Special Education.* London: Sage. 272–279.

Kugelmass, W.J. and Ainscow, M. (2004). 'Leadership for inclusion: A comparison of international practices'. *Journal of Research in Special Education Needs,* 4(3), 133–141.

Ladson-Billings, G. (1998). 'Just what is critical race theory and what's it doing in a nice field like education?' *Qualitative Studies in Education,* 11(1), 7–24.

Lakes, R. and Carter, P. (2011). 'Neoliberalism and education: An introduction'. *Educational Studies,* 47, 107–110.

Lens, W. and Neves de Jesus, S. (1999). 'A psychosocial interpretation of teacher stress and burnout'. In Vandenberghe, R. and Huberman, A.M. (Eds) *Understanding and Preventing Teacher Burnout: A Sourcebook of International Research and Practice.* Cambridge: Cambridge University Press, 192–201.

Levin, B. and Fullan, M. (2008). 'Learning about system renewal'. *Educational Management Administration & Leadership,* 36(2), 289–303.

Liasidou, A. (2007). 'Inclusive education policies and the feasibility of educational change: The case of Cyprus'. *International Studies in Sociology of Education,* 17(4), 329–347.

Liasidou, A. (2008a). 'Critical discourse analysis and inclusive educational policymaking: The power to exclude'. *Journal of Education Policy,* 13(5), 483–500.

Liasidou A. (2008b). 'Politics of inclusive education policy-making: The case of Cyprus'. *International Journal of Inclusive Education,* 12(3), 229–241.

Liasidou, A. (2009). 'Critical policy research and special education policymaking: A policy trajectory approach'. *Journal for Critical Education Policy Studies,* 7(1), 107–130.

Liasidou A. (2011). 'Special education policymaking: A discursive analytic approach'. *Educational Policy,* 25(6), 887–907.

Liasidou, A. (2012a). *Inclusive Education, Politics and Policymaking.* London: Continuum.

Liasidou, A. (2012b). 'Inclusive education and critical pedagogy at the intersections of disability, race, gender and class'. *Journal for Critical Education Policy Studies,* 10(1), 168–184.

Liasidou, A. (2013a). 'Intersectional understandings of disability and implications for a social justice reform agenda in education policy and practice'. *Disability & Society,* 28(3), 299–312.

Liasidou, A. (2013b). 'Bilingual and special educational needs in inclusive classrooms: Some critical and pedagogical considerations'. *Support for Learning,* 28(2), 11–16.

Liasidou, A. (2013c). 'The cross-fertilization of critical race theory and Disability Studies: Points of convergence/divergence and some education policy implications'. *Disability & Society*, 29(5) 724–737.

Liasidou, A. (2014a). 'Disabling discourses and human rights law: A case study based on the implementation of the UN Convention on the Rights of People with Disabilities'. *Discourse: Studies in the Cultural Politics of Education*, DOI: 10.1080/01596306.2014.936928.

Liasidou, A. (2014b). 'Critical disability studies and socially just change in higher education'. *British Journal of Special Education*, 41(2), 120–135.

Liasidou, A. and Antoniou, A. (2013). 'A special teacher for a special child? (Re)considering the role of the special education teacher within the context of an inclusive education reform agenda'. *European Journal of Special Needs Education*. Retrieved from http://dx.doi.org/10.1080/08856257.2013.820484.

Liasidou, A. and Antoniou, A. (in press) Head teachers' leadership for social justice and inclusion. School Leadership and Management.

Liasidou, A. and Svensson, C. (2011). 'Theorizing educational change within the context of inclusion'. In Cornwall, J. and Graham-Matheson, L. (Eds) *Leading on Inclusion: Dilemmas, Debates and New Perspectives*. London: Routledge, 33–44.

Liasidou, A. and Svensson, C. (2013). 'Educating leaders for social justice: The case of special educational needs coordinators'. *International Journal of Inclusive Education*, DOI: 10.1080/13603116.2013.

Lingard, B. and Mills, M. (2007). 'Pedagogies making a difference: Issues of social justice and inclusion'. *International Journal of Inclusive Education*, 11(3), 233–244.

Lloyd, C. (2008). 'Removing barriers to achievement: A strategy for inclusion or exclusion?' *International Journal of Inclusive Education*, 12(2), 221–236.

Long, M., Wood, C., Littleton, K., Passenger, T. and Sheehy, K. (2011). *The Psychology of Education*. London: Routledge.

Low, C. (1997). 'Is inclusivism possible?' *European Journal of Special Needs Education*, 12(1), 71–79.

Luke, A. (1996). 'Text and discourse in education. An introduction to critical discourse analysis'. *Review of Research*, 21, 3–47.

Luke, A. (2002). 'Beyond science and ideology critique: Developments in critical discourse analysis'. *Annual Review of Applied Linguistics*, 22, 96–110.

Madriaga, M., Hanson, K., Kay, H. and Walker, A. (2011). 'Marking out normalcy and disability in higher education'. *British Journal of Sociology of Education*, 32(6), 901–920.

Maguire, M. and Ball, S. (1994). 'Discourses of educational reform in the United Kingdom and the USA and the work of teachers'. *British Journal of In-Service Education*, 20(1), 5–16, DOI: 10.1080/0305763940200102.

Makkonen, T. (2002). 'Multiple, compound and intersectional discrimination: Bringing the experiences of the most marginalized to the fore'. *Institute for Human Rights*, Abo Akademi University. Retrieved from http://www.abo.fi/media/24259/report11.pdf.

Maslach, C., Schaufeli, W.B. and Leiter, M.P. (2001). 'Job burnout'. *Annual Review of Psychology*, 52, 397–422.

Masschelein, J. and Simon, M. (2005). 'The strategy of the inclusive education apparatus: Inclusive education for exclusive pupils'. *Studies in Philosophy and Education*, 24(2), 117–138.

Mavratsas, K. (2003). *Ethniki omopsihia kai politiki omophonia. Hatrophia ths ellinokypriakis koinonias stis aparhes toy 21ou aiona* [in Greek]. [National unity and political consensus: The atrophy of the Greek-Cypriot society in the beginning of the 21st century]. Athens: Katarti.

Mayrowetz, D. and Weinstein, C. (1999). 'Sources of leadership for inclusive education: Creating schools for all children'. *Educational Administration Quarterly*, 35(3), 423–449.

McIntosh, K., Horner, R.H. and Sugai, G. (2009). 'Sustainability of systems-level evidence based practices in schools: Current knowledge and future directions'. In Sailor, W., Dunlap, G., Sugai, G. and Horner, R. (Eds) *Issues in Clinical Child Psychology*. New York: Springer, 327–352.

McLaren, P. (1998). *Life in Schools: An Introduction to Critical Pedagogy in the Foundation of Education* (3rd edn). New York: Longman.

McLaren, P. and Farahmandpur, R. (2001). 'Teaching against globalization and the new imperialism: Toward a revolutionary pedagogy'. *Journal of Teacher Education*, 52(2), 136–150.

McPhillips, T., Bell, S. and Doveston, M. (2010). 'Overcoming barriers to the acquisition of literacy in twenty-first-century inclusive classrooms'. In Rose, R. (Ed.) *Confronting Obstacles to Inclusion. International Responses to Developing Inclusive Education*. London: Routledge, 213–226.

Mercer, G. (2002). 'Emancipatory disability research'. In Barnes, C., Oliver, M. and Barton, L. (Eds) *Disability Studies Today*. Cambridge: Polity, 228–249.

Mesibov, G. and Howley, M. (2003). *Accessing the Curriculum for Pupils with Autistic Spectrum Disorders: Using the TEACCH Programme to Help Inclusion*. London: Dave Fulton Publishers.

Mills, C.W. (1961). *The Sociological Imagination*. New York: Grove Press.

Mitchell, D. (2008). *What Really Works in Special and Inclusive Education. Using Evidence Based Teaching Strategies*. London: Routledge.

Mittler, D. (1999). 'Equal opportunities. For whom?' *British. Journal of Special Education*, 26(1), 3–7.

MOEC (Ministry of Education and Culture). (1999). *The 1999 Special Education Act (N.113(I)/99) and 2001 N.69(I) for the Education of Children with Special Needs*. [In Greek]. Nicosia: Government Press.

MOEC (2008). *National curriculum for the schools of the Greek-cypriot community*. Retrieved from http://www.moec.gov.cy/analytika_programmata/pdf/keimeno_epitropis_analytiko_programma.pdf (accessed 19 August 2013).

MOEC (2010). *Curricula for pre-primary, primary and secondary education*. Retrieved from http://www.moec.gov.cy/analytika_programmata/programmata_spoudon.html (accessed 19 August 2013).

Moreau, M.P. (Ed.) (2014). *Inequalities in the Teaching Profession. A Global Perspective*. Basingstoke: Palgrave Macmillan.

Morris, J. (1991). *Pride against Prejudice: Transforming Attitudes to Disability.* London: The Women's Press.

Morris, J. (1996). *Encounters with Strangers: Feminism and Disability.* London: The Women's Press.

Morrison, W. (2001). 'Emotional/behavioral disabilities and gifted and talented behaviors: Paradoxical or semantic differences in characteristics?' *Psychology in the Schools,* 38(5), 425–431.

Muijs, D. (2010). 'Changing classroom learning'. In Hargreaves, A., Lieberman, A., Fullan, M. and Hopkins, D. (Eds) *Second International Handbook of Educational Change.* London: Springer, 857–868.

Muijs, D. and Reynolds, D. (2010). *Effective Teaching: Evidence and Practice.* London: Sage.

Mullen, C. and Jones, R. (2008). 'Teacher leadership capacity-building: Developing democratically accountable leaders in schools'. *Teacher Development,* 12(4), 329–340.

National Joint Committee on Learning Disabilities (2011). *Learning Disabilities: Implications for Policy Regarding Research and Practice.* Retrieved from http://www.ldonline.org/?module=uploads&func=download&fileId=816.

Nayler, J. and Keddie, A. (2007). 'Focusing the gaze: Teacher interrogation of practice'. *International Journal of Inclusive Education,* 11(2), 199–214.

Nevin, A., Smith, R.S. and McNeil, M. (2008). 'Shifting attitudes of related service providers: A disability studies and critical pedagogy approach'. *International Journal of Whole Schooling,* 4(1), 1–12.

Norwich, B. (2002). 'Education, inclusion and individual differences: Recognizing and resolving dilemmas'. *British Educational Research Journal,* 50(40), 482–502.

Norwich, B. (2008a). *Dilemmas of Difference, Inclusion, and Disability.* London: Routledge.

Norwich, B. (2008b). 'Perspectives and purposes of disability classification systems: Implications for teachers and curriculum and pedagogy'. In Florian, L. and McLaughlin, M. (Eds) *Disability Classification in Education.* London: Sage. 131–149.

Norwich, B. (2010). 'A response to special educational needs: A new look'. In Terzi, L. (Ed.) *Special Educational Needs: A New Look.* London: Continuum, 47–113.

Norwich, B. and Lewis, A. (2001). 'Mapping a pedagogy for special educational needs'. *British Educational Research Journal,* 27(3), 314–329.

Norwich, B. and Lewis, A. (2007). 'How specialized is teaching children with disabilities and difficulties?' *Journal of Curriculum Studies,* 39(2), 127–150.

Oliver, M. (1990). *The Politics of Disablement.* London: Macmillan.

Oliver, M. (1996). *Understanding Disability: From Theory to Practice.* Basingstoke: Palgrave.

Oliver, M. (2002). 'Emancipatory research: A vehicle for social transformation or policy development'. Paper presented at *1st Annual Disability Research Seminar,* The National Disability Authority and the Centre for Disability Studies, University College, Dublin. Retrieved from http://

disability-studies.leeds.ac.uk/files/library/Oliver-Mikes-paper.pdf   (accessed 3 December 2002).

Oliver, M. (2013). 'The social model of disability: Thirty years on'. *Disability & Society*, 28(7), 1024–1026, DOI: 10.1080/09687599.2013.818773.

Oliver, M. and Barton, L. (2000). 'The emerging field of Disability Studies: A view from Britain'. Paper presented at *Disability Studies: A Global Perspective*, Washington, DC, October 2000.

Pather, S. (2007). 'Demystifying inclusion: Implications for more sustainable inclusive practice'. *International Journal of Inclusive Education*, 11(5&6), 627–643.

Phtiaka, H. (2003). 'The power to exclude; facing the challenges of inclusive education in Cyprus'. *International Journal of Contemporary Sociology*, 40(1), 139–152.

Pihlaja, P. (2007). 'Behave yourself! Examining meanings assigned to children with socio-emotional difficulties'. *Disability and Society*, 23(1), 5–15.

Polat, F. and Kisanji, J. (2009). *Inclusive Education: A Step towards Social Justice*. London: EdEqual. Retrieved from http://r4d.dfid.gov.uk/Output/182023.

Pollard, A. (2012). *Reflective Teaching. Evidence-Informed Professional Practice* (3rd edn). London: Continuum.

Powell, J.J.W. (2011). *Barriers to Inclusion: Special Education in the United States and Germany*. London: Paradigm.

Power, S. (1992). 'Researching the impact of education policy: Difficulties and discontinuities'. *Journal of Education Policy*, 7(5), 493–500.

Priestley, M. and Miller, K. (2012). 'Educational change in Scotland: Policy, context and biography'. *Curriculum Journal*, 23(1), 99–116.

Race, R. (2015). *Multiculturalism and Education*. (2nd edn). London: Bloomsbury.

Race, R. and Lander, V. (Eds) (2014). *Advancing Race and Ethnicity in Education*. Basingstoke: Palgrave Macmillan.

Raffo, C.A., Dyson, H., Gunter, D., Hall, Jones, L. and Kalambouka, A. (2009). 'Education and poverty: Mapping the terrain and making the links to educational policy'. *International Journal of Inclusive Education*, 13(4), 341–358.

Rayner, S. (2009). 'Educational diversity and learning leadership: A proposition, some principles and a model of inclusive leadership'. *Educational Review*, 61(4), 433–477.

Riddell, S., Tinklin, T. and Wilson, A. (2005). 'New Labour, social justice and disabled students in higher education'. *British Educational Research Journal*, 31(5), 623–643.

Riehl, C. (2000). 'The principal's role in creating inclusive schools for diverse students: A review of normative, empirical and critical literature on the practice of educational administration'. *Review of Educational Research*, 70(1), 55–81.

Rioux, M. (2002). 'Disability, citizenship and rights in a changing world'. In Barnes, C., Oliver, M. and Barton, L. (Eds) *Disability Studies Today*. Cambridge: Polity, 210–227.

Rioux, M. (2010). Disability rights in education. In Florian, L (Ed.) *The Sage Handbook of Special Education*. London: Sage 107–116.

Roaf, C. and Bines, H. (1989). 'Needs, rights and opportunities in special education'. In Roaf, C. and Bines, H. (Eds) *Needs, Rights and Opportunities*. London: The Falmer Press, 5–15.

Rose, D.H. (2001). 'Universal design for learning: Deriving guiding principles from networks that learn'. *Journal of Special Education Technology*, 16(1), 66–70.

Rose, D.H. and Meyer, A. (2002). *Teaching Every Student in the Digital Age: Universal Design for Learning*. Alexandria, VA: Association for Supervision and Curriculum Development.

Rose, R. and Howley, M. (2007). *The Practical Guide to Special Educational Needs in Inclusive Primary Classrooms*. London: Sage.

Ross, J.A. and Berger, M. (2009). 'Equity and leadership: Research-based strategies for school leaders'. *School Leadership & Management*, 29(5), 463–476.

Rothstein, L. and Johnson, S. (2010). *Special Education Law*. London: Sage.

Rouse, M. (2009). 'Developing inclusive practice: A role for teachers and teacher education'. *Education in the North*, 16, 6–13.

Roulstone, A. and Prideaux, S. (2008). 'More policies, greater inclusion? Exploring the contradictions of New Labour inclusive education policy'. *International Studies in Sociology of Education*, 18(1), 15–29.

Rowe, D., Horsley, N., Thorpe, T. and Breslin, T. (2011). *School Leaders, Community Cohesion and the Big Society*. Reading: CfBT.

Ryan, J. (2006a). 'Inclusive leadership and social justice for schools'. *Leadership and Policy in Schools*, 5, 3–17.

Ryan, J. (2006b). 'Exclusion in urban schools and communities'. In Armstrong, D and McMahon, B (Eds) *Inclusion in Urban Educational Environments: Addressing Issues of Diversity, Equity, and Social Justice*. Greenwich, CT: Information Age, 3–30.

Sachs, D. and Schreuer, N. (2011). 'Inclusion of students with disabilities in higher education: Performance and participation in students' experiences'. *Disability Studies Quarterly*, 31(2), 1–19.

Sahlberg, P. (2010). 'Educational change in Finland'. In Hargreaves, A. Lieberman, A. Fullan, M. and Hopkins, D. (Eds) *Second International Handbook of Educational Change*. London: Springer, 119–130.

Sargis, J. (2005). 'Education, paideia and democracy: Experiences of the U.S. educational system'. *The International Journal of Inclusive Democracy*, 2(1), 1–10. Retrieved from http://www.inclusivedemocracy.org/journal/vol2/vol2_no1_sargis.htm.

Sayed, Y. Soudien, C. and Carrim, N. (2003). 'Discourses of exclusion and inclusion in the South: Limits and possibilities'. *Journal of Educational Change*, 4(3), 231–248.

Scarlett, W.G., Ponte, I.C. and Singh, J.P. (2009). *Approaches to Behaviour and Classroom Management. Integrating Discipline and Care*. Thousand Oaks: Sage.

Schwab, R.L. (1983). 'Teacher burnout: Moving beyond "Psychobabble."' *Theory into Practice*, 22(1), 21–26.

Shakespeare, T. (1997). 'Cultural representation of disabled people: Dustbins or disavowal?' In Barton, L. and Oliver, M. (Eds) *Disability Studies: Past, Present and Future*. Leeds: Disability Press, 217–233.

Shakespeare, T. (2006). *Disability Rights and Wrongs*. Oxford: Routledge.

Shakespeare, T. and Watson, N. (2001). 'The social model of disability: An outdated ideology?' In Barnartt, S.N. and Altman, B.M. (Eds) *Research in Social Science and Disability, Volume 2, Exploring Theories and Expanding Methodologies*. Bingley: Emerald, 9–28.

Shepherd, K. and Brody Hasazi, S. (2010). Leadership for social justice and inclusion. In Florian, L. (Ed.) *The Sage Handbook of Special Education*. London: Sage, 475–485.

Shields, C.M. (2004). 'Dialogic leadership for social justice: Overcoming pathologies of silence'. *Educational Administration Quarterly*, 40(1), 109–132.

Shields, C.M. and Mohan, E. (2008). 'High-quality education for all students: Putting social justice at its heart'. *Teacher Development*, 12(4), 289–300.

Sindelar, P., Shearer, D., Yendol-Hoppey, D. and Liebert, T. (2006). 'The sustainability of inclusive school reform'. *Exceptional Children*, 72(3), 317–331.

Singal, N. and Miles, S. (2009). 'The education for all and inclusive education debate: Conflict, contradiction or opportunity'. *International Journal of Inclusive Education*, 14(1), 1–15.

Slee, R. (2001). 'Social justice and the changing directions in educational research: The case of inclusive education'. *International Journal of Inclusive Education*, 5(2/3), 167–177.

Slee, R. (2006). 'Limits to and possibilities for educational reform'. *International Journal of Inclusive Education*, 10(2–3), 109–119.

Slee, R. (2008). 'Beyond special and regular schooling? An inclusive education reform agenda'. *International Studies in Sociology of Education*, 18(2), 99–116.

Slee, R. (2010). 'Inclusive schooling as a means and end of education?' In Florian, L. (Ed.) *The Sage Handbook of Special Education*. London: Sage, 160–170.

Slee, R. (2012). 'How do we make inclusive education happen when exclusion is a political predisposition?' *International Journal of Inclusive Education*, 17(8), 895–907. DOI: 10.1080/13603116.2011.602534.

Slee, R. (2014a). 'Beyond a psychology of student behaviour'. *Emotional and Behavioural Difficulties*, DOI: 10.1080/13632752.2014.947100.

Slee, R. (2014b). 'Evolving theories of student disengagement: A new job for Durkheim's children?' *Oxford Review of Education*, 40(4), 446–465.

Sleeter, C. (2008). 'Equity, democracy and neo-liberal assaults on teacher education'. *Teaching and Teacher Education*, 24(8), 1947–1957.

Smith, E. (2012). *Key Issues in Education and Social Justice*. London: Sage.

Smith, E. and Douglas, G. (2014). 'Special educational needs, disability and school accountability: an international perspective'. *International Journal of Inclusive Education*, 18(5), 443–458.

Stainback, S. and Stainback, W. (1998). 'Curriculum in inclusive classrooms: The background'. In Stainback, S. and Stainback, W. (Eds) *Inclusion: A Guide for Educators*. Baltimore: Brookes, 36–45.

Stonemeier, J., Trader, B., Richards, C., Blank, R. East, B. and Toson, A. (2013). *Delivering on Equity: Implications for Decision-Makers*. Lawrence, KS: SWIFT Center.

Sullivan, M. (2005). 'Subjected bodies: Paraplegia, rehabilitation and the politics of movement'. In Tremain, S. (Ed.) *Foucault and the Government of Disability*. Michigan, IL: University of Michigan Press, 27–44.

Symeonidou, S. and Mavrou, K. (2013). 'Deconstructing the Greek-Cypriot new national curriculum: To what extent are disabled children considered in the 'humane and democratic school' of Cyprus'. *Disability and Society*, 29, 303–316. DOI: 10.1080/09687599.2013.796879.

Talmor, R., Reiter, S. and Feigin, N. (2005). 'Factors relating to regular education teacher burnout in inclusive education'. *European Journal of Special Needs Education*, 20(2), 215–229.

Taylor, S. (2004). 'Researching educational policy and change in "new times": Using critical discourse analysis'. *Journal of Educational Policy*, 19(4), 433–451.

The Economist (2014) Teacher tenure Brown v Board, the sequel 14 June 2014. Available online at: http://www.economist.com/news/united-states/21604201-stunning-defeat-teachers-unions-california-brown-v-board-sequel.

The Economist (2014). 'Politics'. 14 June 2014. p. 8. Retrieved from http://www.economist.com/news/international/21590494-countries-ratify-human-rights-accords-often-delete-bits-they-dislike-mightier.

The Guardian (2013). 'Schools should be fined for illegally excluding pupils, inquiry finds Children's commissioner says illegal exclusions are "source of shame to education system"'. Retrieved from http://www.guardian.co.uk/education/2013/apr/24/schools-illegally-excluding-pupils-inquiry?CMP=twt_fd.

Theoharis, G. (2007). 'Social justice educational leaders and resistance: Toward a theory of social justice leadership'. *Educational Administration Quarterly*, 43(2), 221–258.

Theoharis, G. and Causton, J. (2014). 'Leading inclusive reform for students with disabilities: A school- and systemwide approach'. *Theory into Practice.*, 53(2), 82–97.

Theoharis, G. and Causton-Theoharis, J. (2008). 'Oppressors or emancipators: Critical dispositions for preparing inclusive school leaders'. *Equity & Excellence in Education*, 41(2), 230–246.

Theoharis, G. and Sebastian, J. (2006). 'Toward a framework for preparing leaders for social justice'. *Journal of Educational Administration*, 44(3), 209–224.

The Persons with Intellectual Disability Law of 1989 (17/87). (1989). Retrieved from http://www.cpmental.com.cy/epnka/page.php?pageID=16.

Thomas, C. (1999). *Female Forms*. Buckingham: Open University Press.

Thomas, C. (2004). 'How is disability understood?' *Disability and Society*, 19(6), 569–583.

Thomas, G. and Loxley, A. (2007). *Deconstructing Special Education and Constructing Inclusion*. Buckingham: Open University Press.

Thousand, J.S., Villa, R.A. and Nevin, A.I. (2007). *Differentiating Instruction: Collaborative Planning and Teaching for Universally Designed Learning*. Thousand Oaks, CA: Corwin Press.

Thuneberg, H., Hautamaki, J., Ahtiainen, R., Lintuvuori, M. Vainikainen, M.P. and Hilasvuori, T. (2014). 'Conceptual change in adopting the national special education strategy in Finland'. *Journal of Educational Change*, 15, 37–56.

Tokuhama-Espinosa, T. (2012). *Why Mind, Brain, and Education Science Is the 'New' Brain-Based Education*. Retrieved from http://education.jhu.edu/PD/newhorizons/Journals/Winter2011/Tokuhama1.

Tomlinson, S. (1982). *A Sociology of Special Education*. London: Routledge and Kegan Paul.

Tomlinson, S. (2012). 'The irresistible rise of the SEN industry'. *Oxford Review of Education*, 38, 267–286.

Tomlinson, S. (2013). 'Social justice and lower attainers in a global knowledge economy'. *Social Inclusion*, 1(2), 102–112.

Tomlinson, S. (2014). *The Politics of Race, Class and Special Education: The Selected Works of Sally Tomlinson*. London, New York: Routledge.

Topping, K. (2012) 'Conceptions of inclusion: Widening ideas'. In Boyle, C. and Topping, K. (Eds) *What Works in Inclusion*. Maidenhead: Open University Press, 9–19.

Tremain, S. (Ed.). (2005). *Foucault and the Government of Disability*. Michigan, MI: The University of Michigan Press.

UNICEF UK (2013) *Rights Respecting Schools Award: A Best Practice Review* London: UNICEF UK. Retrieved from http://www.unicef.org.uk/Documents/Education-Documents/RSSA_Good_Practice_Review.pdf (accessed 27 February 2015).

United Nations (UN) (2008). *Convention on the Rights of Persons with Disabilities*. New York: UN.

Van Kampen, M. Van Zijverden, I.M. and Emmett, T. (2008). 'Reflections on poverty and disability: A review of literature'. *Asia Pacific Disability Rehabilitation Journal*, 19(1), 19–37.

Vislie, L. (2003). 'From integration to inclusion: Focusing global trends and changes in the western European societies'. *European Journal of Special Needs Education*, 18(1), 17–35.

Vlachou, A. (1997). *Struggles for Inclusive Education*. Buckingham: Open University Press.

Warnock, M. (2005). *Special Educational Needs: A New Look*. London: Philosophy of Education Society of Great Britain Publications, Impact Series No. 11.

Warnock, M. (2010). 'Special educational needs: A new look'. In Terzi, L. (Ed.) *Special Educational Needs a New Look*. London: Continuum. 11–46.

Watson, K. (2001). 'Introduction: Rethinking the role of comparative education'. In Watson, K. (Ed.) *Doing Comparative Education Research*. Oxford: Symposium Books, 9–22.

Watts, I.E. and Erevelles, N. (2004). 'These deadly times: Reconceptualizing school violence by using critical race theory and disability studies'. *American Educational Research Journal*, 41(2), 271–299.

Webb, T.P., Neumann, M. and Jones, L.C. (2004). 'Politics, school improvement, and social justice: A triadic model of teacher leadership'. *The Educational Forum*, 68(3), 254–262.

Wedell, K. (2008). 'Confusion about inclusion: Patching up or system change?' *British Journal of Special Education*, 35(3), 127–135.

Welch, A. (1998). 'The cult of efficiency in education: Comparative reflections on the reality and the rhetoric'. *Comparative Education*, 34(2), 157–175.

Westwood, P. (2001). 'Differentiation as a strategy for inclusive classroom practice: Some difficulties identified'. *Australian Journal of Learning Disabilities*, 6(1), 5–11.

Wilkinson, L. (2003). 'Advancing a perspective on the intersections of diversity: Challenges for research and social policy'. *Canadian Ethnic Studies/Études Ethniques au Canada*, 35(3), 26–38.

Wilson, B. (2007). 'Social justice and neoliberal discourse'. *Southeastern Geographer*, 47(1), 97.

Winzer, M.A. and Mazurek, K. (2011). 'Canadian teachers' associations and the inclusive movement for students with special needs'. *Canadian Journal of Educational Administration and Policy*, (116), 18 January 2011.

Woods, P. (2011). *Transforming Education Policy: Shaping a Democratic Future*. Bristol: Policy Press.

Wright, N. (2001). 'Leadership, bastard leadership and managerialism: Confronting twin paradoxes in the Blair Education Project'. *Educational Management Administration Leadership*, 29(2), 275–290.

Youdell, D. (2006). 'Diversity, inequality, and a post-structural politics for education'. *Discourse: Studies in the Cultural Politics of Education*, 27(1), 33–42.

Zajda, J. (2011). 'Globalisation and schooling: Equity and access issues'. *Cultural Studies of Science Education*, 6(1), 143–152(10).

Index

able-bodied order, 46, 123, 130–1, 153, 161
accountability, 10–12, 16, 23, 47, 55, 58, 91, 110–12, 148–50
action research, 105, 108–9
applied behavioural analysis (ABA), 102
archer, 30
assessment for learning, 103
assimilationist, 15, 30, 32, 34, 37, 48, 86, 119–20, 153
attention deficit hyperactivity disorder (ADHD), 80, 98

bilingual special education, 75, 100
bio-psychosocial model of disability, 79
brain-based learning, 98
burnout (professional), 51, 64–5

capacity building, 107–9
citizenship, 6, 27, 36–7, 68, 76, 85, 88, 144
collaborative professional practice, 55, 70, 72, 101
communities of learning, 52, 95
communities of practice, 136
compensatory measures of support, 32, 34, 38, 41, 145
co-teaching, 75, 113
critical disability studies, 117, 123, 133
critical pedagogy, 2, 37, 120–3, 144
critical race theory, 2, 120, 129
Critical theory (ies), 118–19
cross-cultural, 4, 35–6, 166
culturally and linguistically informed instruction, 103

data (transparency of), 53
deficit-oriented approach, 41
democratic and egalitarian communities, 6
democratic entrepreneurialism, 27
difference and diversity, 3, 20, 28–9, 37, 42–3, 68, 75, 96, 110, 116, 129–30, 133, 164
dilemma of difference, 61, 132
disability activism, 156, 159, 161–2
disability politics, 154, 161
disabled people's movement, 159–60
disabled people's organization, 157, 161
disabling discourse, 43
disablism, 124, 130, 151, 159
disciplinary power, 15, 34, 49
discourse around values, 7, 9, 24, 33
discourse of equity, 82
discourse of safety, 82
discourses of inclusion/exclusion, 34, 44

early intervention, 10, 59, 70, 85
economic crisis, 27
    see also fiscal crisis
economy (global/globalised), 20–1, 82, 147
Education, Health and Care plan (EHC), 52
Education for All (EFA), 42
educational accessibility, 38, 102
educational differentiation, 75, 102
effective teaching, 70, 103
equality of opportunity, 14, 28, 88
ethics, 27, 33, 144
evidence-based instruction, 70, 74–5
exclusion, 31–2, 34–5, 41, 44–5, 48, 87, 123–4, 127, 142, 145, 158, 161, 166

feminist analyses, 123–5, 155
Finland, 4, 10, 59, 71, 84–7
fiscal crisis, 6, 9, 27, 32
Foucault
    'docile bodies', 14
    implicit systems, 50
    'progressive politics', 50
    regimes of truth, 57
    technologies of power, 62
    technologies of self, 62
    'will to truth', 29
full service school, 53, 129

gaming strategies, 16
Giddens, 30
globalization, 6, 11, 147

human rights approach to disability,
    35, 42–3, 49

IDEA (Individuals with Disabilities
    Act), 70
identity politics, 46
impaired self, 41
inclusion backlash, 21, 40, 164
inclusive cultures, 37, 68
inclusive pedagogies, 57, 73, 89, 92,
    96, 100
inclusive policies and practices,
    25, 29, 35, 38, 64, 105, 109,
    137
Index for Inclusion, 56, 58, 105
individual deficit, 41, 78, 163
inequality, 5, 9, 13, 39, 121, 122,
    126, 150, 156–7
institutionalization, 34
instructional leadership, 136, 138,
    158
international human rights law,
    43–5, 48
international politics, 2
intersectionality, 43, 80, 120, 125–6,
    133
intra-professional collaboration,
    52–3

language (symbolic power of), 43,
    44, 63
learning organization, 109, 136
learning support, 47, 59, 69, 114,
    145

maindumping, 40
marketizing meta-governance,
    7–8, 27
medical model of disability, 152–3,
    158
multi-tiered intervention
    strategies, 71

neoliberal ideologies, 5, 7, 14, 24, 73
neoliberal reforms, 5, 7
neoliberal understandings (of
    inclusion), 17, 42, 133
neo-special education paradigm, 105
No Child Left Behind (NCLB), 11
non-ideal students, 14
normalcy, 46, 61, 86, 97, 122, 130–1,
    152–3
normalizing practices, 37, 43, 153

OFSTED, 16, 54

policymakers, 29–30, 56, 144, 150,
    159
policy networks, 5
political action, 6, 36, 40, 152, 157–8
political nature of inclusion, 35
politics of difference and diversity, 3,
    116
post-modern/post-structural, 79,
    154, 155
power inequities and discriminatory
    regimes, 37–8, 140, 154–5
Programme for International
    Student Assessment (PISA), 11
pupils referral units, 79

reductionism, 4
reflection, 2, 61–2, 64, 96, 105, 114,
    144, 146–8
Response to Intervention (RTI), 70

school change, 72, 83, 105
school development, 47, 56, 76, 105, 108
school effectiveness research, 30, 90, 128
school improvement, 83, 108, 140, 143, 146
school improvement movement, 83
Schools for the Future, 129
segregated forms of provision, 28, 31
self-advocacy, 155–9
social and emotional aspects of learning, 76–7
social constructionist (analyses of disability), 154
social, emotional and behavioural difficulties (SEBD), 77–82
social injustices, 14
socially just change, 39, 49, 61, 69, 117, 135, 143
social model of disability, 119, 125, 129, 151–2, 154–6, 160
social oppression, 37, 153, 158
socio-cultural theories of learning, 92, 100
Special Educational Needs and Disability Code of Practice, 53, 54
special educational needs coordinator (SENCO), 52
special education industry, 15

special education status quo, 1, 30, 33, 48, 51, 57
special education strategy (SPES), 71
structuration theory, 30
structure and agency, 30
sustainability of inclusive education reforms, 111–12, 115

TEACCH, (Treatment and Education of Autistic and other Communication handicapped Children), 102
teaching to the test, 11, 17, 93
theories of change, 68, 91, 107
transformative educational change, 3

United Nations Convention on the Rights of People with Disabilities (UNCRPD), 42, 45
Universal Design for Learning (UDL), 38
US Department of Education, 70, 71

Vygotsky, 99, 101, 104

welfare state, 83–4, 86
whole-school approach, 78–9, 91, 104

zero-tolerance policies, 51, 78, 82

CPSIA information can be obtained at www.ICGtesting.com
Printed in the USA
LVOW11*1803060715

445146LV00009B/42/P